INKSCAPE DRAWING COMPLETE 2024 GUIDE FOR BEGINNERS

HETTIA SORTHAW

Copyright © 2023 Hettia Sorthaw

All rights reserved.

INTRODUCTION

Welcome to the "Inkscape Drawing Complete 2024 Guide for Beginners," a comprehensive resource designed to guide you through the fascinating world of Inkscape. Whether you are an aspiring graphic designer, a creative hobbyist, or someone looking to delve into the realm of vector graphics, this guide is your gateway to mastering Inkscape, a powerful, open-source vector graphics editor.

In the realm of digital art and design, Inkscape has emerged as a formidable tool, offering a diverse range of features and capabilities. Its user-friendly interface, coupled with an extensive array of tools, makes it an ideal choice for beginners and professionals alike. As you embark on this journey, this guide aims to not only introduce you to Inkscape but also to deepen your understanding and enhance your skills in vector graphics.

The Evolution and Importance of Inkscape

Inkscape's journey, from its inception to becoming a staple in the graphic design industry, is a testament to its robustness and versatility. Originating as a fork from the Sodipodi project, Inkscape has evolved significantly over the years. This section will explore its development history, highlighting key milestones and how they have shaped Inkscape into the software it is today.

Understanding the software's evolution provides context and appreciation for its capabilities. It also offers insights into how Inkscape has remained relevant and continued to grow in a rapidly evolving digital landscape.

Navigating the World of Inkscape

Inkscape is not just a tool; it's a landscape of creativity waiting to be explored. The guide will walk you through the process of obtaining Inkscape – from subscription and purchase options to installation methods. It will also delve into the price and accessibility aspects, ensuring you have all the necessary information to get started.

This section aims to ease your initiation into Inkscape, making the transition from installation to utilization as smooth as possible. It serves as a primer, setting the stage for the exciting journey ahead.

Embarking on a Creative Journey

The heart of Inkscape lies in its design concepts and mindset. This guide will introduce you to the fundamental principles of vector graphics and how Inkscape leverages these principles. Understanding these concepts is crucial in harnessing the full potential of the software.

As you progress, you will learn about the expectations and future uses of Inkscape. This foresight not only prepares you for immediate projects but also equips you with knowledge and skills that are future-proof, ensuring that your learning remains relevant and valuable in the years to come.

Mastering the Basics and Beyond

Our journey through the chapters will start with familiarizing you with the Inkscape interface, followed by a deep dive into the core features and tools. From fundamental shapes and transformations to mastering paths and curves, each chapter is meticulously crafted to build your skills progressively.

Color theory, gradients, effects, and text handling are more than just features; they are the building blocks of compelling designs. This guide will provide you with a strong foundation in these areas, allowing you to create intricate and visually stunning artwork.

Expanding Your Horizon

As you become more comfortable with the basics, the guide will introduce you to advanced techniques and tools. You will learn about filters, clipping, embedding drawings in webpages, and much more. These chapters are designed to unlock new possibilities, helping you transform your ideas into sophisticated designs.

Specialized applications like fashion design, 3D box creation, and auto tracing images open up new avenues for using Inkscape. These chapters will showcase the versatility of Inkscape, illustrating how it can be adapted to various creative needs.

Integration and Professional Insights

In today's interconnected world, the ability to integrate with other software is crucial. This guide covers how Inkscape works in tandem with programs like Paint.Net and X3D, enhancing your workflow and productivity.

Finally, the book culminates with professional insights, offering a glimpse into the life of a graphic designer. This section is not just about skills and techniques; it's about understanding the role, challenges, and opportunities in the field of graphic design.

Embracing the Digital Canvas

Inkscape is not just a tool; it's a canvas where your digital artistry comes to life. This guide will take you beyond the basics, exploring how Inkscape can be used to create complex and intricate designs. You'll learn how to manipulate shapes, create stunning patterns, and bring your artistic visions to fruition. This journey through Inkscape is akin to learning a new language, one that speaks in lines, curves, colors, and textures.

The Power of Vector Graphics

At the heart of Inkscape's functionality is the power of vector graphics. Unlike raster graphics, vectors are not made up of pixels but paths, which allows for infinite scalability without loss of quality. This section of the guide will delve into the significance of vector graphics in modern design, highlighting how Inkscape harnesses this power to create versatile and high-quality designs.

Understanding and Utilizing Inkscape's Interface

A major component of mastering any software is understanding its interface. Inkscape's interface, with its multitude of tools and options, might seem daunting at first. This guide will break down each element of the interface, from toolbars to menus, ensuring you become comfortable and efficient in navigating and utilizing Inkscape's workspace. We'll explore how to customize the interface to suit your workflow, making your design process more intuitive and enjoyable.

Tools and Techniques for Every Designer

Inkscape is equipped with a diverse set of tools, each with its own unique functionality. From simple line drawings to complex bezier curves, each tool in Inkscape has a purpose and a myriad of applications. This guide will provide in-depth explanations and examples of how to use these tools effectively. Whether you're looking to create precise geometric shapes or free-flowing artistic elements, you'll find the techniques and tips you need to bring your ideas to life.

Colors, Textures, and Effects

The magic of a design often lies in its colors, textures, and effects. Inkscape offers a wide range of options to add depth and vibrancy to your designs. This guide will teach you how to select and apply colors, create gradients, and use textures to add realism or artistic flair to your creations. You'll also learn how to apply and customize various effects to enhance the visual appeal of your designs.

Practical Projects and Applications

Learning is most effective when it's applied. Throughout the guide, you'll find practical projects and real-world applications of Inkscape's tools and features. These projects are designed to reinforce the concepts you've learned and provide you with hands-on experience. From creating logos and icons to designing complex illustrations, these projects will challenge and inspire you, helping you apply your skills in meaningful and creative ways.

Beyond the Software: Tips and Best Practices

While mastering Inkscape is a significant part of your journey, understanding the broader aspects of design is equally important. This guide includes tips and best practices that go beyond the software, covering topics like design theory, composition, and color psychology. These insights will help you create designs that are not only technically proficient but also aesthetically compelling and emotionally resonant.

Looking Ahead: The Future of Inkscape and Digital Design

As we conclude the introduction, we'll look towards the future of Inkscape and digital design. The digital design landscape is ever-evolving, with new trends, tools, and techniques emerging regularly. This section will explore what the future may hold for Inkscape and how you can stay updated and adaptable in this dynamic field.

CONTENTS

Chapter 1: Introducing Inkscape 1
- Welcome to Inkscape
- Development History
- Subscription and Purchase
- Price and Accessibility
- Installation Method
- Design Concept and Mindset
- Future Use and Expectations

Chapter 2: Getting Started with Inkscape 17
- The Inkscape Interface

Chapter 3: Fundamental Shapes and Transformations 23
- Basic Shapes
- Squares and Rectangles
- Circles, Ellipses, and Arcs
- Stars and Polygons
- Spirals
- Rotation and Transformation

Chapter 4: Mastering Paths and Curves 38

- Basic Paths
- Bezier Curve Tool
- Add or Delete a Node
- Add or Delete a Segment
- Join Two Segments

Chapter 5: Colors and Gradients 50

- The RGB Color Model
- The HSL Color Model
- The CMYK Color Model
- Basic Fill
- Fill Rule
- Linear Gradients
- Radial Gradients
- Bitmap Fill

Chapter 6: Enhancing Designs with Effects 73

- Shadows and Highlights
- Layers and Z – Order
- Grouping

Chapter 7: Creative Text Handling 84

- Basic Text
- Text Kerning
- Text on Path
- Text in Shape
- Place Greek Letters in Drawing

Chapter 8: Advanced Techniques and Tools 101

- Filters
- Filters That Create Buttons
- Clipping
- Embed Drawing in Webpage
- Export Inkscape Drawing as Image
- Configuring Document Properties
- Configuring Inkscape Preferences

Chapter 9: Specialized Applications 143

- Fashion Design With Inkscape
- Create 3D Boxes Tool
- Auto Trace an Image
- Hand Trace an Image
- Hand Code SVG
- Inkscape's Built-in XML Editor

Chapter 10: Integrating with Other Software 172
- Paint.Net
- X3D

Chapter 11: Professional Insights 190
- What Does a Graphic Designer Do?

Chapter 12: Keyboard shortcuts in Inkscape 195

CONCLUSION... 209

CHAPTER 1: INTRODUCING INKSCAPE

1. WELCOME TO INKSCAPE

1.1 Overview of Inkscape

Inkscape, a renowned vector graphics editor, offers a powerful yet user-friendly platform for creating and editing scalable vector graphics (SVG). What sets Inkscape apart is its commitment to open-source principles, offering a robust, cost-free alternative to commercial software. It's compatible with multiple operating systems, including Windows, macOS, and Linux, making it accessible to a broad range of users.

At its core, Inkscape is designed for artists, illustrators, web designers, and anyone interested in vector imagery. Whether you're crafting logos, icons, diagrams, maps, or complex artworks, Inkscape's comprehensive suite of tools facilitates creativity and precision. Its capabilities extend from basic drawing and shape tools to more complex features like path editing, node alignment, and Boolean operations, suitable for both beginners and experienced designers.

Inkscape's SVG compatibility ensures that designs are scalable to any size without loss of quality, an essential feature in today's multi-device world. Additionally, its ability to import and export various file formats, including AI, PDF, EPS, and PNG, enhances its versatility.

1.2 The Rise of Vector Graphics

The rise of vector graphics in the digital art world can be traced back to the need for scalability and resolution independence, crucial in a variety of applications, from web design to branding. Unlike raster graphics, which are made up of pixels and can lose quality when scaled, vector graphics are composed of paths defined by mathematical equations, allowing them to be resized infinitely without any degradation in quality.

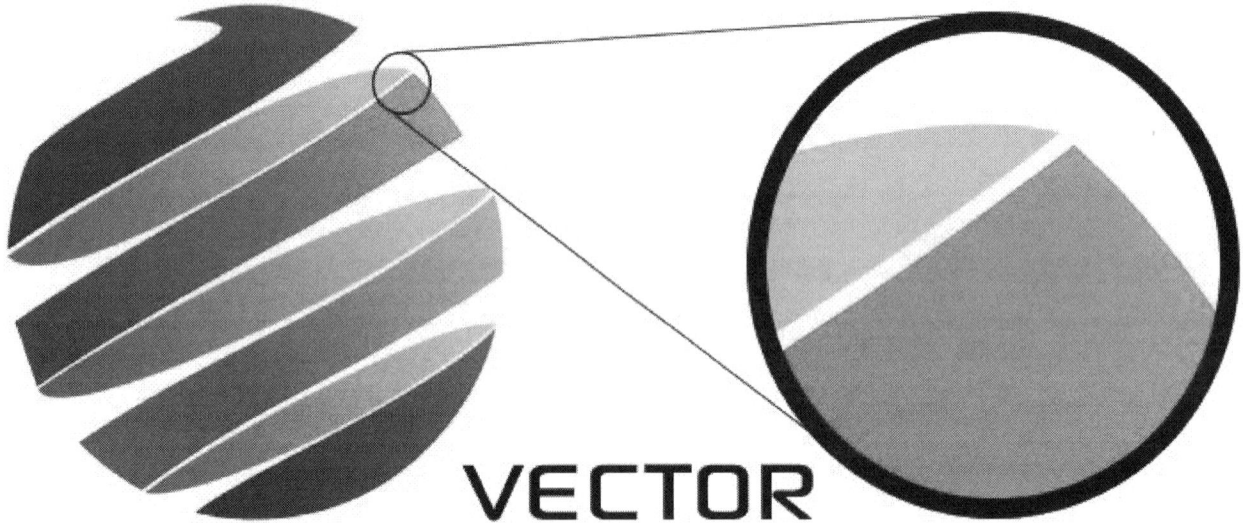

This scalability makes vector graphics ideal for logo design, where a single design must be adaptable to various sizes and mediums. Furthermore, vector graphics consume less disk space, load faster, and are easier to edit and manipulate, making them a preferred choice for designers.

2. WHAT IS INKSCAPE?

2.1 Understanding Vector Graphics

Vector graphics, the backbone of Inkscape's functionality, rely on paths, which are defined by a start and end point, along with other points, curves, and angles. These paths can be filled with colors, patterns, or gradients and outlined with strokes, giving designers immense creative freedom. The key advantage of vector graphics is their scalability; they can be enlarged or reduced without any loss of quality, making them ideal for a variety of applications, from small icons to large banners.

2.2 Key Features of Inkscape

Inkscape boasts an array of features that make it a standout choice in the realm of vector graphics:

- **Path Editing Tools:** Inkscape's path tool allows for the creation and modification of paths, giving users precise control over their designs.
- **Text Support:** It offers extensive text manipulation tools, supporting

various fonts and allowing text to follow along paths.
- **Filters and Extensions:** A wide range of filters and extensions are available, adding effects like blurs, textures, and more to enhance designs.
- **Layer Management:** Inkscape provides robust layer management, enabling complex compositions and easy manipulation of individual elements.
- **Bezier and Spiro Curves:** These tools allow for the creation of complex and smooth curves, essential for intricate designs.
- **Color Management:** Inkscape supports a variety of color models, including RGB and CMYK, for precise color matching in different media outputs.

2.3 Comparing Inkscape with Other Vector Graphics Software

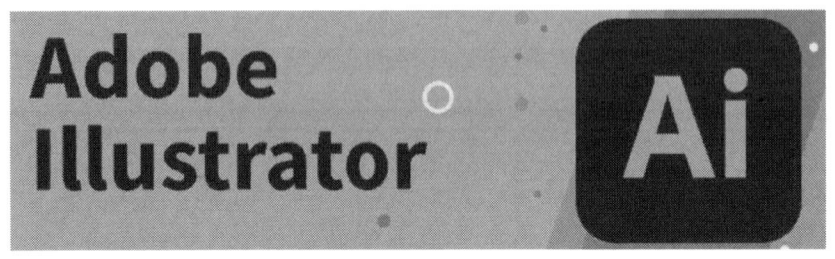

While Inkscape holds a significant position in the world of vector graphics, it's important to compare it with other software like Adobe Illustrator and CorelDRAW:

- **Adobe Illustrator:** A leading vector graphics software, Illustrator is known for its professional-grade tools and wide industry acceptance. However, it comes with a subscription-based pricing model.
- **CorelDRAW:** Another powerful vector editor, CorelDRAW is favored for its ease of use and extensive feature set, suitable for both graphic design and technical illustration.
- **Affinity Designer:** A newer competitor, Affinity Designer, offers a modern, intuitive interface and is gaining popularity for its one-time purchase model and professional capabilities.

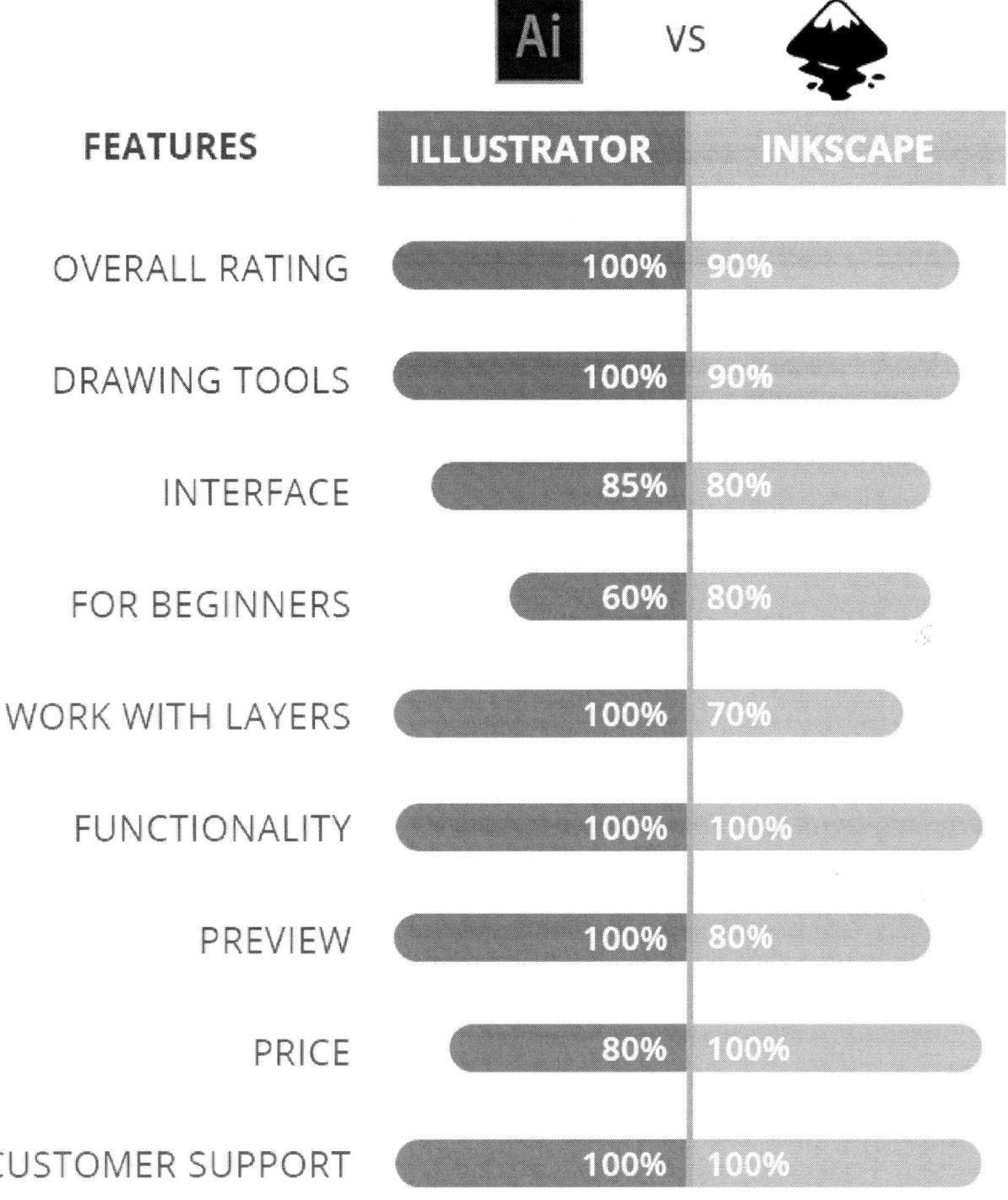

Each of these programs has its strengths, but Inkscape's open-source nature, zero-cost barrier, and a strong community of developers and users make it an accessible and continuously evolving tool, ideal for beginners and professionals alike.

3. DEVELOPMENT HISTORY

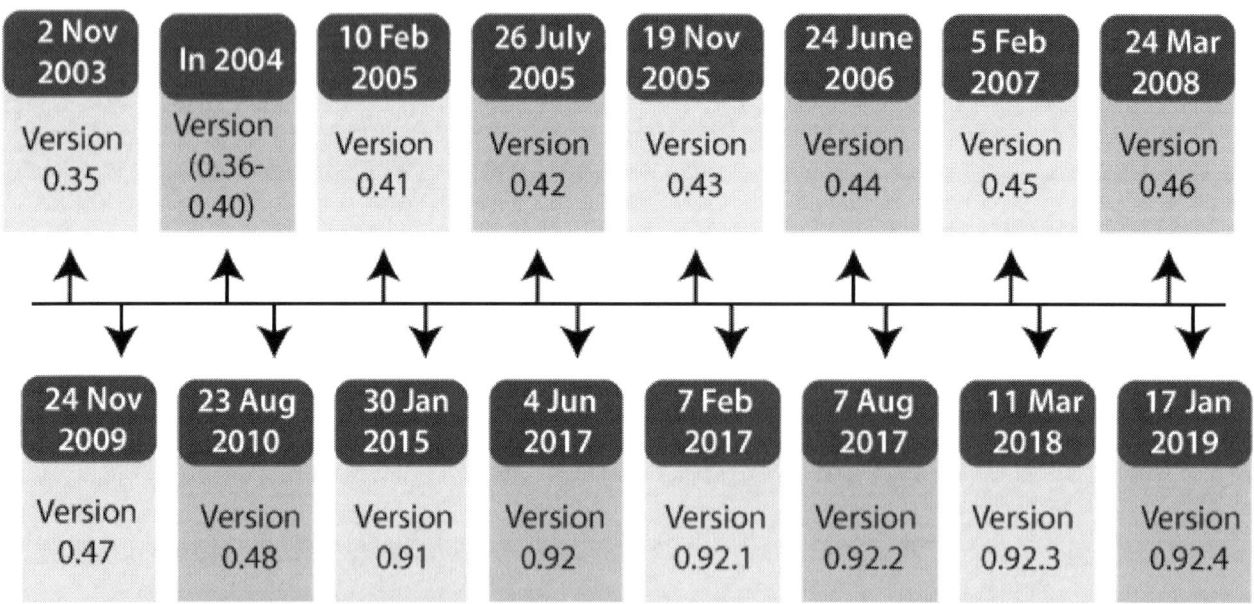

3.1 The Origins of Inkscape

Inkscape's journey began in the early 2000s, emerging from the ashes of Sodipodi, an earlier vector graphics project. The initial drive behind Inkscape's development was to create a fully compliant Scalable Vector Graphics (SVG) editor that was both accessible and open to contributions from a global community of developers. The founders of Inkscape, a group of software enthusiasts and artists, were motivated by the desire to provide a free, user-friendly alternative to the commercial vector editing software available at the time.

3.2 Major Milestones and Updates

Since its inception, Inkscape has undergone significant transformations, marked by key milestones and updates:

- **Initial Release (2003):** The first version of Inkscape was essentially a fork of Sodipodi, but with a stronger focus on SVG compliance and usability enhancements.
- **Version 0.42 (2005):** This release introduced the much-celebrated feature

of path stroking, allowing for more complex and creative vector illustrations.
- **Version 0.91 (2015):** This major update brought performance improvements, a new rendering engine, and the introduction of the much-needed feature of on-canvas gradient editing.
- **Version 1.0 (2020):** A landmark release, Inkscape 1.0, offered a native macOS version, hiDPI support, and a revamped user interface, making it more compatible and user-friendly across different platforms.

3.3 Community and Open Source Contribution

The development of Inkscape has been a testament to the power of community-driven software development. Volunteers from around the world have contributed to its codebase, documentation, translations, and user support. The open-source nature of the project ensures that anyone can contribute, leading to a diverse range of features and enhancements. Regular community meetings, open mailing lists, and participatory decision-making processes have fostered a vibrant and inclusive Inkscape community.

4. SUBSCRIPTION AND PURCHASE

Inkscape	Adobe Photoshop Plans	
Inkscape	Illustrator	All Apps
Free	$20.99/month	$52.99/month
Includes:	Includes:	Includes:
Flexible drawing tools	Step-by-step tutorials	Photoshop
Broad file format compatibility	100GB of cloud storage	10TB of cloud storage
Powerful text tool	Your own portfolio website	Collection of 20+ Apps: Adobe Portfolio, Adobe Fonts, and Adobe Spark with premium features.
Bezier and spiro curves.	Premium fonts.	
BUY NOW	BUY NOW	BUY NOW

4.1 Understanding the Free Software Model

Inkscape is a shining example of the free software model, where "free" refers to freedom rather than price. This model allows users to freely use, study, modify, and distribute the software. In contrast to proprietary software, free software like Inkscape is developed collaboratively, often by a community of users and developers who are motivated by the desire to create high-quality software accessible to everyone.

4.2 Optional Donations and Support

While Inkscape is free to download and use, the project relies on the support of its user community. Donations are encouraged and play a crucial role in sustaining the project. These funds are typically used for web hosting costs, development sprints, and outreach programs like workshops and conferences. Contributors also support Inkscape through code contributions, bug reporting, and participating in community discussions, which are equally valuable.

5. PRICE AND ACCESSIBILITY

5.1 The Cost-Free Nature of Inkscape

One of Inkscape's most significant advantages is its cost-free nature. Unlike many professional graphic design tools that come with high subscription fees, Inkscape offers a full suite of vector editing tools at no cost. This accessibility has made it a popular choice among students, hobbyists, and professionals who seek a budget-friendly yet powerful vector graphics tool.

5.2 Accessibility Features and Cross-Platform Availability

Inkscape's developers have continuously worked to make the software accessible to as many people as possible. This includes features like keyboard accessibility, high-contrast icons, and interface scaling for users with visual impairments. Furthermore, Inkscape's cross-platform availability means it can be used on Windows, macOS, and Linux, ensuring that no matter the user's operating system, they have access to a high-quality vector graphics tool.

6. INSTALLATION METHOD

Inkscape's popularity stems not only from its capabilities as a vector graphics editor but also from its accessibility across different operating systems. This chapter provides detailed installation guides for Windows, macOS, and Linux platforms, ensuring a smooth setup process for users of all technical levels.

6.1 Step-by-Step Installation Guide for Windows

System Requirements: Before installing Inkscape on Windows, ensure that your system meets the minimum requirements. A modern Windows OS (Windows 7 or later) and at least 2 GB of RAM are recommended for optimal performance.

Download Process:

1. Visit the official Inkscape website (inkscape.org) and navigate to the download section.
2. Select the version suitable for Windows. You will typically find options for a 32-bit or 64-bit installer. Choose the one that matches your system's architecture.
3. Click on the download link, and the installer file (.exe) will start downloading.

Installation Steps:

1. Once the download is complete, locate the .exe file and double-click on it to start the installation process.
2. A setup wizard will open. Follow the prompts, agreeing to the license terms and selecting the installation directory (the default location is usually sufficient).
3. Choose the components to install. For beginners, the standard installation options are recommended.
4. Click on the 'Install' button. The installation process will begin, copying files and configuring the settings.
5. Once the installation is complete, you can choose to launch Inkscape immediately or later. Click 'Finish' to close the installer.

Post-Installation Tips:

- It's advisable to restart your computer after installation.
- Upon first launch, Inkscape might take a few moments to initialize its libraries and settings.

6.2 Installation Guide for macOS

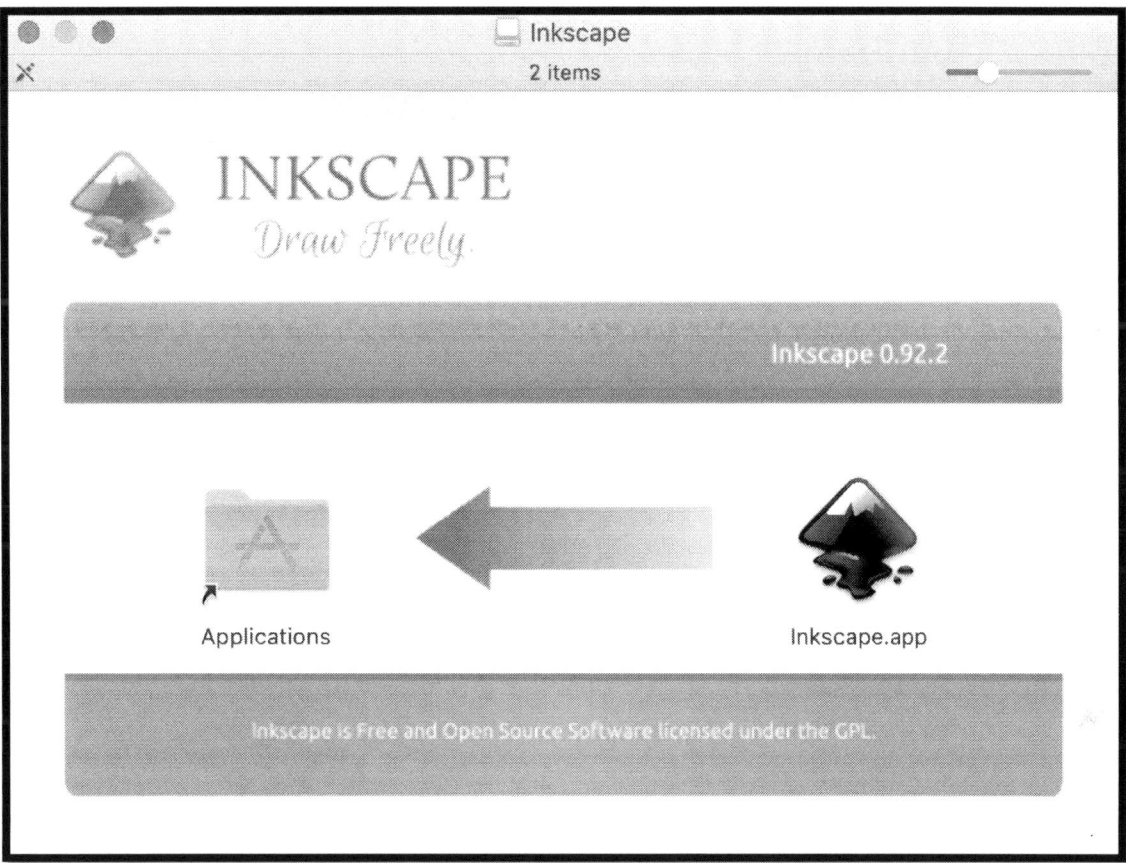

System Requirements: Ensure your Mac runs at least macOS 10.11 (El Capitan) or later. Additionally, having at least 4 GB of RAM will enhance performance.

Download Process:

1. Go to the Inkscape website's download section.
2. Select the macOS version. There will typically be a .dmg file for download.
3. Click the download link, and the file will start downloading to your 'Downloads' folder.

Installation Steps:

1. After downloading, find the .dmg file and double-click on it.
2. A new window will appear showing the Inkscape icon and the Applications folder.
3. Drag the Inkscape icon into the Applications folder. This action copies Inkscape into your Applications.

4. Wait for the copying process to complete, then eject the .dmg file by right-clicking and selecting 'Eject.'

Post-Installation Tips:

- The first time you run Inkscape, right-click on its icon in the Applications folder and choose 'Open' to bypass macOS security settings that block unrecognized apps.
- Some users may need to install XQuartz, an additional software that Inkscape depends on for macOS. If needed, Inkscape will prompt you to install it.

6.3 Setting up Inkscape on Linux

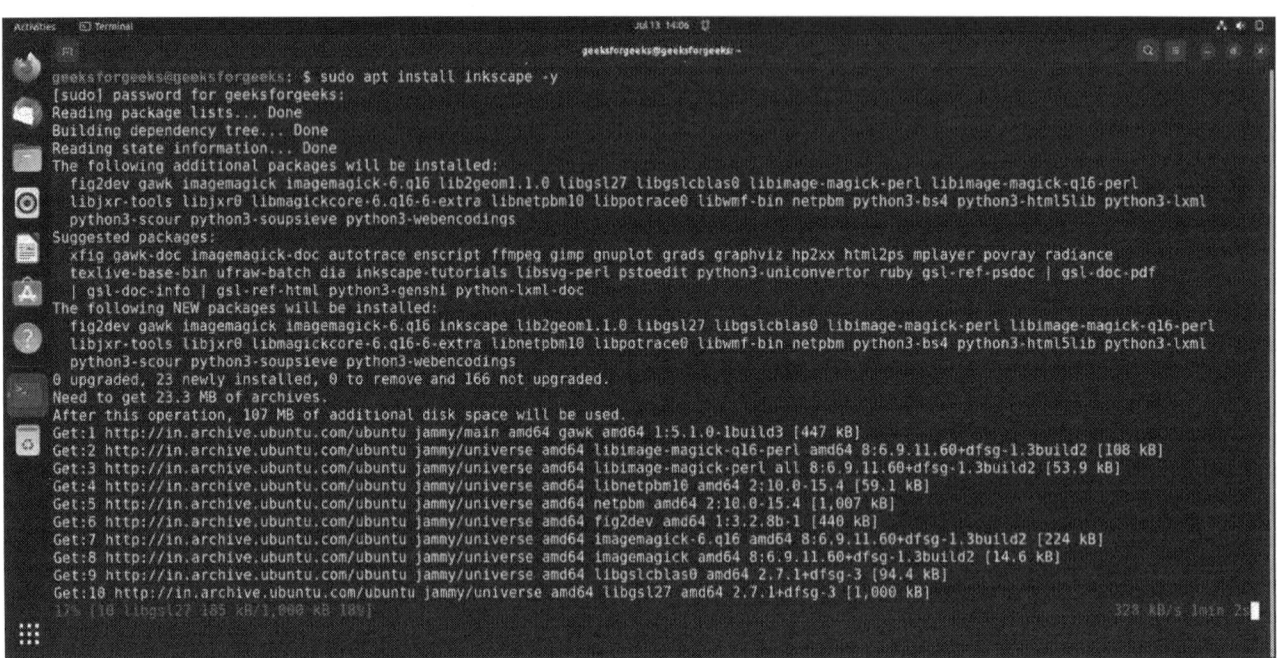

System Requirements: Most modern Linux distributions can run Inkscape. Having at least 2 GB of RAM and sufficient disk space for installation and working files is advisable.

Download Process:

1. Open your terminal.
2. Depending on your Linux distribution, you will use a package manager like APT (for Ubuntu, Debian) or YUM/DNF (for Fedora, CentOS). For instance, on Ubuntu, you would use sudo apt-get install inkscape.

Installation Steps:

1. In the terminal, input the installation command for your specific package manager and hit Enter.
2. You may need to enter your password to authorize the installation.
3. The terminal will download and install Inkscape. Follow any on-screen prompts to complete the installation.
4. Alternative Method: Some users prefer installing software through a GUI package manager or software center available in their Linux distribution. Inkscape can usually be found in these repositories, allowing for an installation process similar to installing apps on Windows or macOS.

Post-Installation Tips:

- After installation, Inkscape can be launched from your application menu or using the terminal.
- Ensure your system is up-to-date with the latest libraries that Inkscape might depend on.

7. DESIGN CONCEPT AND MINDSET

7.1 The Philosophy Behind Inkscape's Design

Inkscape's design philosophy is deeply rooted in the principles of open-source software and community collaboration. This ethos not only defines the development approach but also influences the user experience and functionality of the software. Key aspects of this philosophy include:

- **Accessibility and Inclusivity:** Inkscape aims to be accessible to users of all skill levels and backgrounds. This is reflected in its user-friendly interface, comprehensive tutorials, and active community support forums.
- **Freedom and Flexibility:** As an open-source tool, Inkscape offers users the freedom to modify and customize the software according to their needs. This flexibility encourages experimentation and innovation.
- **Community-Driven Development:** Inkscape evolves through the contributions of its user community. Features are often developed in response to user feedback, ensuring that the software continually adapts to the needs of its users.

7.2 Embracing the Creative Process with Inkscape

Inkscape is not just a tool; it's a medium through which artists and designers can express their creativity. To embrace the creative process with Inkscape, one must understand its potential:

- **Exploring Vector Graphics:** The power of Inkscape lies in its ability to create and manipulate vector graphics. Unlike raster graphics, vectors are scalable and versatile, making them ideal for logos, illustrations, and web graphics.
- **Experimentation:** Inkscape encourages users to experiment with its wide range of tools and features. Exploring different brushes, filters, and effects can lead to unique and surprising creative outcomes.
- **Workflow Integration:** Inkscape seamlessly integrates with other design tools and software, allowing for a fluid and flexible design workflow. This integration is crucial for professionals who use multiple tools in their work.

7.3 Tips for Beginners to Get Started

For beginners, starting with Inkscape can be both exciting and overwhelming. Here are some tips to ease the learning curve:

- **Familiarize with the Interface:** Spend time understanding the layout, toolbars, and menus. Knowing where things are and what they do is the first step in mastering Inkscape.
- **Start with Basic Projects:** Begin with simple projects like creating basic shapes and experimenting with colors and gradients. Gradually move on to more complex tasks.
- **Use Tutorials and Resources:** Inkscape has a vast array of tutorials available online. Utilize these resources to learn new techniques and tools.
- **Practice Regularly:** Like any skill, proficiency in Inkscape comes with practice. Regular use will increase your comfort level and enhance your skills.
- **Join the Community:** Engage with the Inkscape community through forums, social media groups, and local meetups. Learning from and contributing to the community can be incredibly rewarding.

8. FUTURE USE AND EXPECTATIONS

8.1 The Road Ahead for Inkscape

The future of Inkscape is closely tied to the evolving needs of its users and the broader trends in graphic design. Some anticipated developments include:

- **Enhanced Performance and Features:** Continuous improvement in performance, with more advanced features being added, is a constant goal. This includes better compatibility with different file formats and more sophisticated drawing tools.
- **Greater Integration with Other Tools:** As the design ecosystem becomes more interconnected, expect to see Inkscape integrating more seamlessly with other tools, both in terms of workflow and file compatibility.
- **Focus on User Experience:** User experience will remain a priority, with improvements aimed at making Inkscape more intuitive and easier to learn for new users.

8.2 Emerging Trends in Vector Graphics

The world of vector graphics is dynamic, with several emerging trends:

- **Mobile and Web Integration:** With the growing importance of mobile and web platforms, vector graphics tools are increasingly focusing on compatibility and optimization for these platforms.
- **AI and Machine Learning:** The integration of AI into vector graphics could revolutionize how designs are created, with possibilities for automated design suggestions, pattern generation, and more.
- **Augmented Reality (AR) and Virtual Reality (VR):** As AR and VR technologies mature, the demand for vector graphics in these domains is likely to increase, requiring tools like Inkscape to adapt and provide relevant features.

8.3 Preparing for Advanced Use

For users looking to advance their skills in Inkscape, preparation is key:

- **Master Advanced Tools and Features:** Gain proficiency in using advanced tools like Bezier curves, path effects, and extensions. Understanding these tools will open up new possibilities in your designs.
- **Stay Updated with New Versions:** Regularly update your Inkscape software to take advantage of new features and improvements.
- **Experiment with Different Styles and Techniques:** Don't be afraid to step out of your comfort zone. Trying new styles and techniques can lead to a deeper understanding of the software's capabilities.
- **Collaborate and Share Your Work:** Collaboration with other designers can provide new insights and feedback. Sharing your work with the community can also lead to opportunities and constructive criticism.

In summary, this chapter delves into the philosophy and mindset behind using Inkscape, offering guidance for beginners and insights into future trends and advanced use. The focus is on fostering a deep understanding of Inkscape's capabilities and how users can harness its full potential to enhance their creative endeavors.

Chapter 2: Getting Started with Inkscape

The Inkscape Interface

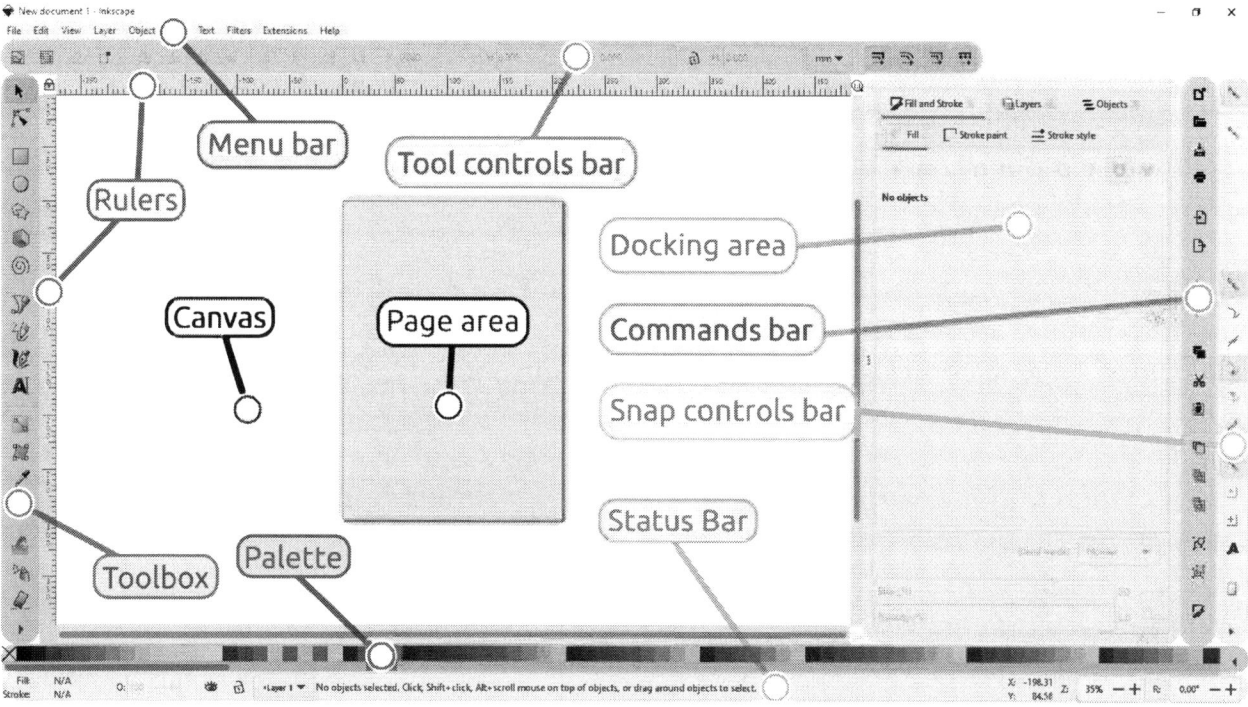

The main window of Inkscape is seen above. The Main Menu bar is located at the top of the window and includes the standard File, Edit, and View menus as well as choices particular to vector graphics, such as Layer, Object, Path, Text, and Effects. There are several excellent tutorials available through the Help menu.

The Commands Bar is located underneath the main menu bar. In contrast to the main menu bar, it offers many of the same operations but in a button style. The Tool Controls Bar is located underneath the Commands Bar and offers you commands specific to the tool that is presently chosen in the toolbox.

The Toolbox is located on the left side of the main window. The buttons in the Toolbox provide you access to the available vector drawing tools. The Select Tool, which is used to select regions and objects, is located at the top of the Toolbox. The Node/Handle tool, which is used to choose and manage nodes and handles, is located below that.

Along with tools to generate calligraphic lines, text, and gradients, the Toolbox also includes icons for drawing various shapes, lines, and curves. Experimenting with these tools is the greatest approach to learn how to use them.

The Drawing Area, which shows the Page border, is at the window's center. The rulers, which let you keep track of where you are drawing, are located at the top and left of the drawing area. Drawing outside the page border is not prohibited.

You may extend your drawing past the edge. I frequently set items, such as drawing components, outside the boundary and then pull them within as needed. However, just the portion of your design that is within the page border will be included in the picture if you choose to export it as a bitmap.

The Palette is located at the bottom of the window. You may alter an object's fill or stroke color using the Palette. The Status bar, which is located below the Palette, has buttons for changing the Fill and Stroke, choosing the Layer, setting the Zoom, and it has a Notification Area with information and support for the current activity.

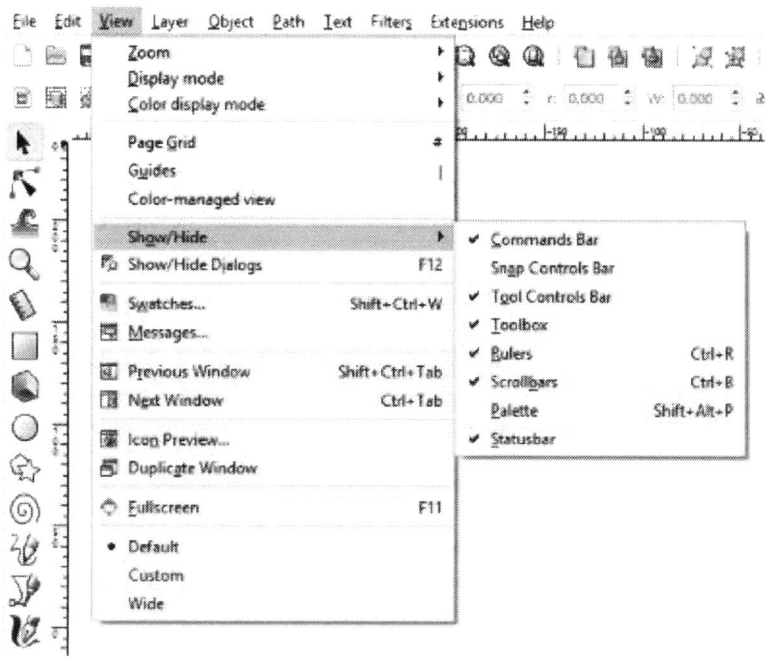

Some individuals enjoy having access to every toolbar on the user interface. This appeals to application designers since it demonstrates the application's strength. Some individuals prefer having as few toolbars as possible displayed because they think they clog up the user interface. I have precise preferences for which toolbars to display, and you can change this by choosing Show/Hide from the View menu.

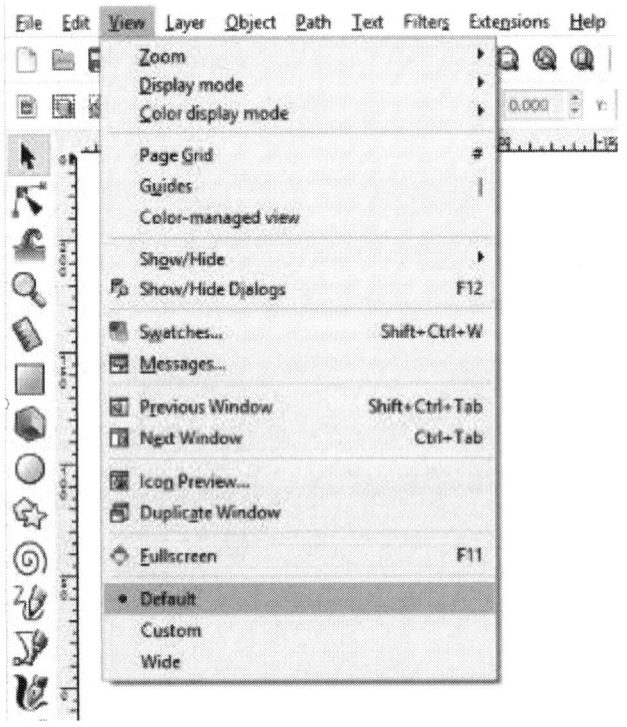

You have some control over the toolbar placements using Inkscape. Select the Default, Custom, or Wide toolbar layouts from the option at the bottom of the View window.

Snap Controls Bar is located vertically on the right side, above the Default Commands Bar and Tool Controls Bar.

Custom Horizontal toolbars at the top for all three.

At the top, there is a horizontal Wide Controls Bar, and to the right, a vertical Tool Controls Bar and Snap Controls Bar.

Inkscape Navigation

Drawing using Inkscape will be challenging if you aren't comfortable with zooming and panning around the drawing area. To assist acquire accustomed zooming and panning you need first sketch a basic form.

Select the rectangles and squares tool from the Toolbox on the left side of the window. Next, position the mouse pointer someplace along the page's edge. Then, while continuing to hold down the left mouse button, move the mouse to create a rectangle. Pull back on the mouse button.

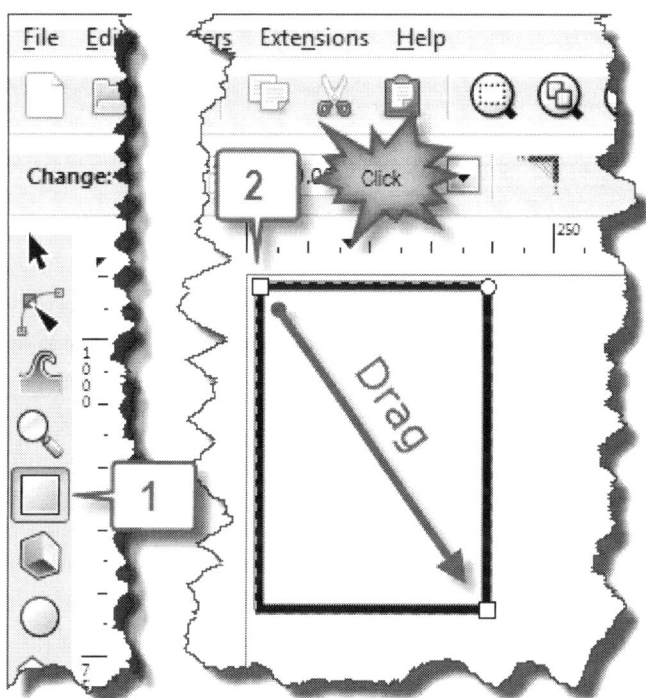

You should have drawn a square as shown above. Of course you can't readily operate at this size. To undertake intricate work, you may need to zoom in on a section of the drawing. Inkscape has several options to zoom. The quickest and easiest way to zoom is to use the keyboard [+] key to zoom in, or press the keyboard [-] key to zoom out.

The difficulty with keyboard zoom is that you zoom into the center of your viewing area, and the exact region that you want to zoom into may not be at the center. The way that you'll probably utilize most is the Toolbox Zoom tool. Click on the Zoom tool and drag a box around the area you wish to zoom into. Inkscape will zoom in on the region inside the box.

You don't actually need to drag a box to zoom, just simply move the Zoom tool pointer to the region that you want to zoom in on and click the left mouse button. To zoom out, move the Zoom tool cursor to the place where you wish to zoom out, then click the right mouse button.

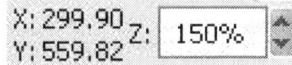

If, for any reason, you need to zoom to a certain level, like 150% zoom, you may utilize the Zoom control situated on the right side of the toolbar positioned at the bottom of the Inkscape window. Click on an up/down arrows to change the precise amount of zoom you want, or write the required zoom level into the control's input box.

Another procedure that will make sketching simpler is panning. Inkscape includes several options to pan the drawing area. The simplest basic approach to pan the drawing is to utilize the scrollbars. Similar to other programs, you may utilize the wheel on your mouse for scrolling up or down. Press and hold the [Shift] key to utilize the wheel on your mouse for scrolling left or right.

If you like using the keyboard [+] key to zoom in, and the [-] key to zoom out, you might also want to scroll by holding down the keyboard [Ctrl] key while hitting one of the arrow keys.

Chapter 3: Fundamental Shapes and Transformations

Basic Shapes

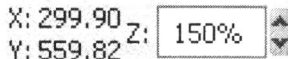

When you open a new Inkscape drawing, the zoom level is set at 35% by default. The first thing I do with any new Inkscape design is utilize the Zoom control found on the right side of the toolbar placed at the bottom of the Inkscape window to set the zoom level to 100%. I just type 100 into the control's input field.

Since, on the Internet, I find numerous complaints about fresh Inkscape drawings starting at 35% zoom rather than 100% zoom, I suppose practically everybody has to make this modification to begin a drawing. Some sites suggest you can get new drawing to open at 100% zoom by default by modifying a template included in the install directory of Inkscape.

Note: While drawing a basic form, you may find that the shape is not an outline but instead a filled shape, or the shape's outline may be a color other than black, or the outline may be dashed or dotted or thicker than the picture. This is because Inkscape has a huge number of configuration parameters and one or more of them is influencing your artwork. This would most likely be caused by a Fill and Stroke setting. You can't learn everything in one instant. My objective is to teach you in a rational step-by-step method. So if the form has some of the impacts indicated, you may either disregard it, or skip ahead in the text to the paragraph about Filling Shapes and Areas.

Squares and Rectangles

▫

Click on the Create rectangles and squares tool in the Toolbox on the left side of the window after adjusting the zoom level. Next, position the mouse pointer someplace along the page's edge. Then, while continuing to hold down the left mouse button, move the mouse to create a rectangle. Pull back on the mouse button.

When the Create rectangles and squares tool is chosen, the cursor in the screenshot above will be the mouse pointer.

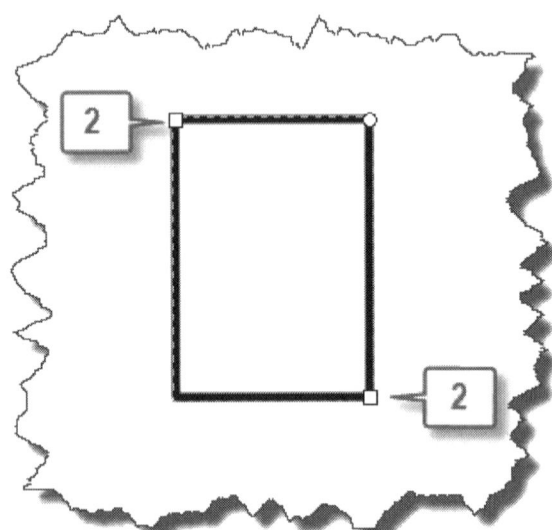

The real rectangle will display the nodes (small boxes on its corners> shown above. To reshape the rectangle position the cursor on one of the square nodes, press and hold the left mouse button and, while holding down the mouse button, drag the mouse to reshape the rectangle.

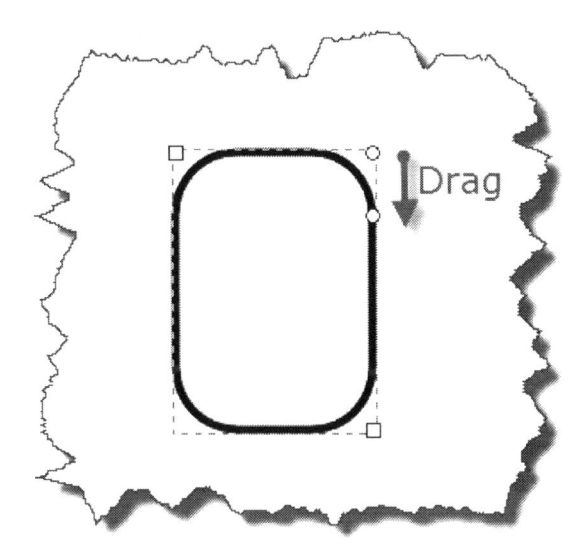

You might be shocked to learn that dragging the round node enables the rectangle to have rounded edges in the upper-right corner.

You can make a perfect square if you press and hold the [Ctrl] key on your keyboard while sketching a rectangle. The form will abruptly change to a new ratio, such as a 2 to 1 ratio or 3 to 1 ratio rectangle, if you move the node too far out of square.

Circles, Ellipses, and Arcs

You may draw circles, ellipses, and arcs with the Create circles, ellipses, and arcs tool. In the toolbox, select the Create circles, ellipses, and arcs tool.

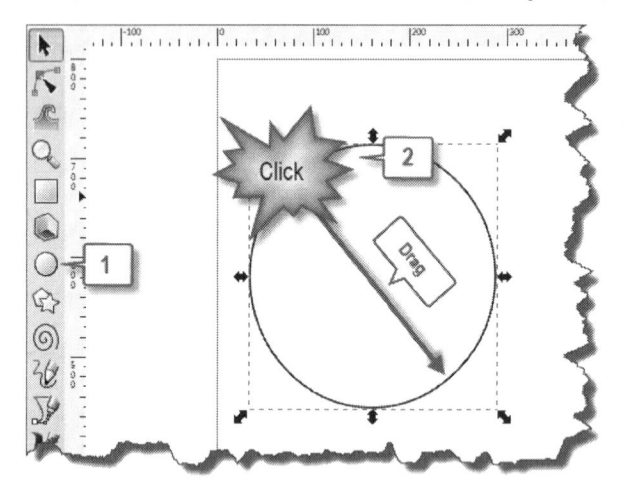

Press and hold the left mouse button while dragging the mouse cursor in the Inkscape drawing area. To finish the ellipse, let go of the left mouse button. After you let off of the left mouse button, the ellipse should still be chosen and surrounded in a rectangle. Two tiny square handles and one tiny circle handle will be on the rectangle.

In Inkscape, handles may only be added to selected objects. Click anywhere on the ellipse after selecting the Edit pathways by nodes tool if the item is not already chosen. When the tool to Edit pathways by nodes is chosen, The mouse cursor will change into a skinny arrow. Press and hold the left mouse button while dragging the tiny square handle with the arrow tip on it. Pull back on the mouse button.

The width of the ellipse may be altered using one of the little square knobs. The second little square handle is used to change the ellipse's height.

You may make a complete circle by holding down the [Ctrl] key on your keyboard while sketching an ellipse. Up until you move the node too far from the center, at which point the form will suddenly change to an ellipse with a ratio of about 2:1 or 3:1.

Drawing an Arc

You may make an arc with the little circle handle. The tiny circle handle really consists of two identical small circle handles stacked on top of one another. Drag one of the little circle handles off the top of the other one to form an arc. This is tough, though:

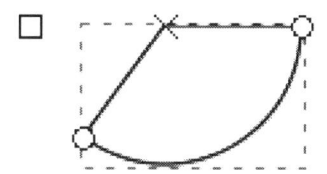

The arc will be a closed wedge with sides that extend to the center of the ellipse if you click on a tiny circle handle and then slide the mouse cursor slightly outside the curve while holding down the mouse button.

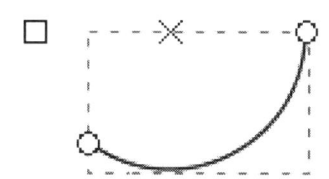

The arc will be an open arc with no discernible sides if you click on a tiny circle handle and then drag the mouse while continuing to hold down the mouse button.

I find you have to zoom in close and arrange the arc handles precisely on top of each other in order to get rid of them if you accidentally drag a little circle handle, which causes the arc sides to show.

Stars and Polygons

You may draw stars and polygons with the Stars and polygons tool. In the toolbox, select the Stars and polygons tool.

In essence, the Stars and polygons tool produces polygons. A star is a concave polygon in Inkscape, whereas a polygon is a convex polygon. This is the key distinction between the two shapes. In any scenario, you'll need to set up this tool's Tool Controls Bar, which gives you access to commands for the tool that is presently chosen in the toolbox.

You must first decide whether you want a polygon or a star in the Stars and Polygons Tool Controls Bar. If you choose polygon, the number of sides for your polygon will be determined by the Corners: spin box. The Corners: spin box will determine the number of points your star will have if you choose star.

The Spoke ratio: spin box in the star setting controls the depth of the star's points, which can range from 0.010 to 1.000; the lower the value, the deeper the points. The corners' roundness is determined by the Rounded: spin box.

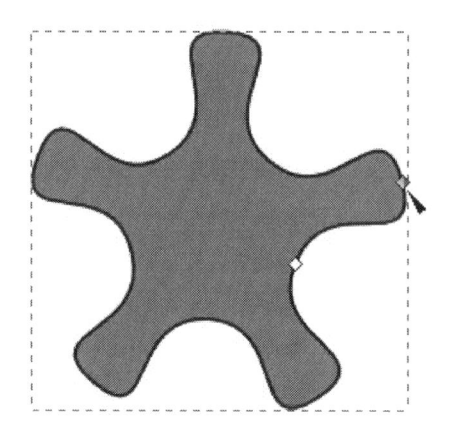

Shown above is a star with 6 corners, Spoke ratio: set to 0.200, Rounded: set to 0.450.

In the polygon setting, the Randomized: spin box randomizes the placement of the polygon's vertexes.

Shown above is a polygon with 6 sides, Randomized: set to 1.767. If you click on the Edit pathways by nodes button in the toolbox, a little square node box will emerge near the polygon. If you drag this node, even the tiniest, the polygon will go insane.

If you need some ideas for abstract painting, playing with the Stars and polygons Tool Controls Bar can supply you with limitless concepts, however I don't see this being useful in reqular sketching.

Spirals

With the Create spirals tool you'll need to configure the Tool Controls Bar which gives you with instructions linked to the presently chosen tool in the toolbox.
In the Create Spirals Tool Controls Bar, the spins: spin box sets the number of spins the spiral will have. The Divergence: spin box sets separation of the turns. When set to 1, the spacing of the turns will be uniform. The smaller the number, the greater the spacing of the turns towards the center of the spiral. The higher the number the larger the spacing between the turns on the exterior of the spiral. Setting the Inner radius: spin box seems to subtract turns from the center of the spiral.

Shown above is a spiral with Turns: set to 5.00, Divergence: set to 1.000, and Inner radius: set to 0.500.

You may assume that you would get little use out of the Create spirals tool, but fact spirals are fairly prevalent in nature, for example a snails shell or the arrangement of seeds in a sunflower head. Drawing spirals or organizing objects in a spiral would be incredibly difficult without this tool.

Rotation and Transform

You've previously learnt how to draw a rectangle in an earlier phase. This time, in the Toolbox on the left side of the window, click on the select and transform objects tool. Then locate the mouse pointer somewhere within the rectangle that you made and click the left mouse button.

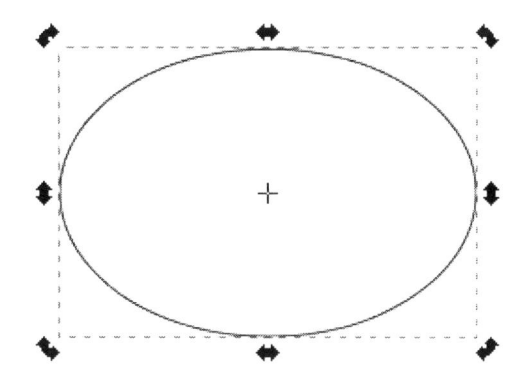

The rectangle will be picked, as evidenced by the appearance of selected handles on the edges and corners of the rectangle. Once an item is selected, Inkscape pays it complete attention to that object, and most instructions that you provide will be applied to the selected object. If you position your mouse cursor within a chosen item, the move cross will appear with the pointer. While the move cross is displayed, you may press and hold the left mouse button to drag the item to a new spot.

If you set your mouse cursor within a selected item and the move cross is visible, you may hit the right mouse button to see a popup menu of actions that you can apply to that selected object.

Rotation

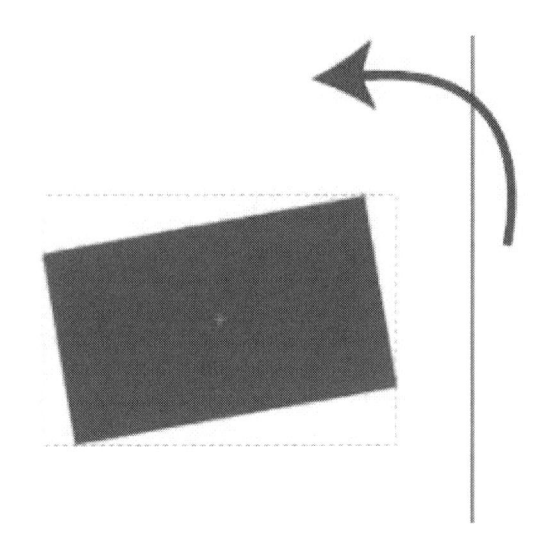

The rotate handles will show up if you click on an item that is already chosen. You can rotate the rectangle by positioning the mouse pointer on one of the corner rotate handles, pressing and holding the left mouse button, and dragging. This only works while the rotate handles are visible.

Object Menu

| Object | Path | Text | Filters | Extensions | He |

	Fill and Stroke...	Shift+Ctrl+F
	Object Properties...	Shift+Ctrl+O
	Symbols...	Shift+Ctrl+Y
	Group	Ctrl+G
	Ungroup	Shift+Ctrl+G
	Clip	▶
	Mask	▶
	Pattern	▶
	Objects to Marker	
	Objects to Guides	Shift+G
	Raise	Page Up
	Lower	Page Down
	Raise to Top	Home
	Lower to Bottom	End
	Rotate 90° CW	
	Rotate 90° CCW	
	Flip Horizontal	H
	Flip Vertical	V
	Unhide All	
	Unlock All	
	Transform...	Shift+Ctrl+M
	Align and Distribute...	Shift+Ctrl+A
	Arrange...	

The *Object* selection in the main menu gives you a large choice of functions that you can apply to a selected object, including *Rotate 90 degrees CW>*, *Rotate 90 degrees CCW, Flip Horizontal, Flip Vertical,* or *Transform*.

Transform

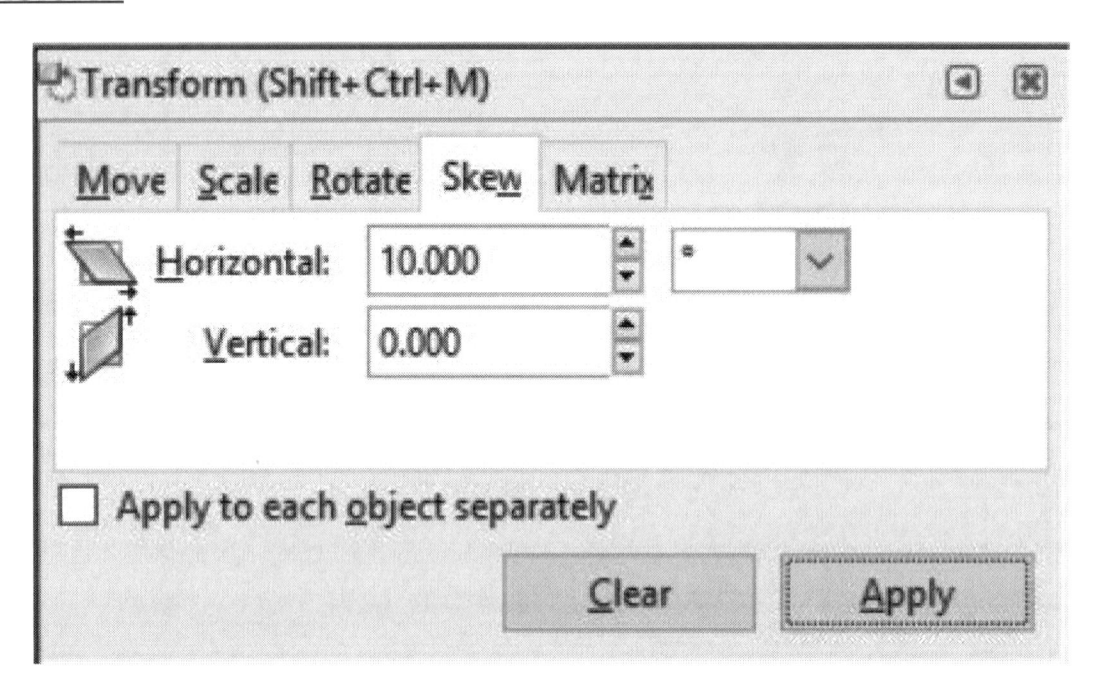

If you choose *Transform*, the *Transform dialog box* will appear. Transforms are an extremely powerful way of modifying the shape of objects. That's an advanced subject that we'll get into at a later time.

Fill and Stroke

For now, let's select the rectangle, place the mouse pointer inside, and press the right mouse button to open the popup menu of commands that you can apply to that selected object. In that menu, select *Fill and Stroke....* This will open the *Fill and Stroke* dialog box.

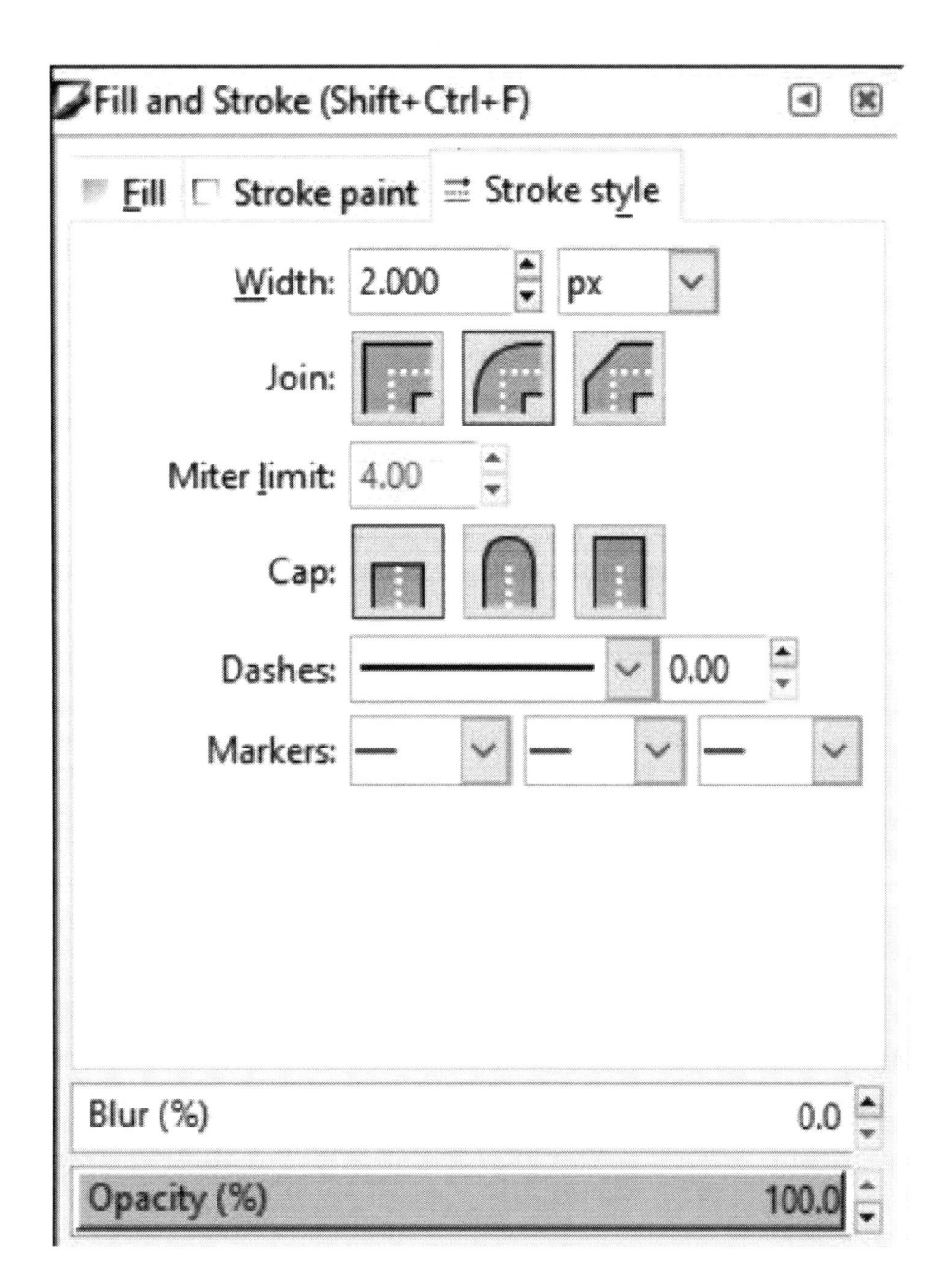

The *Fill and Stroke* dialog box lets us set many visual aspects of the selected object. For example if we select the *Stroke style* tab and change the *width* form 1.000 to 2.000, the width of the rectangle's border will increase.

Edit Paths

One last thing I want to cover is the *Edit paths by nodes* tool. In the *Toolbox* on the left side of the window, click on the *Edit paths by nodes* tool. Then locate the mouse pointer somewhere within the rectangle that you drew and click the left mouse button.

This will cause the rectangle's nodes to be selected. With the *node* tool pointer over the round node in the upper-right corner of the dialog box, press the left mouse button and drag the node downward away from the corner.

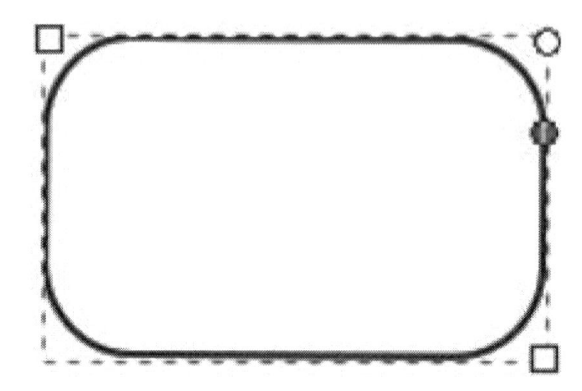

This will allow you to adjust the roundness of the rectangles corners. This method adjusts all four corners equally, you can not set separate radius for each corner. At least not with this method.

You can do quite a bit of ellipse shaping with the *Select and transform objects* tool. Select the *Select and transform objects* tool in the toolbox and then click on the ellipse. Eight double-arrow handles will appear. You can drag one of those handles to change the size of the ellipse.

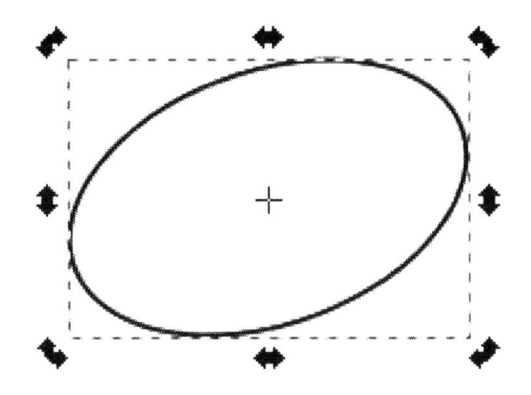

If you click on the edge of the ellipse, the four corner double-arrow handles of the ellipse container box will change into rotation handles. Click on one of the rotation handles, and while holding down the mouse button, drag the handle. This way you can rotate the ellipse.

Of course there are many more things you can do with circles, ellipses, and arcs. But this gives you the basic method of creating and control their size and shape.

Chapter 4: Mastering Paths and Curves

Basic Paths

Inkscape provides tools for drawing standard shapes like rectangles and squares, circles ellipses and arcs, and stars and polygons. In this article, we'll focus on the tools for drawing paths. A path is basically a straight or curved line, or line containing a combination of straight and curved parts. The path drawing tools are the *Freehand* tool, the *Calligraphic* tool, and the *Bezier* tool.

The *Freehand* tool is selected by clicking on the toolbar's "pencil" icon. To start a freehand path, press the mouse button in the drawing area to start your path, while holding down the mouse button drag the mouse to create the desired shape, double click to end the path. While the path is still selected, select the toolbar's *Node* tool.

Clicking on the Node tool will cause the path's nodes to become visible. Click on one of the nodes and that node's control handles will become visible.

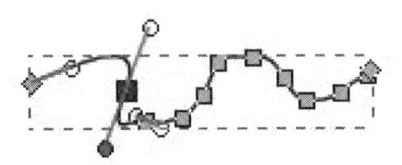

Use the mouse to drag a node, or to move a control handle to reshape the path.

The Calligraphic Tool

The *Calligraphic* tool is selected by clicking on the toolbar's "fountain pen" icon. To start a calligraphic path, press the mouse button in the drawing area to start your path, while holding down the mouse button drag the mouse to create the desired shape, double click to end the path.

To select a path, click on the toolbar's *Select*" tool. With the path selected, clicking on the node tool will make the calligraphic path's nodes visible.

Note that a calligraphic path consists of two paths with a fill area between them. The basic method of shaping a calligraphic path is the same as with a freehand path. Click on one of the nodes and that nodes control handles will become visible. Then use the mouse to drag a node, or to move a control handle to reshape the path.

As interesting as the freehand tool and the calligraphic tool are, they have only limited use. You could create an entire drawing, or a large part of a drawing, with one large freehand path. But then you would be spending a long time moving nodes and adjusting control handles to make the drawing look smooth.

Bezier Curve Tool

CONTENTS

To make nice neat drawings you'll find the *Bezier Curve* tool to be the most useful. For that reason, in this article I'll focus on creating vector drawings with the Bezier Curve Tool.

A "bezier curve" is a curved line whose shape is based on a mathematical formula. Bezier curves are great for drawing because they create nice smooth curves. fortunately, to use bezier curves in Inkscape, we don't need to know anything about mathematics. We control the formula's variables visually by using the mouse to drag the paths nodes and control handle.

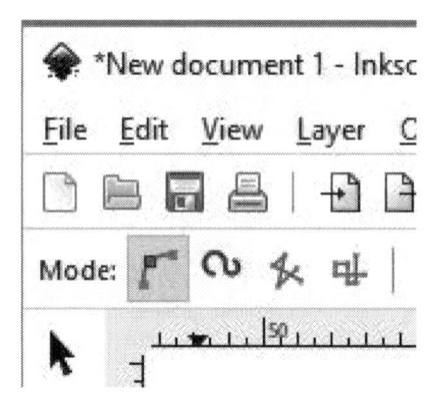

• When you select the *Bezier Curve Tool*, the *Tool Controls Bar* will change to provide you with controls related to the Bezier Curve Tool. The first control on the left side of the Controls Bar sets the *mode* of the Bezier Curve Tool. This control is more of an annoyance than useful because if you accidentally set any button other than the first one; "Create regular Bezier path", you will not be able to shape your Bezier curve line and will have no clue as to why not. Just be aware to check this control if you have a problem.

Select the bezier tool by clicking on the toolbar's "pen" icon. To start a bezier curve, press the left mouse button in the drawing area, while holding down the mouse button drag the mouse to create a short line, release the mouse button to end the line, then move the mouse a bit to the side and double-click to end the bezier curve.

- If you single-click to end the bezier curve, Inkscape will start a new bezier curve beginning at the end of the previous curve. This is fine if you are an experienced vector artist, but this article is for beginners.

While the path is still selected, select the toolbar's node tool. Note: if a path loses the selection, you can always click on the toolbar's select tool and drag a box around the path to select it. With the node tool selected to make the paths nodes and control handle visible, use the mouse to drag a node, or to move a control handle to reshape the path.

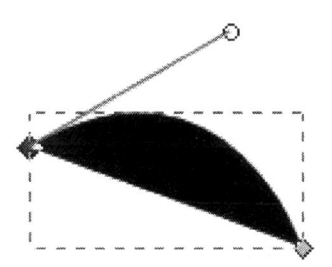

Note that the bezier curve shown above is filled with the color black. We can understand the bezier curve better if we remove the fill. To remove the fill, while the path is selected, choose *Object | Fill and stroke...* in the main menu. In the *Fill and Stroke* dialog box that appears, select the *Fill* tab, and set R, G, and B to 255. Set A to 00.

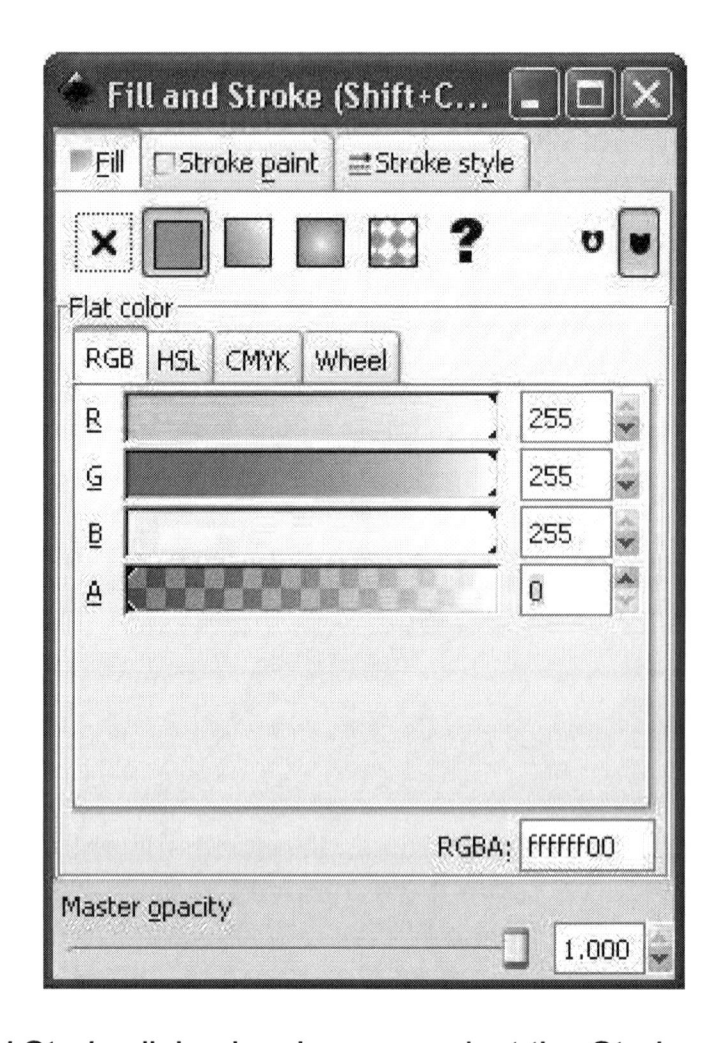

While the *Fill and Stroke* dialog box is open, select the *Stroke paint* tab, and make sure the R, G, and B controls are set to 0, and *Master opacity* is set to 1.000. Then click on the red [x] button to close the dialog box.

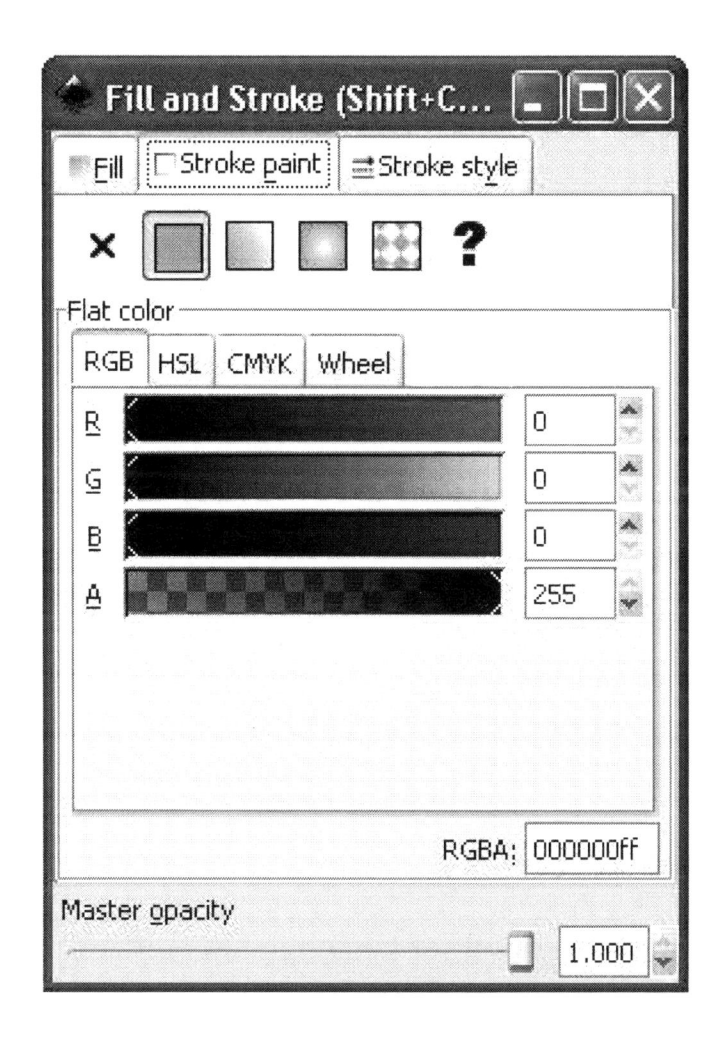

Now, with the fill color gone, you can use the mouse to drag a node, or to move a control handle to see how to control the shape of a bezier curve. The path shown above is the same bezier curve as before. By moving a node and the control handle, I have made it into an entirely different curve.

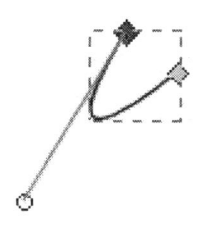

Add or Delete a Node

CONTENTS

Add a New Node on a Segment

To add a new node on a segment use the *Insert new nodes* button on the *Edit path nodes* tool control bar. These steps assume that you have already drawn a segment e.g. using the *Bezier Curves and straight lines tool*.

1. Click on the *Edit path nodes* tool button and then click on the segment to select the segment.

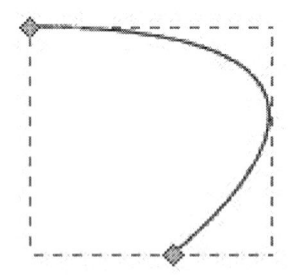

2. Drag a box around the segment (or two adjacent nodes on the segment) to select both nodes.

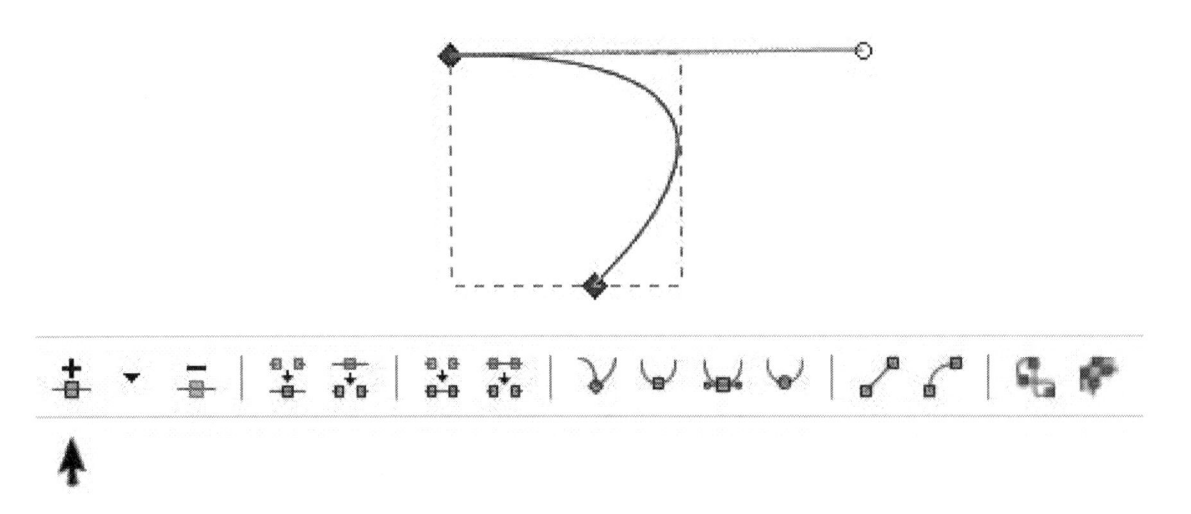

3. Click on the *Insert new nodes* button on the tool bar to insert a new node between the two selected nodes.

44

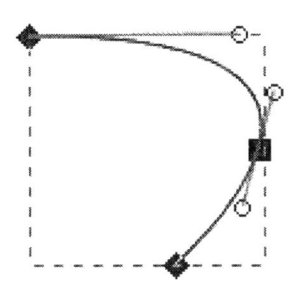

- Clicking on the *Insert new nodes* button with three nodes selected will add two new nodes to the segment between the three selected nodes. Clicking on the *Insert new nodes* button with four nodes selected will add three new nodes to the segment between the four selected nodes, and so on.

- Immediately after creating a new node, while it's still selected, you may as well click on the menu button to change it to a *corner node*, which is more flexible than the default *symmetric* node, which can be used to avoid kinks in your multi-segment lines.

Delete a Node on a Path

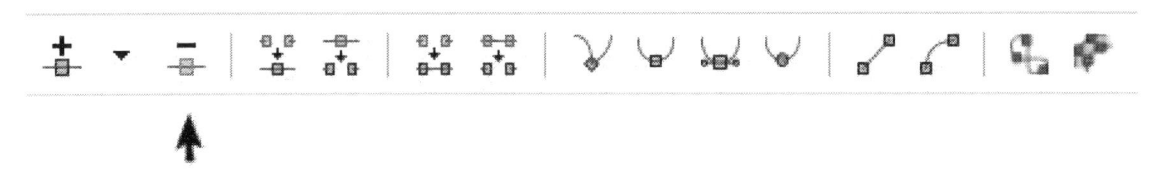

To delete a node on a path, again click on the *Edit path nodes* tool button and then click on the object to display the nodes. Click on the specific note you wish to delete, and then on the *Edit path nodes* tool *Tool Controls Bar* click on the *Delete selected nodes* icon.

Add or Delete a Segment

CONTENTS

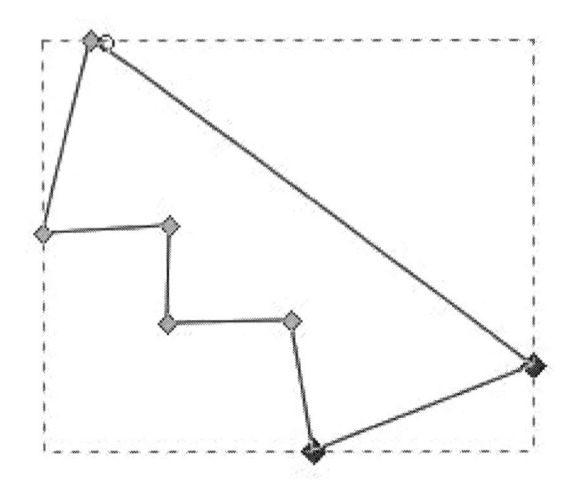

To delete a segment of a path, in the toolbar select the *Edit paths by nodes* tool. Click on one node of the segment to select it. Press and hold the keyboard [Shift] key and click on the other node of the segment to select it.

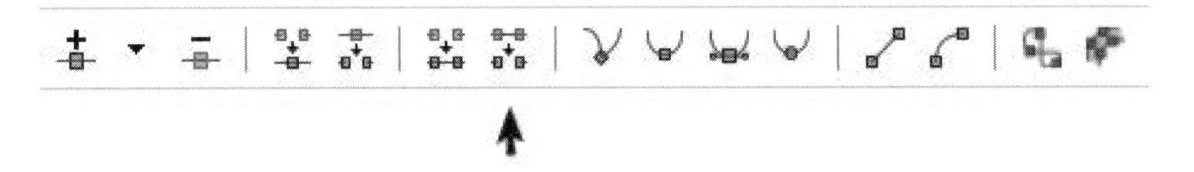

With both nodes selected, in the *Edit paths by nodes Controls Bar*, click on the *Delete segment between two non-endpoint nodes* icon. The segment will be deleted.

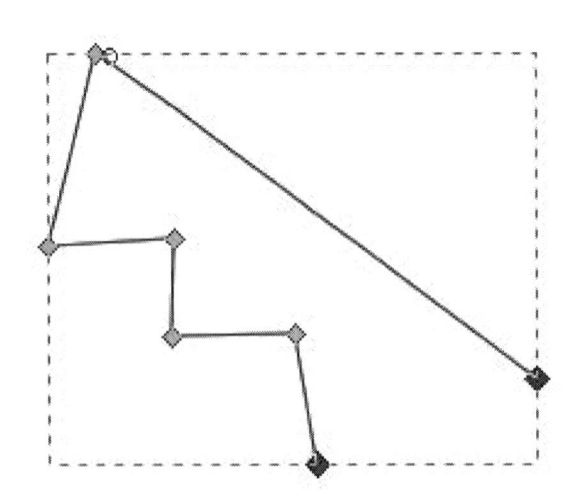

To add a segment to a path, in the toolbar select the *Edit paths by nodes* tool. Click on the node where you want of the segment to select it. Press and hold the keyboard [Shift] key and click on the other node where you want the segment to select it.

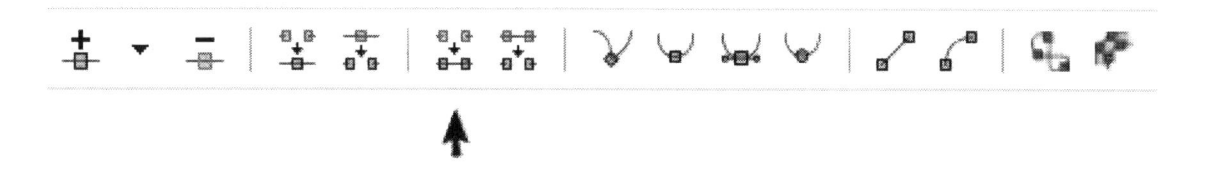

With both nodes selected, in the *Edit paths by nodes Controls Bar*, click on the *Join selected endnodes with a new segment* icon. A segment will be added between the selected nodes.

Join Two Segments

CONTENTS

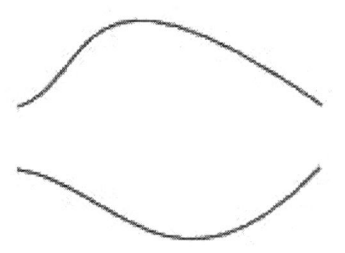

To combine two different paths into one path, you need to join the endnode of one path to the endnode of the other path. To join two endnodes, overlap the two endnodes on top of each other, then combine the paths, then join the endnodes. These steps assume that you have already drawn two line segments e.g. using the *Bezier Curves and straight lines tool*.

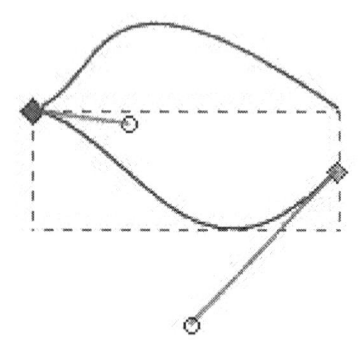

1. Use the *Edit path nodes* tool to overlap the endnode of one path on top of the endnode of the other path. The more accurately they overlap the more successful the node joining will be. You may need to zoom in to get greater accuracy.

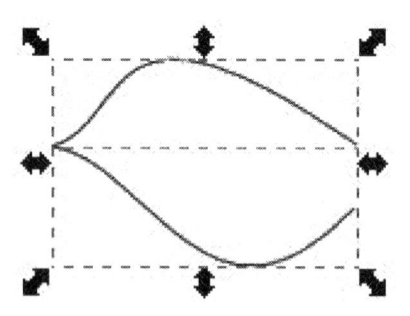

2. Use the *Select objects* tool to draw a box around both segments.

3. In the main menu select *Path | Combine*.

4. With the combined segments still selected, click on the *Edit path nodes* tool to display all nodes in both segments.

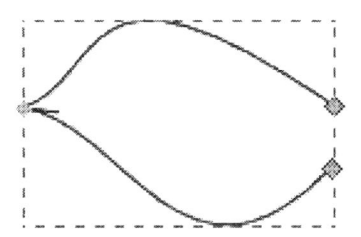

5. With the *Edit path nodes* tool still selected, draw a box around the nodes that you want to join. (The box outline may not appear, but the endnodes have been selected).

6. Click on the *Join selected endnodes* button in the toolbar.

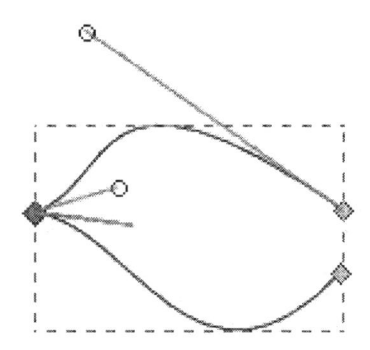

- The *Join selected endnodes* button almost never properly joins two endnodes, no mater how accurately you overlap both endnodes (even if you set snap to grid). It almost always joins the two endnodes with a new segment, as if the *Join selected endnodes* was wired to the same function as the *Join selected endnodes with a new segment* button. The solution is to, after joining the nodes, delete one of the nodes.

7. With the *Edit path nodes* tool selected, click on the "joined" node and click on the *Delete selected nodes* button.

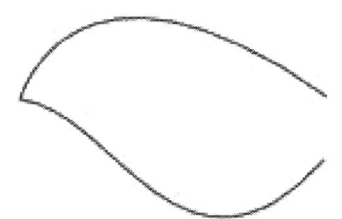

The two segments will now be properly joined.

Chapter 5: Colors and Gradients

The RGB Color Model

Although the color wheel is the easiest way to select a color, it's the most difficult way to exactly specify a color. To exactly specify a color, you have to use an *RGB triplet*. An RGB triplet specifies a color based upon the amounts of red, green, and blue, on a scale from 0 to 255, required to create the color. For example, to create the color cornflowerblue you need red=100, green=149, and blue=237. Shown below is the RGB triplet for the color cornflowerblue.

6495ED

You are probably wondering what happened to the 100,149,237. Well, graphics programs often specify numbers using the *hexadecimal* number system. That's because that's how computers store numbers in their memory. One byte of memory (four bits) can store 16 different values. Whereas the decimal numbering system uses the characters 0 through 9 to get 10 different values, the hexadecimal numbering system uses the characters 0 through f to get 16 different values. (After 9 the characters a, b, c, d, e and f are used, as shown below.)

Decimal Hexadecimal Equivalents

Decimal	Hexadecimal
0	0
1	1
2	2
3	3
4	4
5	5
6	6
7	7
8	8
9	9
10	A
11	B
12	C
13	D
14	E
15	F

On first appearance, this looks pretty simple but you need two hexadecimal characters to represent all decimal values from 0 to 255. When you increment decimal 9 by 1, you change the 9 to 0 and put 1 in the ten's place. When you increment hexadecimal F by one, you change the F to 0 and put 1 in the "sixteens" place. Sometimes it's not easy to convert between decimal and hexadecimal in your head.

RGB Triplet for Cornflowerblue

	decimal	hexadecimal
red	100	64
green	149	95
blue	237	ED

We need this brief introduction to RGB color code because when we select to use the RGB color coding method, sometimes the colors will be specified using the decimal number system, and sometimes the colors will be specified using the hexadecimal number system. There is no need to be confused if you know what's going on.

Specifying Colors With the RGB Coding Method

Click on the [RGB] button to select the RGB method of color coding. Note that there are four bars indicating the value of Red, Green, and Blue in the color that you have selected.

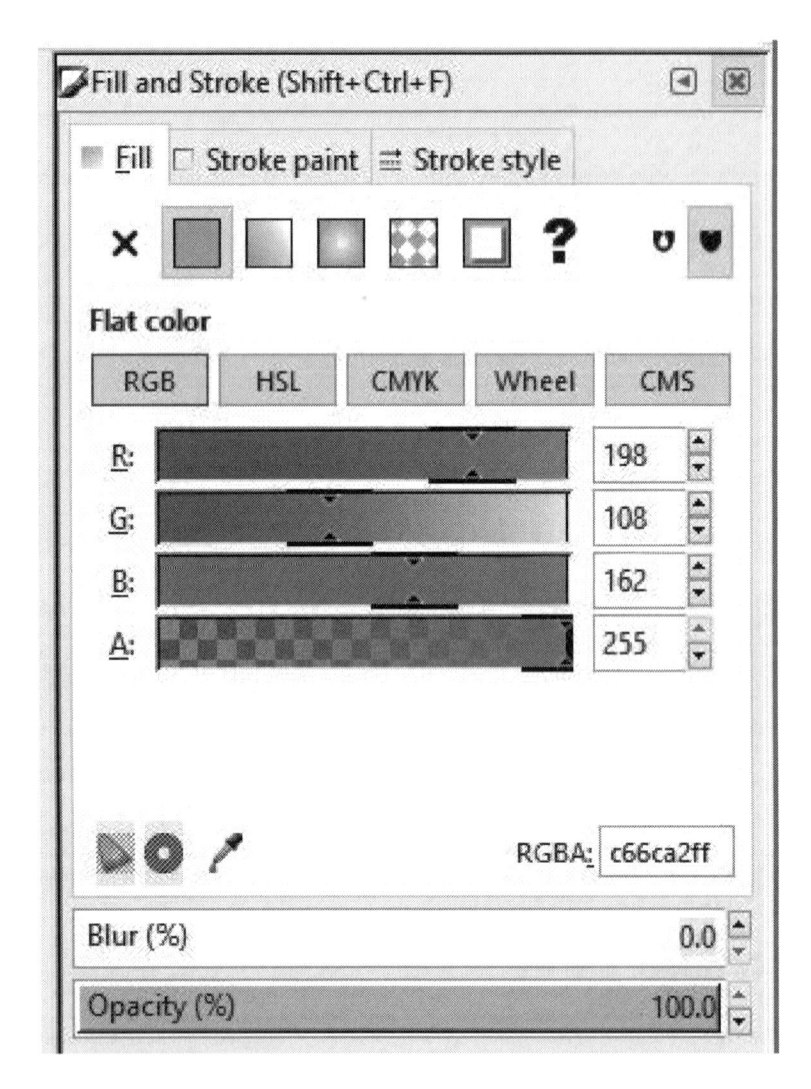

Each color bar has a tracker control that you can drag to adjust the amount of red, green, and blue from 0 to 255. Just below the three color bars is another bar labled A:. A stands for *alpha* and it is the amount of opacity (or transparency if you prefer) of the color.

You can set the alpha value between 0 (fully transparent) and 255 (fully opaque). Any value less than 255 will allow some of the color of an object below your shape to show through. The color specification with the alpha value included is sometimes called an *RGBA quadruplet*.

Below the color bars you will note some small buttons that we are not going to discuss right now, and a box containing the exact RGBA code of the color that you have created.

Below that you will see two more bars labeled *Blur%* and *Opacity%*. These controls are adjusted using the up-down arrows on their right side, or alternately, you can drag inside the bars. Later we will discuss using the Blur slider bar to create shadows and highlights. The Opacity slider is just another way to set transparency.

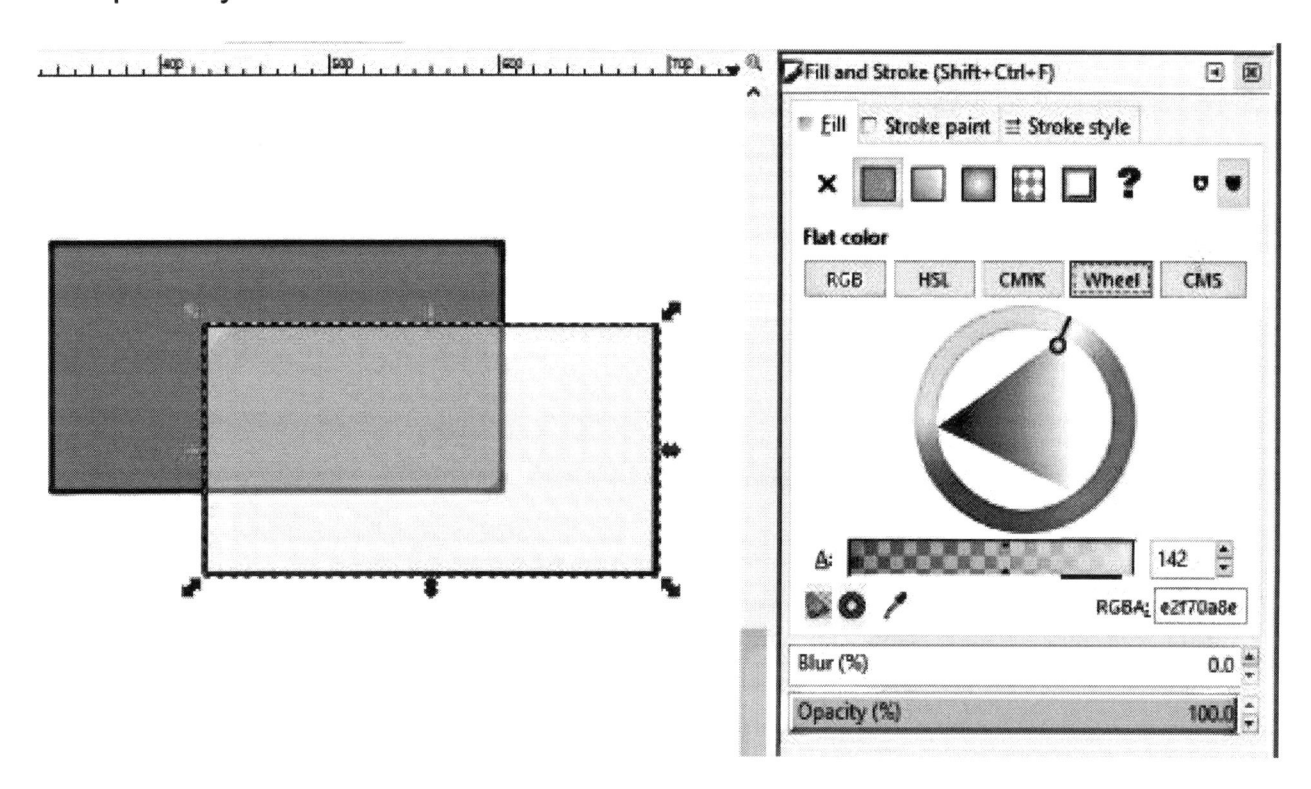

You'll also find an *alpha* adjustment bar with the *wheel* color selector. Shown above, tow objects overlap and the alpha for the top object is set to 142, allowing some of the color of the bottom object to show though.

The HSL Color Model

CONTENTS

Computers use the RGB (Red, Green, Blue) color model. This model is based upon the fact that the retina in the back of the human eye has three different types of photoreceptor cells called cones, those that are sensitive to green, those that are sensitive to red, and those that are sensitive to blue.

The RGB color model, however, does not take into consideration that the vast majority of photoreceptor cells on the retina are not cones, they are another type of cell called rods. Rods are much more sensitive to light than cones, however, they cannot perceive color. That's why at night everything looks gray.

In the 1970s computer graphics designers wanted a color model more aligned with the way the human vision perceives color. They developed the HSL (Hue, Saturation, Lightness) model. In the HSL color model, sometimes called "color space", H stands for hue, which means the color.

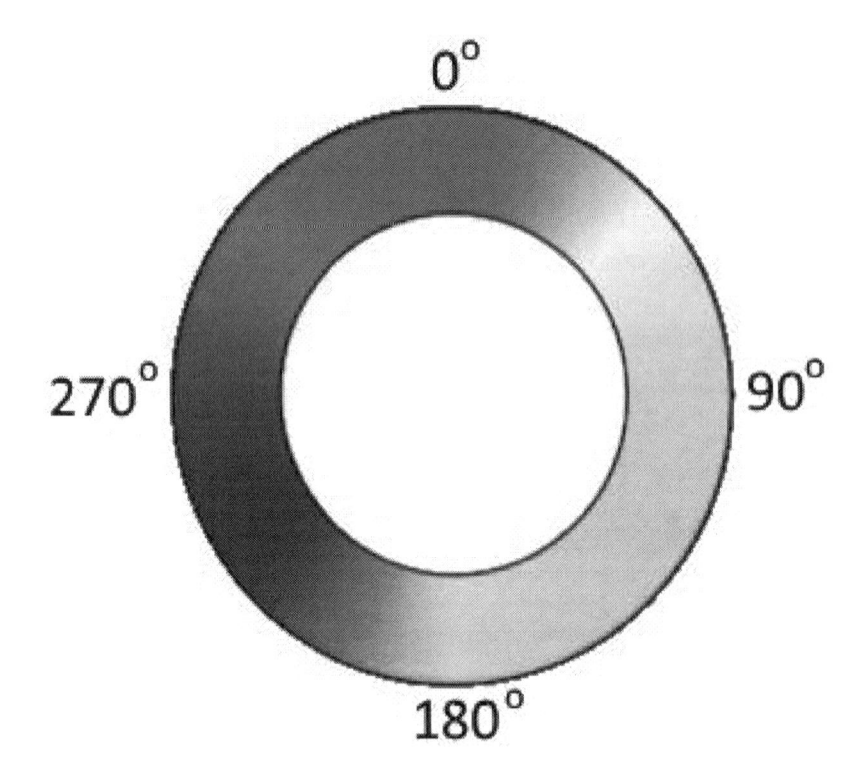

The hue is specified by an angle around the color wheel. It ranges from red at 0 degrees, through all the colors of the rainbow; yellow, green, blue, violet, and back to red at 360 degrees.

Saturation (S) specifies the purity of the color in a range from 0 (low saturation) to 100 (pure color). A color with less than 100 saturation has another color mixed in with it, usually gray. Luminance (L) specifies the lightness in a range from 0 (black) to 100 (white).

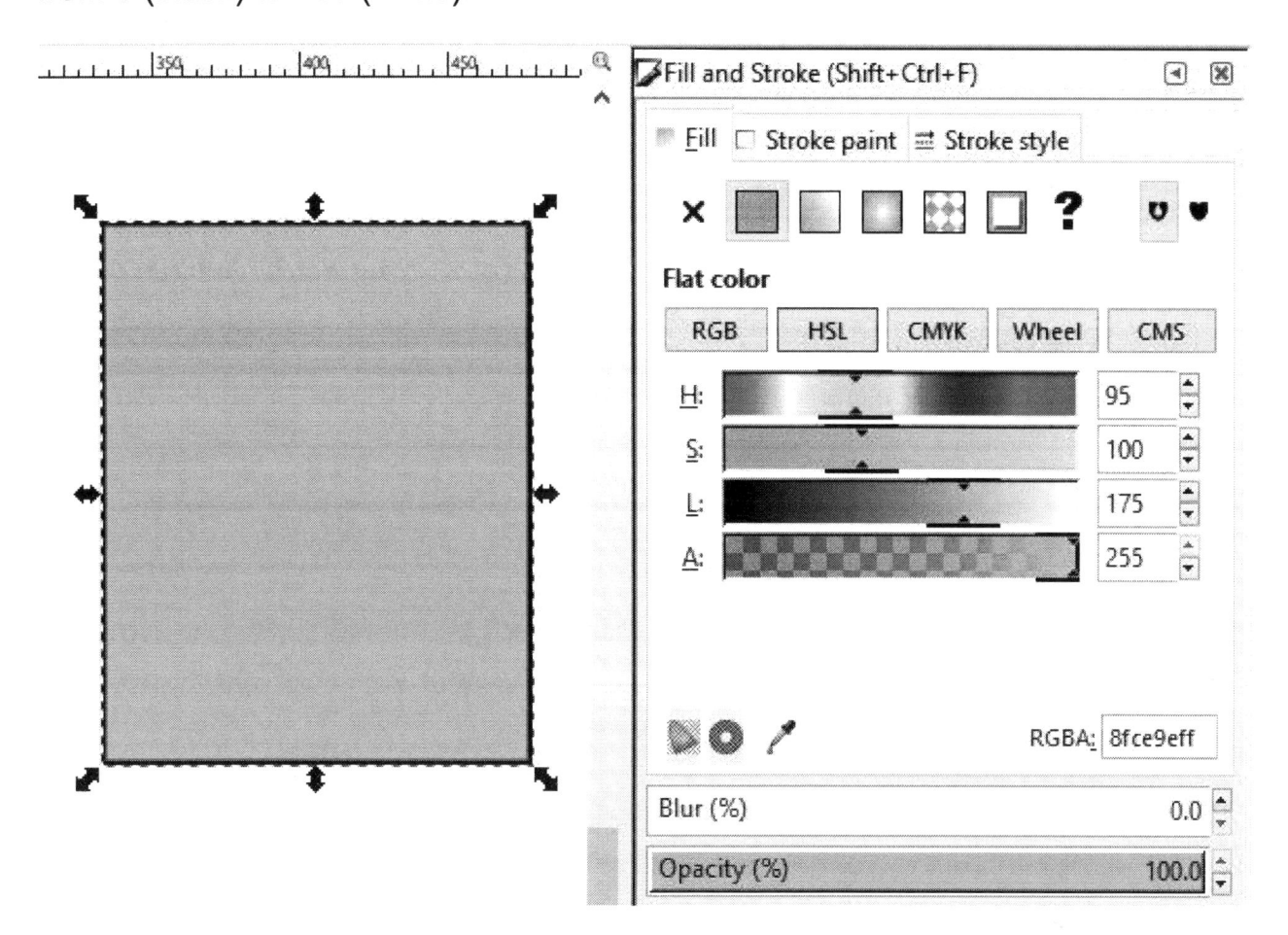

Many artists feel they have more control of their colors using the HSL color model. Inkscape's *Fill and Stroke* dialog box allows you to choose colors using the HSL color model, and also provides the ability to set the alpha channel which controls the degree of transparency (or opacity) of a color. However, the computer ultimately has to convert the HSL values into RGB values to display on the screen.

The CMYK Color Model

CONTENTS

The CMYK color model is used for offset printing. CMYK refers to the four ink colors used in printing: cyan, magenta, yellow, and k for black.

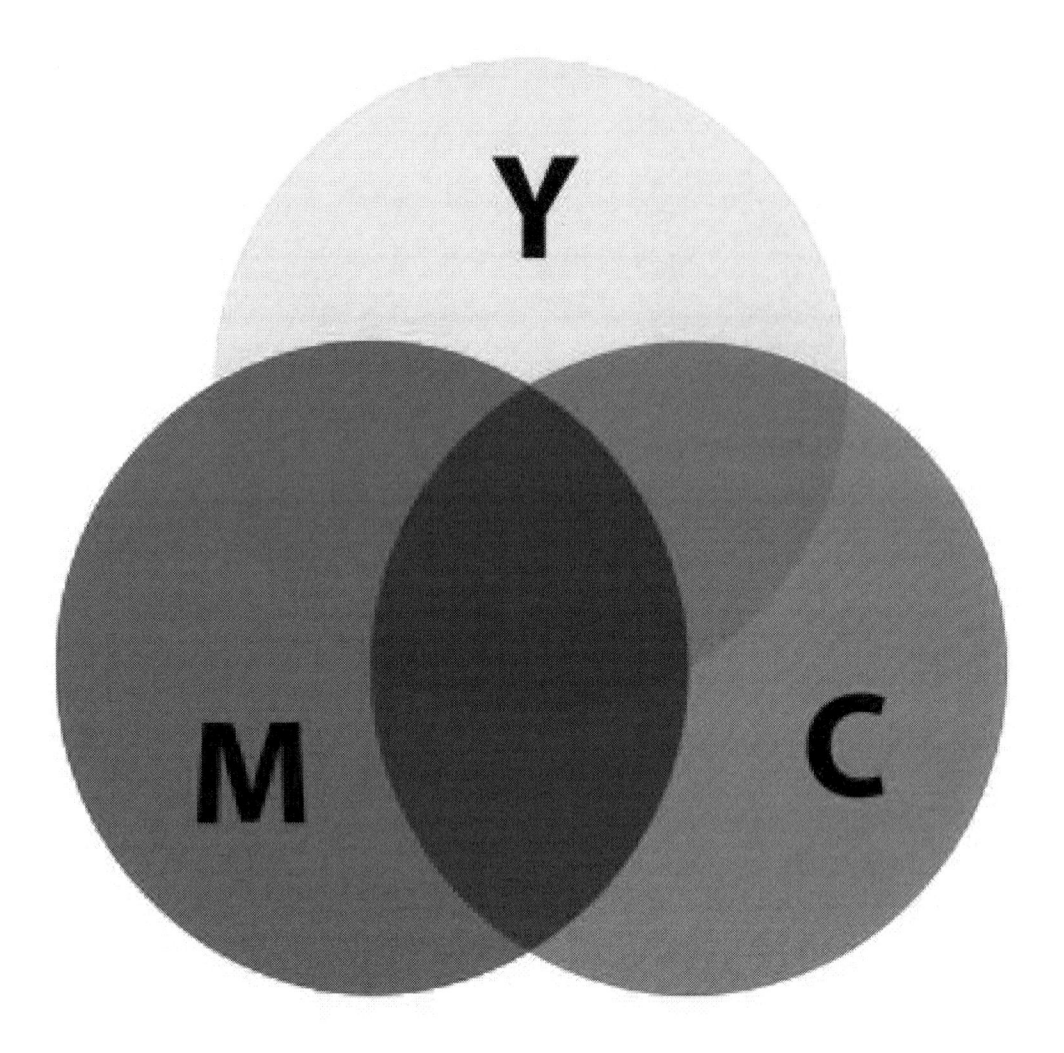

CMYK is described as a *subtractive* color model as compared to a computers display which uses the RGB *additive* color model. In other words, a computer screen starts out black and different amounts of red, green, and blue light are added to form the image. With printing, the paper starts out white, so any color you add to it can only reduce the brightness.

In fact, the more ink you put on a paper, the blacker it gets. CMYK values are expressed in percentages. For example white is C=0, M=0, Y=0, K=0. Putting no ink leaves the paper white.

The typical photograph may contain millions of different colors. In order to print a photograph on paper it would require a printing machine to either mix these colors during the printing process or to have millions of different color inks in the machine. To avoid this a photograph is converted to a grid of tiny cyan, magenta, yellow, black dots. The spacing of the dots is typically 120 lines per inch.

Seeing the image depends on an optical illusion. The dots and their surrounding spaces are beyond the resolving limit of the human eye, so the eye averages out the tone of the dots into a solid color. Of course the dots can be seen using a magnifying glass. Tints and tones of different densities are achieved by varying the size of dot compared to the surrounding non-inked area.

Basic Fill

CONTENTS

You can fill a shape with just about any color, texture, or pattern that you desire. In this chapter we discuss how to fill a shape with a basic color.

In order to fill a shape, it must be selected. To select a shape, click anywhere inside the shape. Double-pointed arrows around the shape's boarder indicate that it is selected.

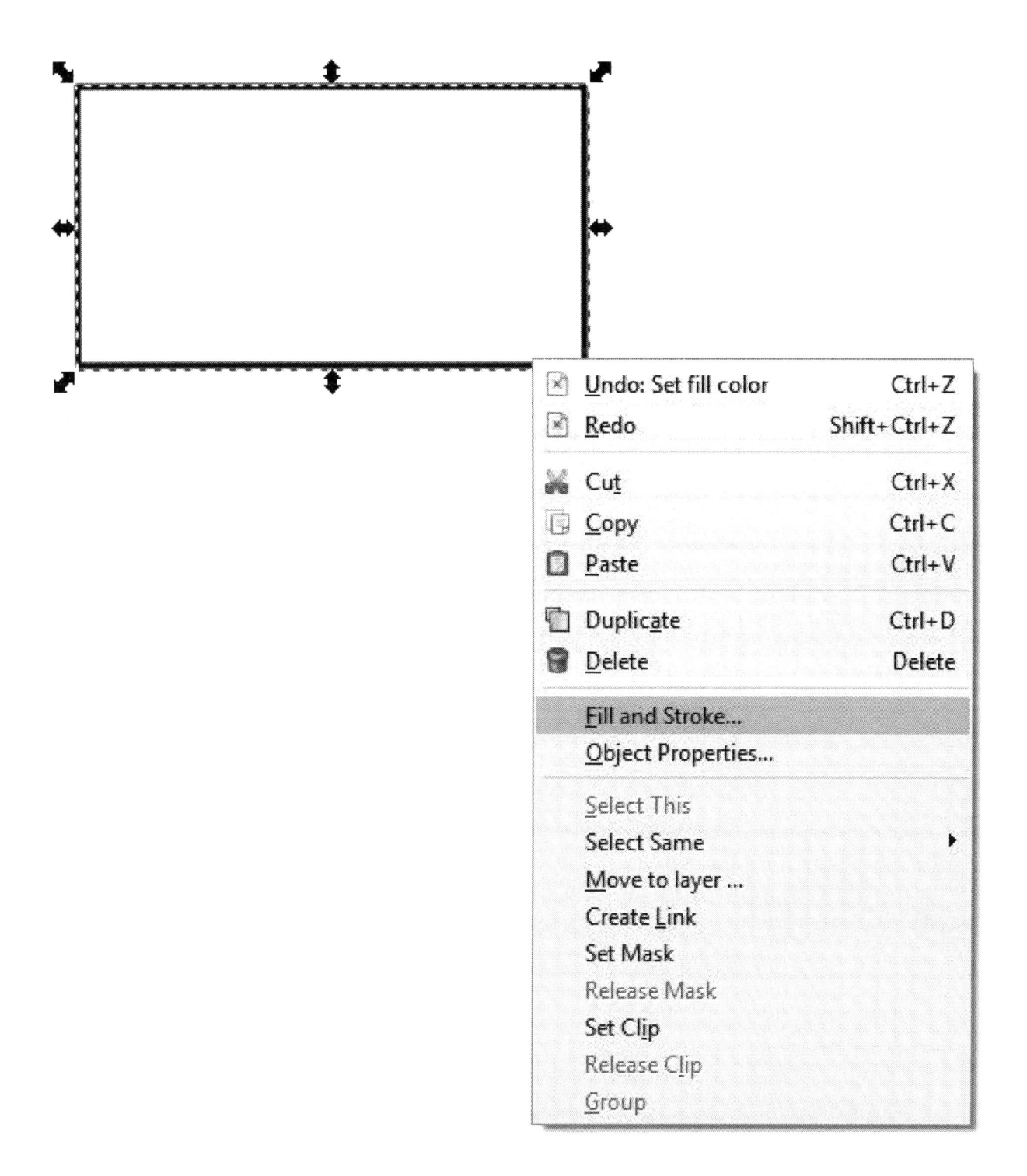

When youm right-click on a shape, a popup menu will appear. If the *Fill and Stroke* dialog box is not visible, select *Fill and Stroke ...* in the popup menu.

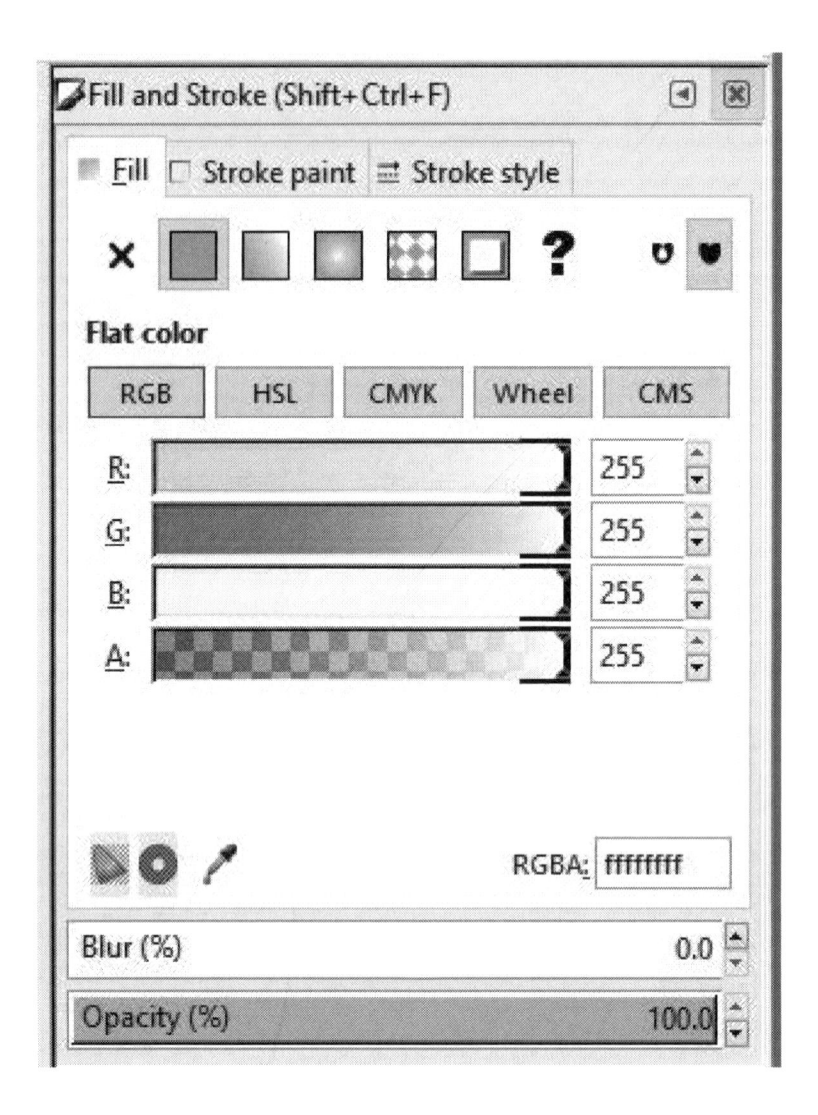

In the *Fill and Stroke* dialog box, make sure the *Fill* tab is selected. Note that at the top of the dialog box are buttons to select the type of fill. The first button, with the [X] is for *No Paint*. Personally, I have never used that button. For now we are interested in only the second button, *Flat Fill Color*.

Just below the buttons to select the type of fill are five buttons to select the color coding method to be used. The first is the [RGB] coding button. The second is the HSL (Hue, Saturation, Luminosity) coding button. The third is the CMYK (Cyan, Magenta, Yellow, Black) coding button. HSL and CMYK are color coding methods sometimes used by professional artists.

In this chapter we are primarily concerned with *RGB* and *Wheel*. Wheel refers to the color wheel. The color wheel is the easiest way to select a color.

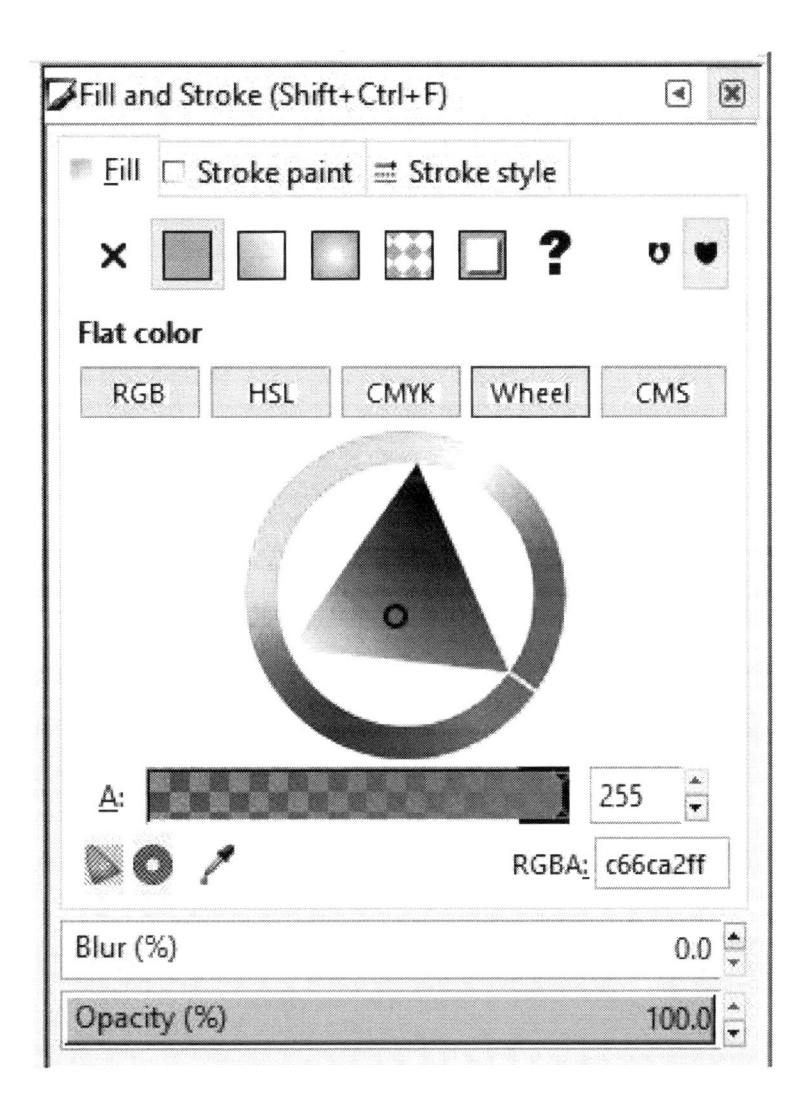

Click on the [Wheel] button to select the color wheel. Noe that the color wheel appears as a rainbow colored circle with a triangle inside. Note the white line emanating from one of the triangle's corners. You can drag this line around the circle with your mouse pointer. As you drag the line, the color just below the line appears in the triangle.

Note that the triangle is filled with a graduation of shades of the selected color. A *shade* is the color with a certain amount of black or white added. As you drag the white line around the circle, and move the tiny circle within the triangle, the selected color is immediately transferred to the inside of your selected shape. This is the easiest way to select a fill color.

Fill Rule

CONTENTS

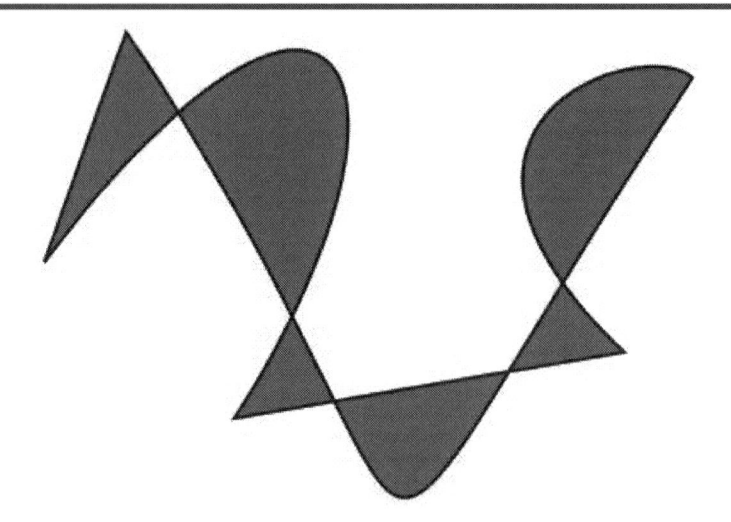

No, the above is not my attempt to create abstract art, although this technique might render some impressive abstract art. Actually, it is the result with the way Inkscape determines how to fill an area. The function is to fill the inside of a shape, but if you move or distort line segments so that they cross each other, you may get unexpected fill results.

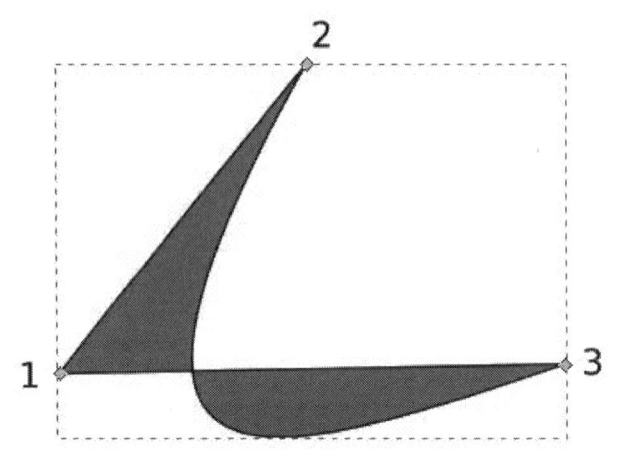

Shown above is a simple triangular shape created with three line segments and three nodes. I dragged a curve in the line segment between node 2 and node 3. Since I dragged the segment such that the inside of the shape crossed the line segment between node 1 and node 3, the fill area at the bottom of the shape was created.

The bottom line is, as you're shaping paths, Inkscape must determine which areas are "inside" the shape so that it can apply the fill to those areas. This may, or may not, be what you expected. You may need to readjust the shape or use several shapes to achieve your desired result.

Linear Gradients

CONTENTS

A gradient is a gradual transition form one color to another color. But before we get deeper into gradients, lets briefly describe how colors are defined by computers.

Computers create colors by defining the amount of red, green, and blue the color contains. Because computers are binary, and because the first computers had small data storage capabilities, each color is defined on a scale from 0 to 255. So, for example, the color blue would be encoded as 0,0,255 and the color white would be 255,255,255.

In Inkscape the beginning color and ending color of a gradient are each called a "stop". You can transition from one color to another, and then to a third color. This requires three stops. You can have any number of stops in a gradient.

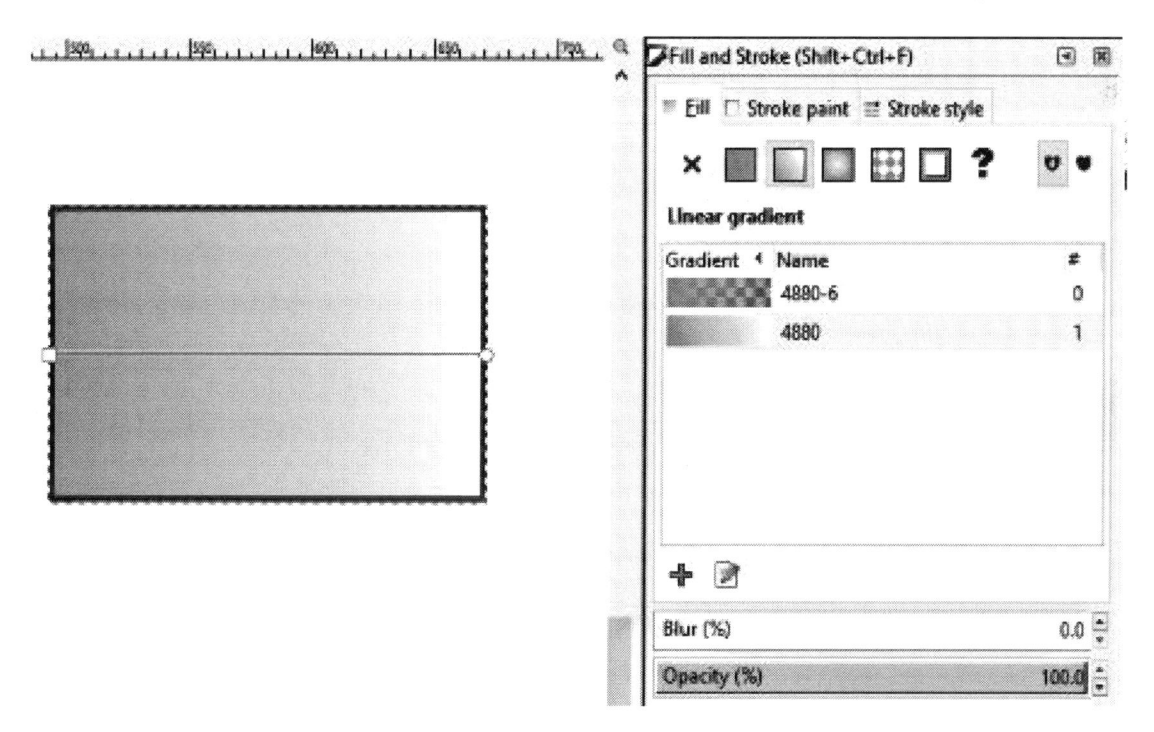

To fill an object with a gradient, right-click with the mouse pointer inside the object, and in the popup menu that appears, select "Fill and Stroke". In the "Fill and Stroke" dialog box that appears, select the "Fill" tab. On the "Fill" tab, click on the "Linear gradient" button. At the top of the "Linear gradient" section that appears you'll see a drop-down list of all the linear gradients that have been defined.

You can click on one of the pre-defined linear gradients to apply it to your object or you can create a new gradient by selecting a pre-defined gradient (there is always one default pre-defined gradient) and clicking on the [Duplicate] button (the blue cross near the bottom of the Fill and Stroke dialog box. Then click on the duplicate gradient to select it, then click on the [Edit Gradient] button (the pencil and tablet near the bottom of the Fill and Stroke dialog box.

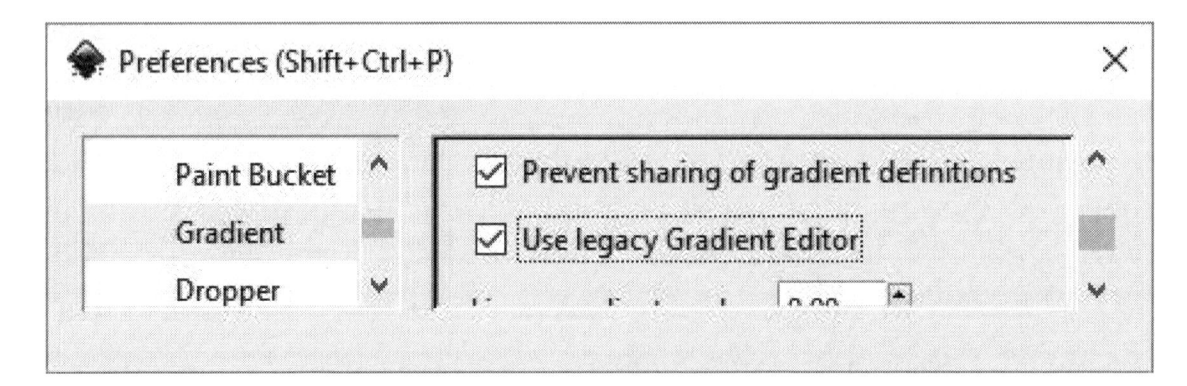

Unfortunately, in some versions of Inkscape, the *Gradient editor* dialog box has been disabled by default. Double click the *Create and edit gradients* tool, and in the *Preferences* dialog box that appears, in the left box, scroll down to *Gradient* and click on it. In the right box, scroll down to *[] Use legacy Gradient Editor* and set the check box.

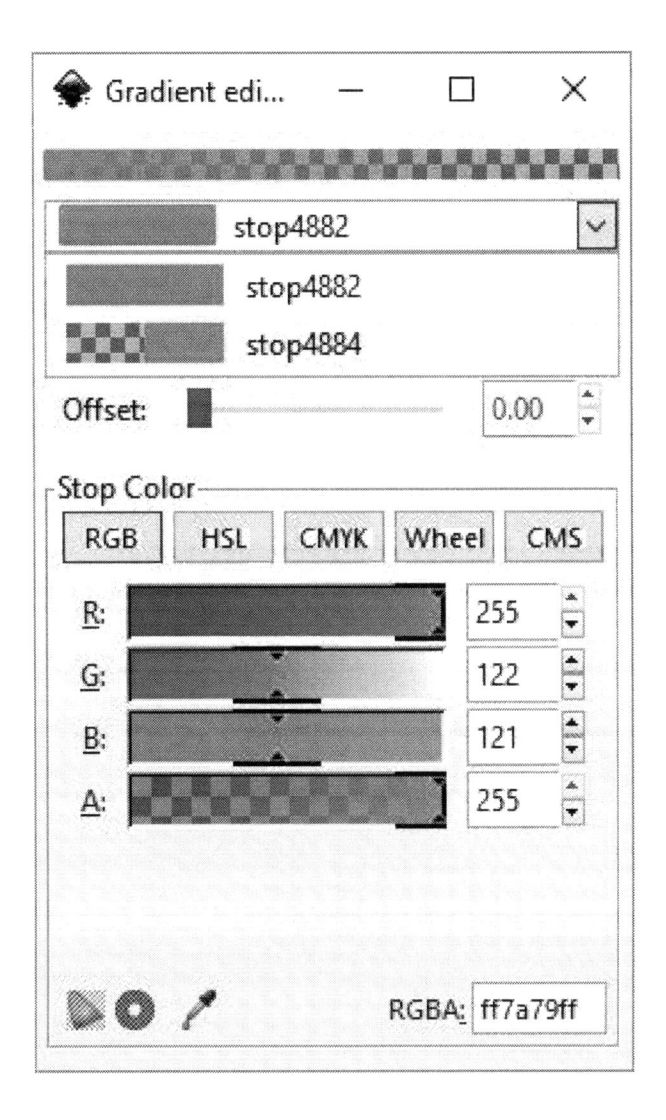

In the *Gradient editor* dialog box, in the drop-down list, select the duplicate gradient that you created, and adjust the color and transparency of the stop using the color and transparency bars, just a s you would for any fill color.

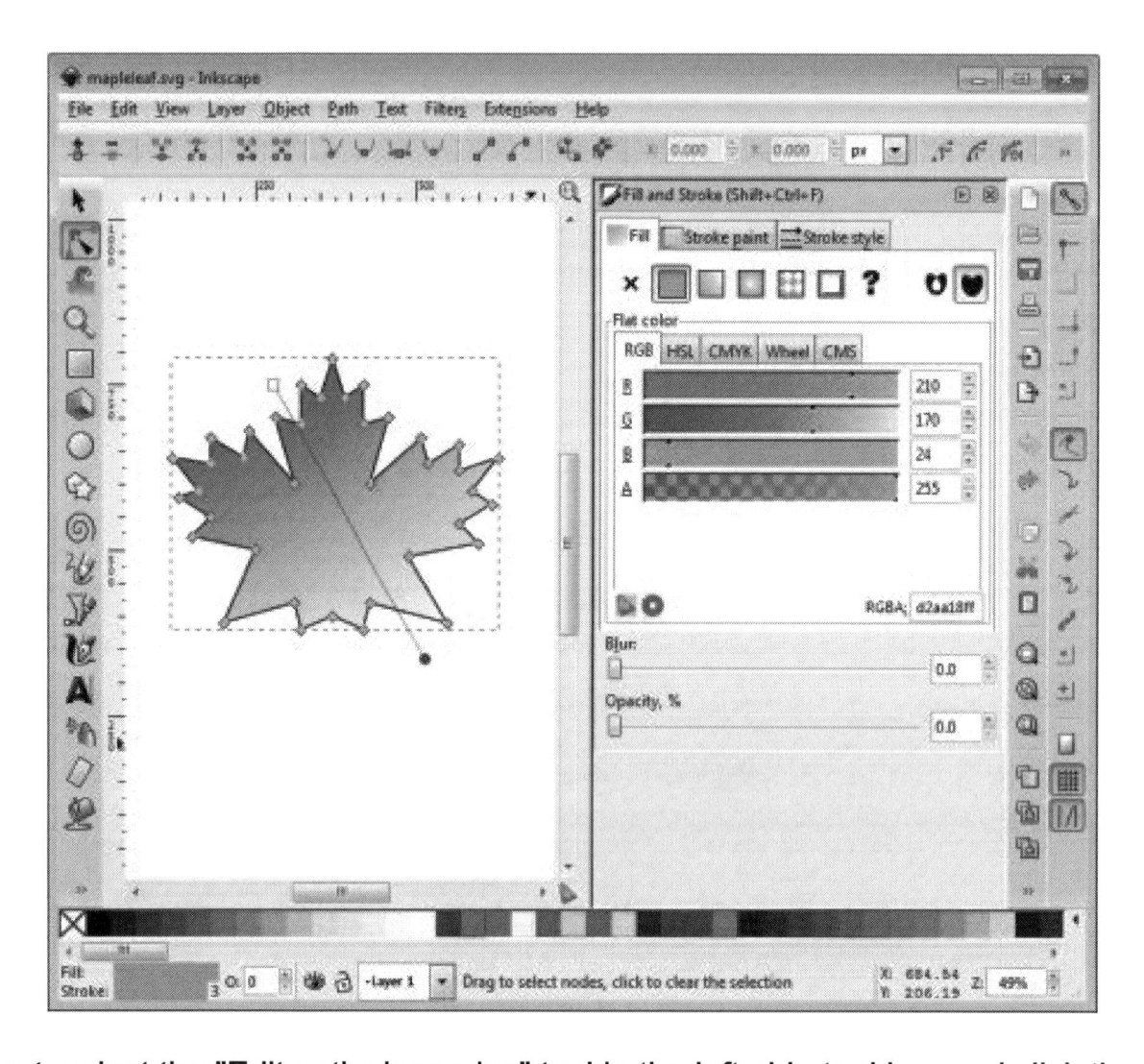

Next, select the "Edit paths by nodes" tool in the left-side tool box and click the object that you applied the gradient to. On the object you'll see the gradient line with a small square at one end and a small circle at the other end. Use your mouse pointer to drag the ends of this gradient line around on the object and the drawing area to see the affects of the gradient.

Clicking on the small square at one end or the small circle at the other end brings up the Fill and Stroke dialog box, where you can also edit the stop. With the tool box *Create and edit gradients* tool selected, if you double-click on the gradient line, you will add another stop, where you can edit it's colors in the Fill and Stroke dialog box.

Gradients are a very powerful effect you can use to make your drawings look more professional. As you learned from this section, gradients are very easy to use in the amazing, powerful, and free Inkscape vector graphics drawing application.

Radial Gradients

CONTENTS

Radial gradients work similar to linear gradients except that one color stop is at the center of the radius and the other color stop is at the circumference of the radius. A radial gradient has three handles allowing you to define an elliptical gradient. If you want to make a radial gradient non-linear, having the effect of moving the center color to one side without changing the color at the circumference, press the [Shift] key while dragging the gradients center square handle.

Here's how to use a radial gradient:

1. To set a radial gradient, right-click on the object, and in the menu that appears, select Fill and Stroke.

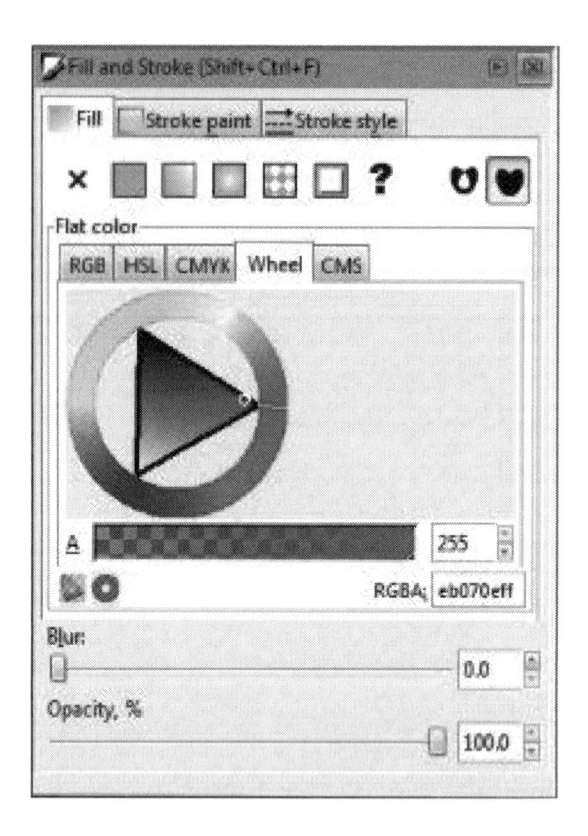

2. In the *Fill and Stroke* dialog box that appears, select the *Fill* tab. Under the *Fill* tab you'll see 5 buttons; [Flat color], [Linear gradient], [Radial gradient], [Pattern], and [Swatch]. Click on the [Flat color] button.

3. In the *Flat color* section of the dialog box, set one of the colors of the radial gradient. The easiest way to set a color is to select the *wheel* tab.

4. In the *Fill and Stroke* dialog box , click on the [Radial gradient] button.

5. Then while the object is still selected, click on the [Create and edit gradients] button in the toolbox. This will cause the radial gradient's stop nodes to appear. The center of the radial gradient is marked by a tiny square node. The outer edges of the radial gradient are marked by tiny round nodes.

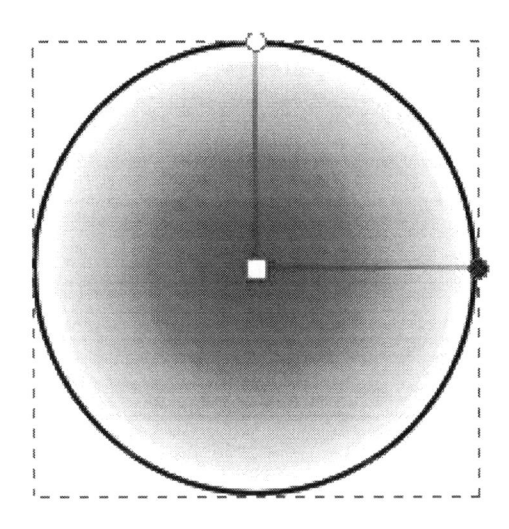

6. Click on one of the nodes to select it. The node should turn blue. Note that the [Flat color] tab is selected. In the *Flat color* section of the dialog box, set the color of the selected stop.

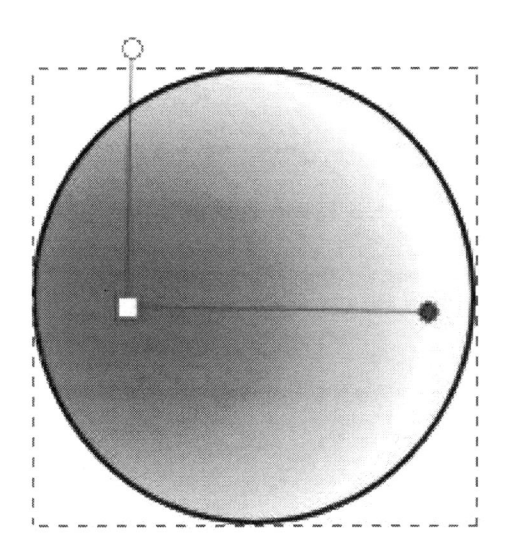

7. You can drag the center node to relocate the center of the radial gradient. You can drag an edge node to set the size or shape of the radial gradient.

• To reverse a radial gradient, with the object and the [Create and edit gradients] tool selected, press the keyboard [Shift] + [R] combination. I find that sometimes I have to do this several times before Inkscape actually reverses the radial gradient, selecting the object and [Create and edit gradients] tool in different orders.

Bitmap Fill

CONTENTS

Rather than just a plain color or gradient, you can fill an object with a bitmap pattern. A bitmap image can be a photograph or an image created in a graphics application, it can be in the .png, .jpg, .gif, or .bmp file format. Assuming that you have an Inkscape file open, and that you have a bitmap file that you wish to use as a fill pattern, here are the steps required:

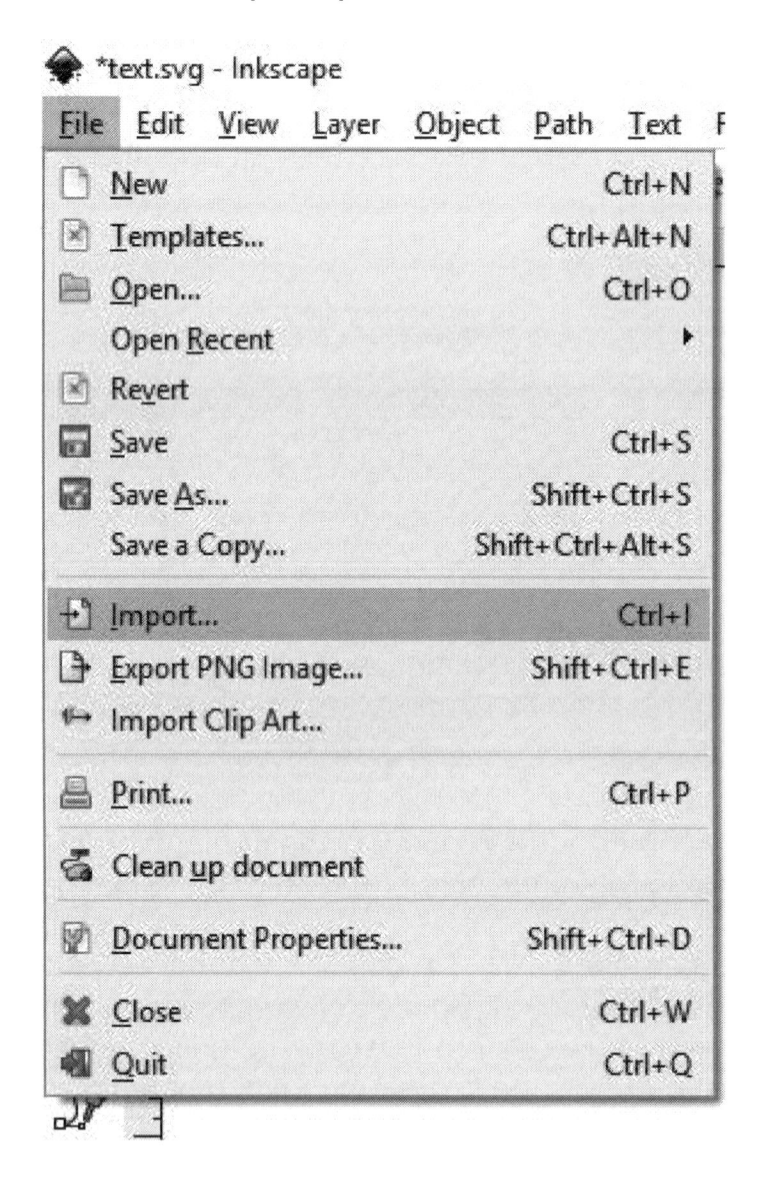

1. In Inkscape's main menu select *File | Import*, and in the *Select file to import* dialog box that appears, navigate to and select the pattern image file. Then click on the [Open] button.

In the *Link or embed image* dialog box that appears, with the embed radio button set, click on the [OK] button. The fill pattern will appear in the drawing area.

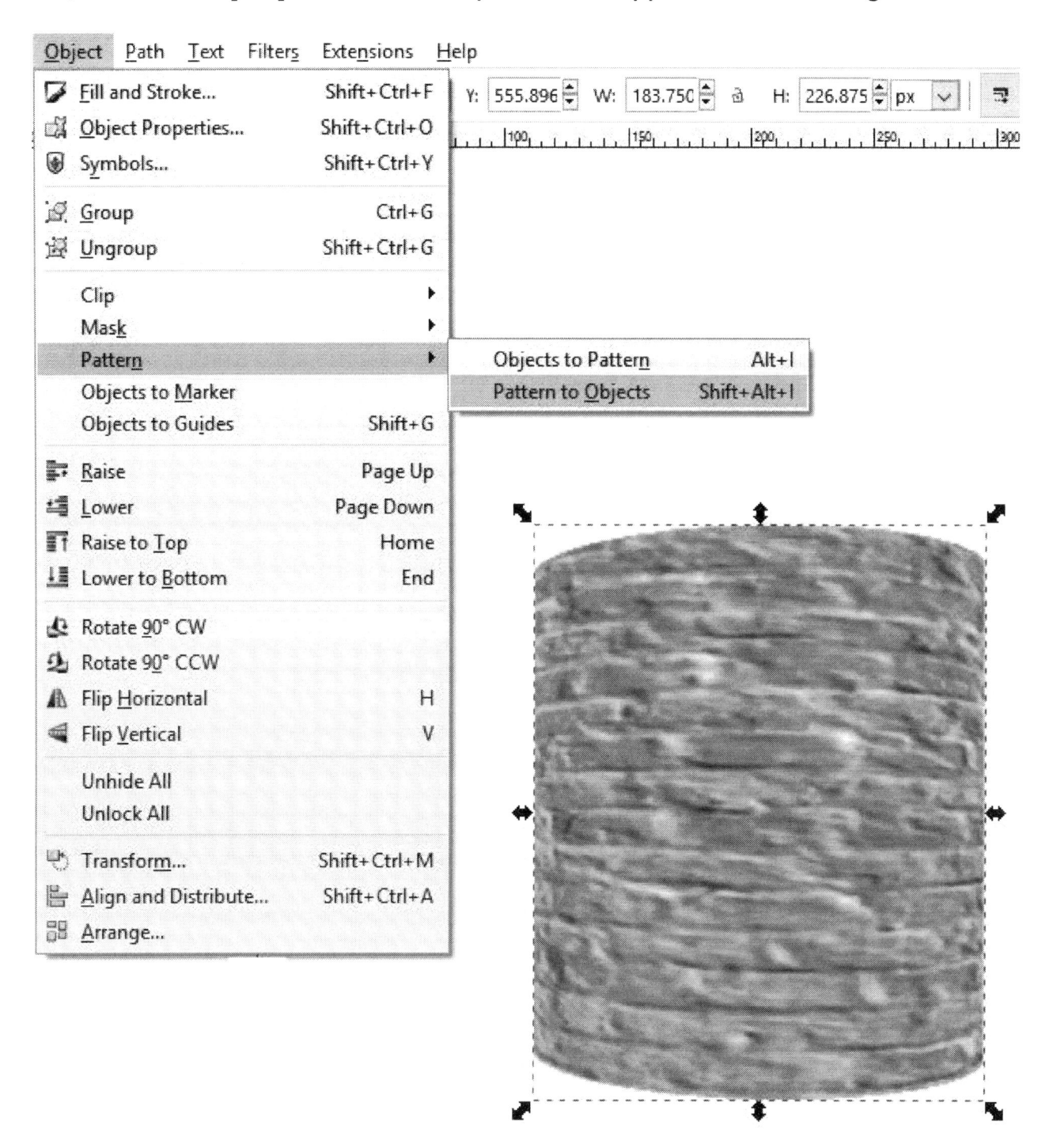

2. In Inkscape's drawing area, select the bitmap, then in the main menu, select *Object | Pattern | Objects To Pattern*.

3. Select the object you want to fill with the bitmap image. If the *Fill and Stroke* dialog box is not open, right-click inside the selected object. In the *Fill and*

Stroke dialog box select the *Fill* tab, then click on the [Pattern] button. The [Pattern] button is the small diamond filled square. The pattern appears to fill the selected object.

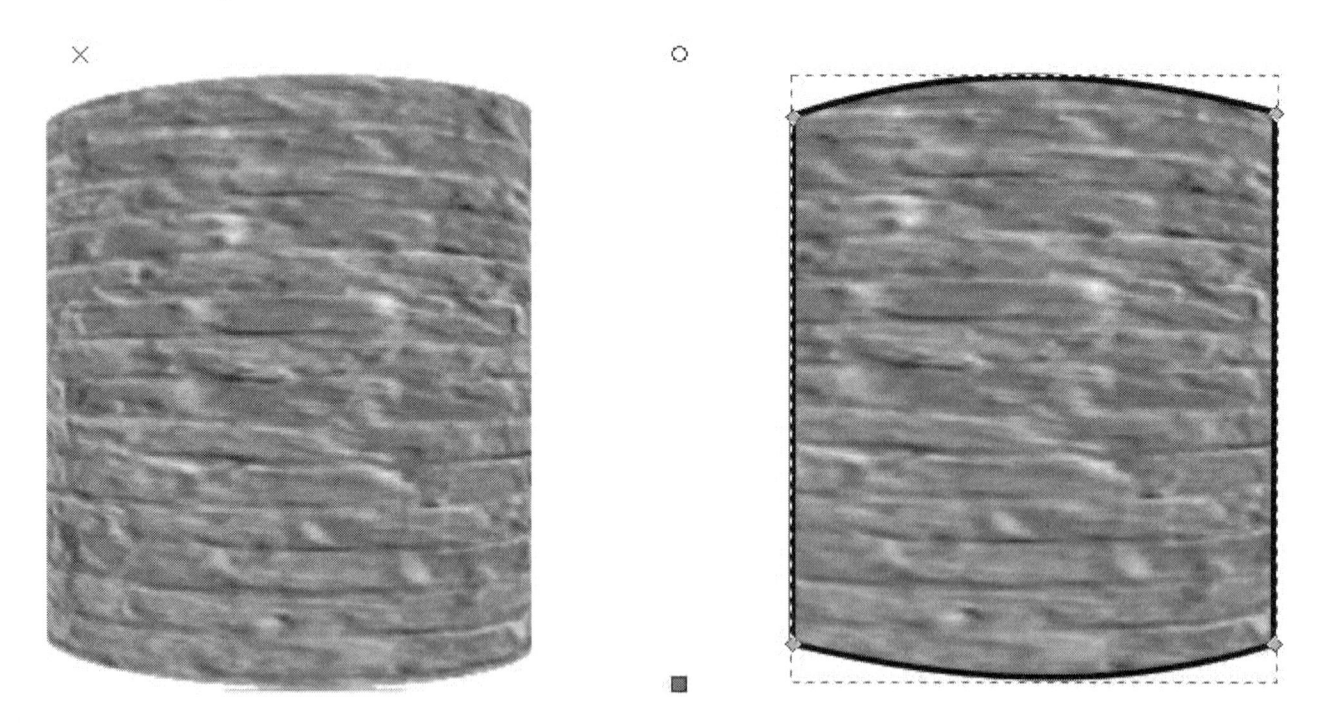

In the *Pattern fill* text box, you'll see the name of the pattern. Use the *Edit paths by nodes* tool to scale and position the pattern on the object.

Chapter 6: Enhancing Designs with Effects

Shadows and Highlights

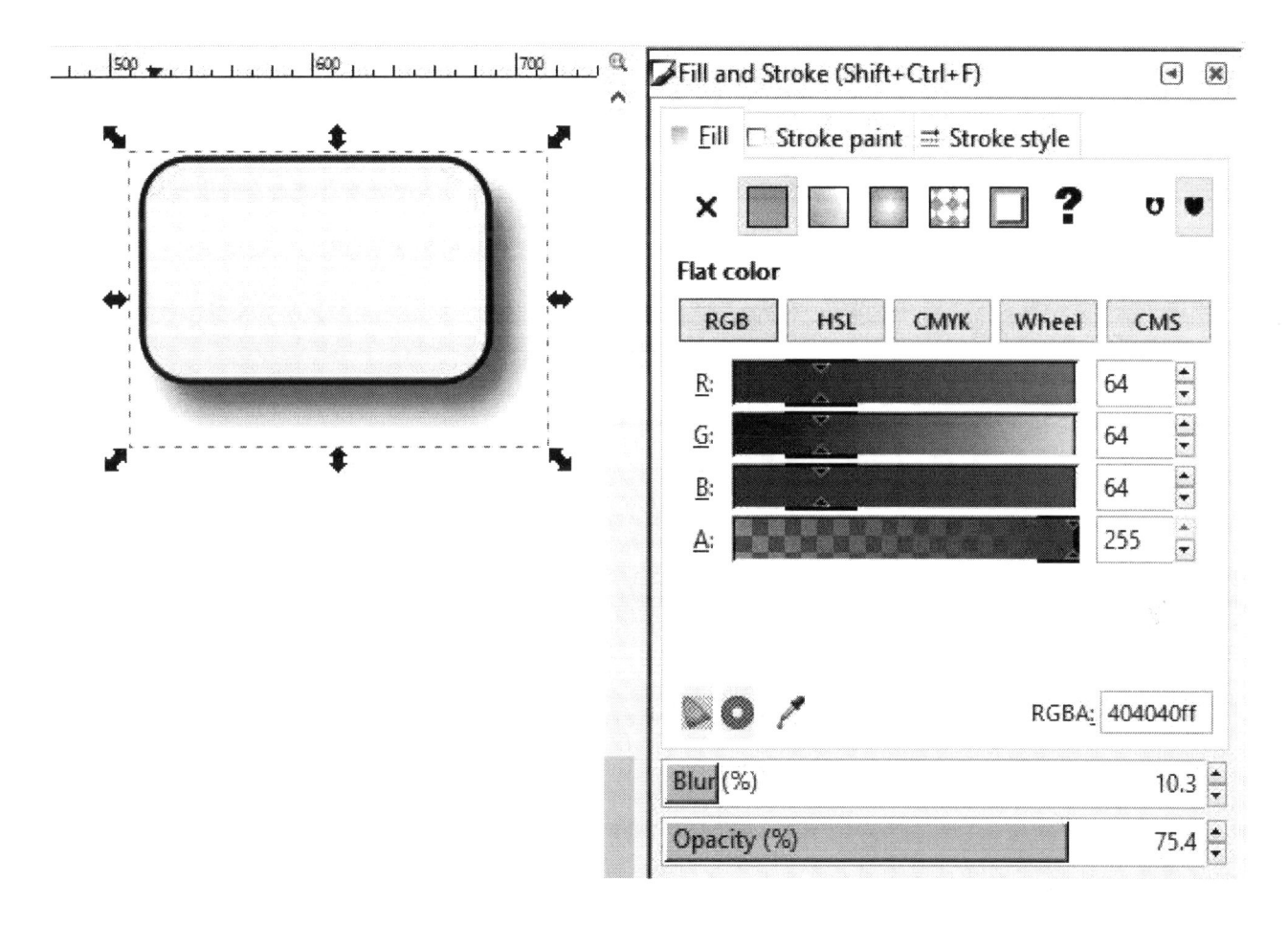

Adding shadows and highlights to your drawings can create a touch of realism. This can be accomplished by creating a copy of the object for which you want the shadow, filling that copy with a darker or lighter color, and positioning it in relationship to the original object.

In the example shown above, I removed the boarder of the copy by, in the *Fill and Stroke* dialog box, setting the Stroke Width to 0. Next, in the same dialog box, I set the fill color to gray. It's easy to create any shade of gray by using the RGB color bars to set red, green, and blue to equal (and low) values.

Then I set the *Blur* bar to 10% and the Opacity bar to 75%. Blur sets the width of the shadow object's "fuzzy" border. Opacity sets how much of the background shows through the shadow. In the real world shadows do not usually totally obscure the object that they fall upon.

The last step is to move the shadow to underneath the object that is casting it. In with the shadow object selected, in the main menu select *Object | Lower* to get the shadow under the object.

All of these parameters; blur, opacity, and relative position can be adjusted to get the exact effect that you desire.

The example above shows what you can do with a shadow using perspective. To create this shadow I used the same steps as before, except this time I rotated the shadow object and then used the *Edit paths by nodes* tool (in the toolbox) to reshape the shadow object to give it a perspective look.

In the picture shown above, I have placed construction lines to aid in showing how I reshaped the shadow object to give it a perspective look. It helps to display the grid. To display the grid, in the main menu select *View | Page Grid*.

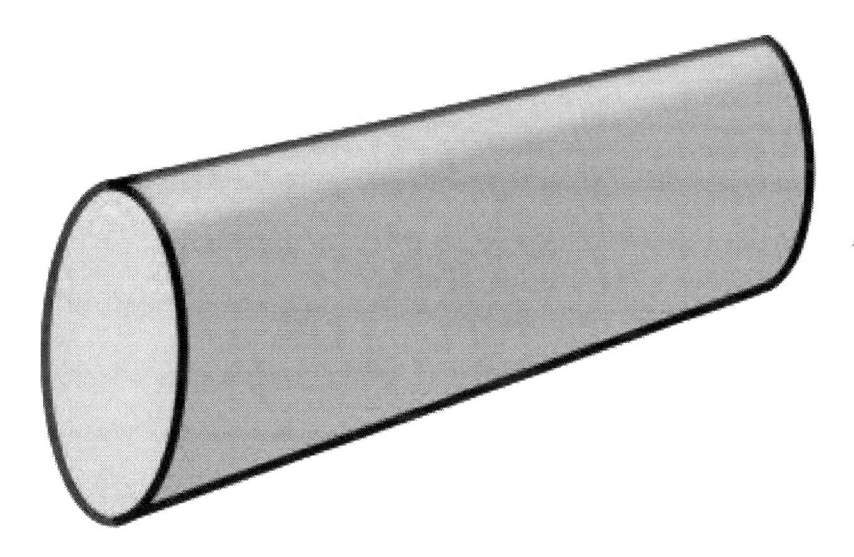

Shown above is an example of highlighting. A highlight is a bright reflection off the surface or a corner of an object. A highlight is the same as a shadow except that its color is lighter than the surface of the object receiving the highlight, and you usually place the highlight up on the object rather than below it.

Shown above is an exploded view of the highlighted cylinder. Note that it is composed of three parts, an ellipse, a shape created using the *Draw Bezier Curves and Straight Lines* tool, and another shape used for the highlight. The highlight is created using similar steps as a shadow, set the path width to 0, set the blur, and possibly set the opacity.

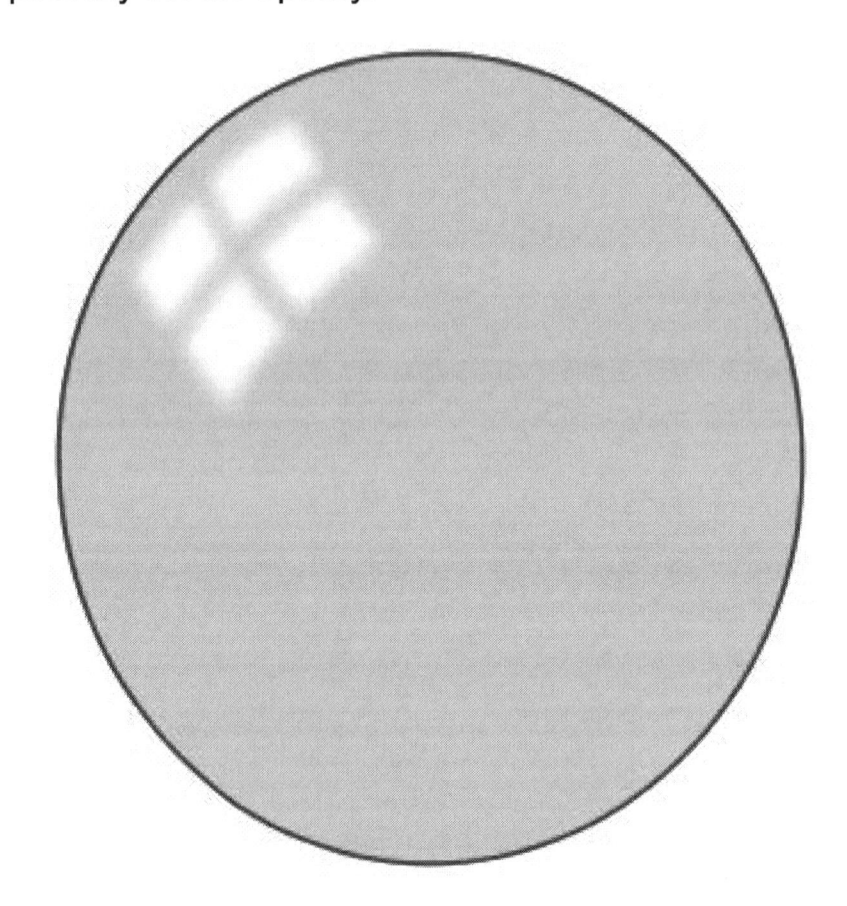

Shown above is a sphere with highlighting. This time the highlight represents the reflection of a window. For greater realism, I would put a shadow on the right side of the sphere and another shadow underneath.

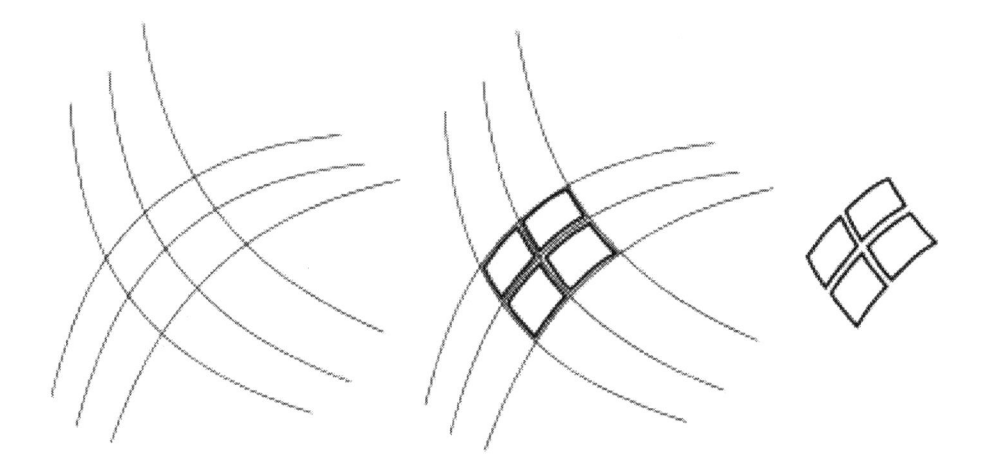

Shown above is how I constructed the highlight for the sphere. First I drew some construction lines. You could use more geometrically accurate construction lines, but I just winged it. Then I drew the window panes within the construction lines. Then I removed the construction lines. Then I applied the same settings to all the windows panes as with any highlight; set the stroke width to 0, set the fill color, set the blur, position the highlight on top of the sphere.

If the sphere used a textured fill, or it had some other visible features on it, you would want to set the the highlight's opacity to let that show through.

Layers and Z-Order

CONTENTS

Inkscape is a 2D vector drawing program. The location of any point on the canvas is defined by its X (horizontal location from left to right), and Y (vertical location from top to bottom) coordinates. Applications that render in 3D also use the Z axis, (location from in to out). Inkscape's use of the Z axis is represented by *layers* and is called *z-order*.

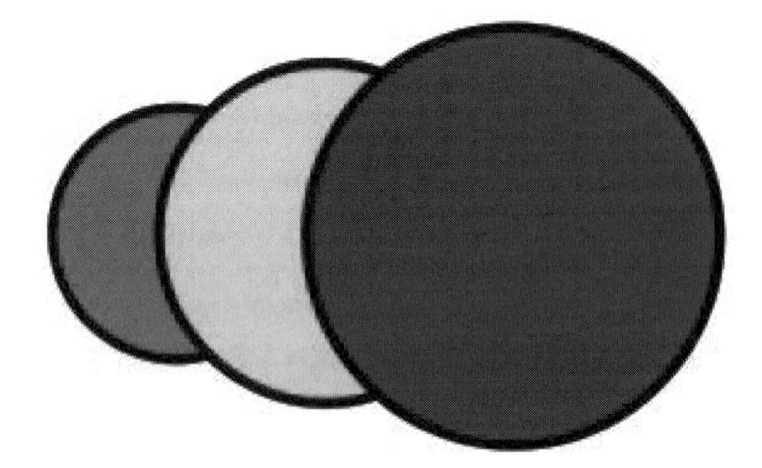

When you first draw an object on an empty canvas, it has a z-order of 1. If you draw a second object, it has a z-order of 2. If you move the second object so that it occupies some of the same canvas area as the first object, it will overlap the first object. If you draw a third object, it has a z-order of 3 and if it occupies some of the same canvas area as the first or second object, it will overlap them. And so on.

When you click on an object to select it, Inkscape will select the object under the mouse pointer that has the highest z-order. If you want to select an object lying below the top object, you can't just click on it.

Selecting Objects in the Z-Order

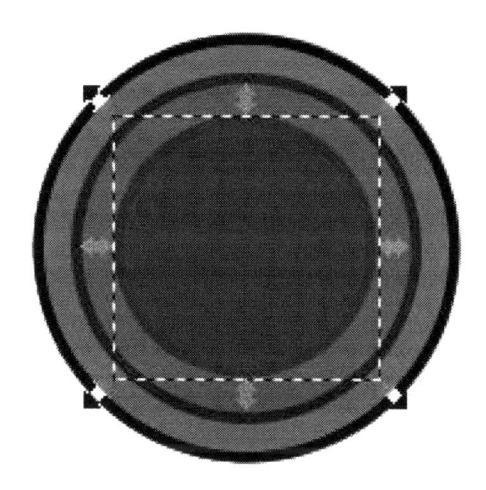

There are several methods of selecting objects that are lying below objects that have higher z-order. You could use buttons on the *Tools Control Bar* or the you could use the *Layers dialog* but the easiest method is to press and hold the [Alt] button while repeatedly clicking over the area where the object you want to select is located. Each time you click, the next lower object in the z-order will be selected.

If you press and hold [Shift][Alt] the objects that you click on in the z-order stack will stay selected, allowing you to select multiple objects in the stack.

An alternative method of selecting objects in the z-order of the *entire* drawing is to repeatedly press the [Tab] key. This will select objects in order from the bottom of the z-order to the top of the z-order. [Shift][Tab] will select objects in order from the top of the z-order to the bottom of the z-order. However, using this method you will need to use the arrow keys to move the selected object.

Changing an Object's Z-Order

As with everything in Inkscape, there are several methods of changing an objects location in the z-order. In any case, you have to select the object first. The easiest method may be to use one of the keys as listed below.

Key	Move Selected Object
[PgUp]	up one layer
[PgDn]	down one layer
[Home]	to top
[End]	to bottom

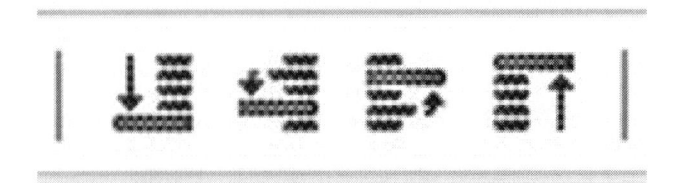

Another easy method to of changing an objects location in the z-order is to use the z-order buttons in the *Tools Control Bar*. Or you could use the *Raise, lower, Raise to Top*, or *Lower to Bottom* selections in the main menu's *Object* menu.

Selecting Multiple Objects

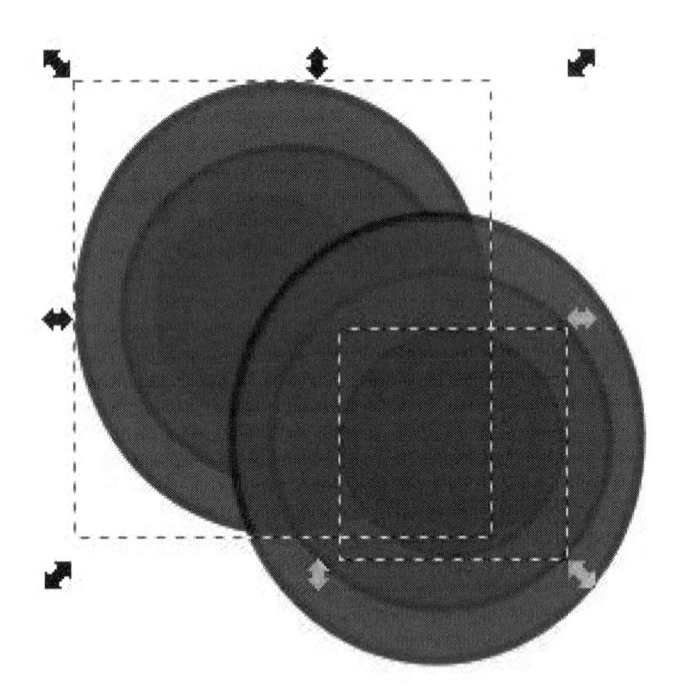

To select multiple objects, click on the first object, then hold down the [Shift][Alt] keys while selecting additional objects. To unselect a previously selected object in a group of selected objects, just click on it again while still holding down the [Shift][Alt] keys.

While multiple objects are selected, you can use the menu to change all their z-orders simultaneously.

One thing I find useful when doing work that involves changing objects z-orders is setting transparencies. being able to see through objects makes it easier to see exactly what you're doing.

Grouping

CONTENTS

One function in Inkscape that is very handy is grouping. To demonstrate let's make the simple example shown above. It's an exploded view of all the shapes you would need to create a simple drawing of a rocket.

Shown above, we have assembled all the shapes into the rocket and placed it a background with some clouds and a moon or planet. In order to reposition the rocket over the background, we would need to select all its pieces. This could be done, as mentioned previously, by pressing and holding the [Alt] key while clicking on each piece, or by drawing a selection box around the entire rocket.

The problem with this is that it's difficult to select all the rocket shapes while avoiding selecting any background shapes. Also, if you decide to relocate the rocket relative to the background several times, it could get tedious.

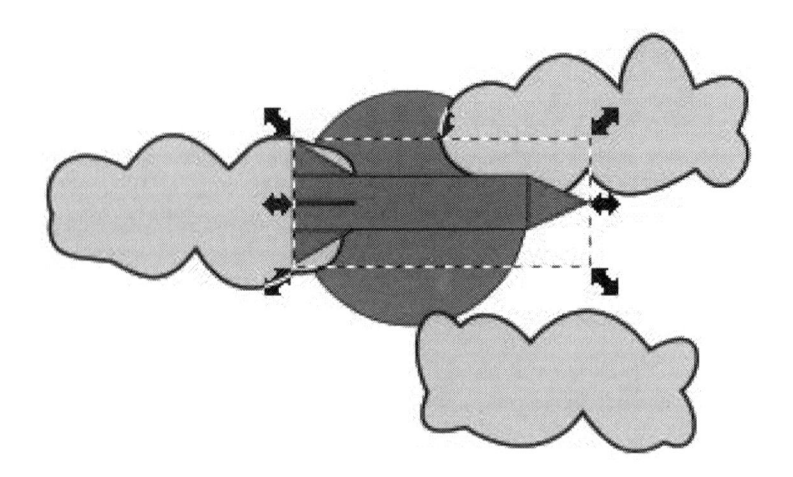

Instead we could "group" all the rocket shapes. To group the pieces, select them all, preferably before you place them over the background, then in the main menu select *Object | Group*. When we group all the pieces, we need only click anywhere on the rocket to select the entire rocket.

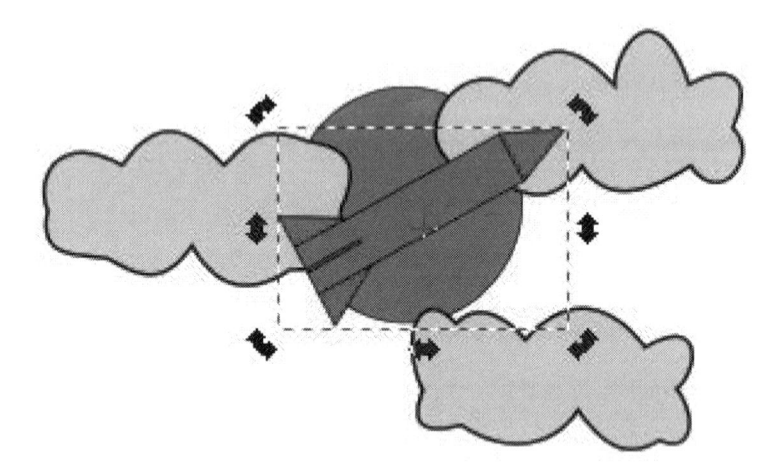

Now the rocket behaves like a single object and we can easily move the rocket relative to the background. If you were to select all the pieces of the rocket individually and then tried to rotate the rocket, each piece would rotate around it's individual axis and you would get some very surprising results. However, with the pieces grouped, the rocket behaves as a single object and rotates nicely.

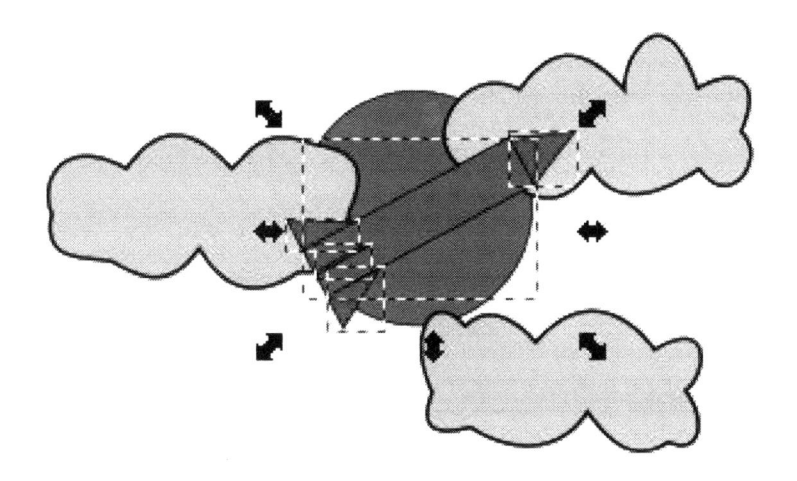

Grouping doesn't effect the *Edit path by nodes* tool, so you can still change the shape of any part of the object. However, if you really need to make some serious changes, you can select the object and in the main menu select *Object | Ungroup*. You may preferably want to move the object off the background before ungrouping it.

Chapter 7: Creative Text Handling

Basic Text

Putting text into an Inkscape drawing is as easy as it is in any word processing application.

Just click on the *Create and edit text objects* tool in the Toolbox, click on the canvas where you want the text to appear, and in the text *Tool Controls Bar* select the *font, font size*, and *font style* (Normal, Italic, Bold) that you want.

In Inkscape, text is both *text*, that is you can select the font and font properties, and an *object*. As an object you use the *Select and transform objects* tool to select and move the text and perform other operations similar to regular non-text objects.

As an object, the most interesting thing you can do is set the *Stroke* and *fill*. This makes it very easy to create colored, outlined text.

When selected as an object, you can click on it again to get the rotation handles and easily rotate the text to any angle you desire. Note that i said "click on it again" rather than double-click, because if you double-click on text selected with the *Select and transform objects* tool, the text will change to the *font, font properties*, and *type entry* mode.

You can also return to the *font, font properties*, and *type entry* mode by selecting the text and clicking on the *Create and edit text objects* tool.

If you click again on text selected with the *Select and transform objects* tool, to get the rotation handles and you rotate the object, it might seem a little weird while using the arrow keys to step through the characters of the text, and the backspace key to remove characters. For example if you rotate the text 180 degrees, the right-arrow key will move the insertion point left, and the backspace key will remove the character to the right of the insertion point.

Similarly, if you flip the object horizontally, the right-arrow keys and the backspace key will appear to be working backwards. I'm not complaining, this is what you would want. And if you enter more characters with the text flipped, they will be inserted to the right of the insertion point, and they will have all the properties (stroke style and fill color) that you set for the rest of the text.

This article just touches on the basics of using text in Inkscape. Through the use of gradients, filters, and textured fills, what you can do with text in Inkscape is just about unlimited.

Text Kerning

CONTENTS

Actually *Text Kerning* is not a good title for this article because in it I will cover all the different typographical adjustments you can make in Inkscape. Shown below is a list of what we will cover.

leading	space between lines
tracking	space between all letters
kerning	space between two letters
vertical shift	vertical offset of part of line
character rotation	rotation one character

The easiest way to make typographical adjustments in Inkscape is to use the controls on the *Tool Controls bar*.

Shown above is text without any typographical adjustments. There is a huge debate online as what the definition of "font size" is. Most people think it is the height of a character. But you can clearly see above that the space between lines is not 1.2 times the height of a character.

Since we are mostly concerned about the graphical look of our work, we can choose to ignore whatever actual dimensions Inkscape provides and just use the up-down arrow buttons to visually set the spacing between lines. Shown above, I have set the spacing between lines so that the lines overlap.

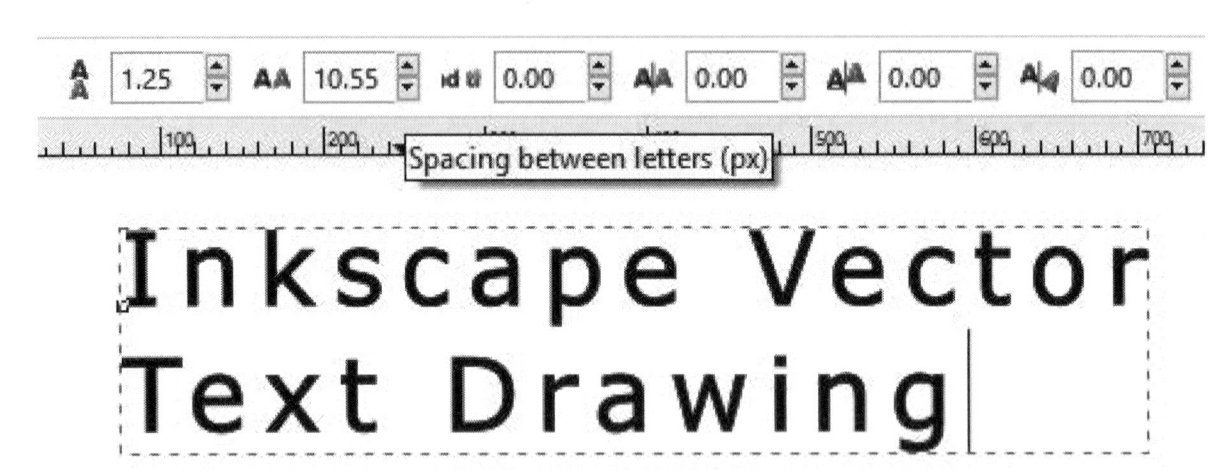

The second typographical control allows you to adjust the spacing between characters. This is called *tracking*. Shown above, I have increased the spacing between characters.

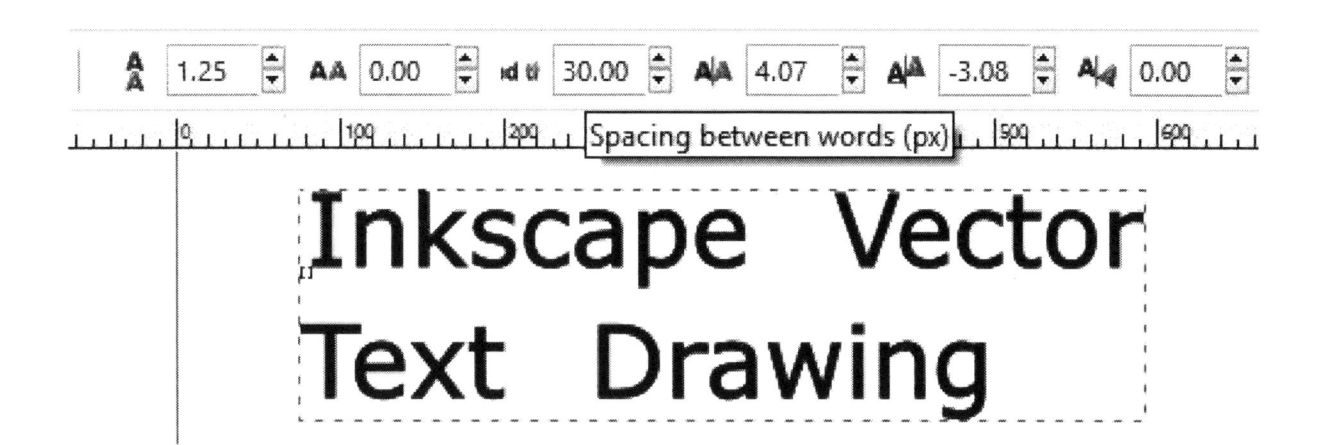

The third typographical control allows you to adjust the spacing between words. Shown above, I have increased the spacing between words.

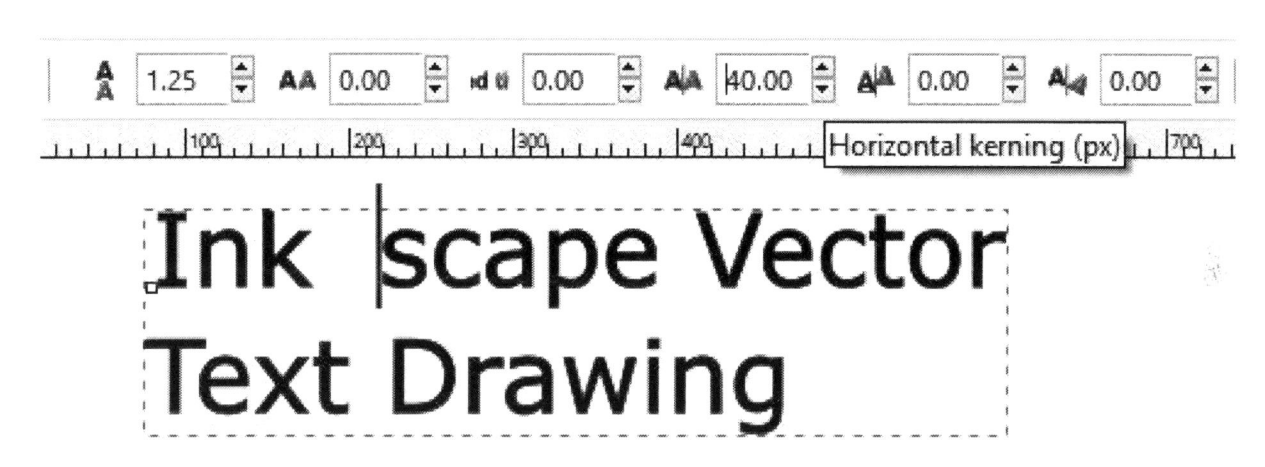

The fourth typographical control allows you to adjust the spacing between two characters. This is called *kerning*. It adjusts the spacing at the point of the insertion point. Shown above, I have increased the spacing between the characters k and s in the word "Inkscape".

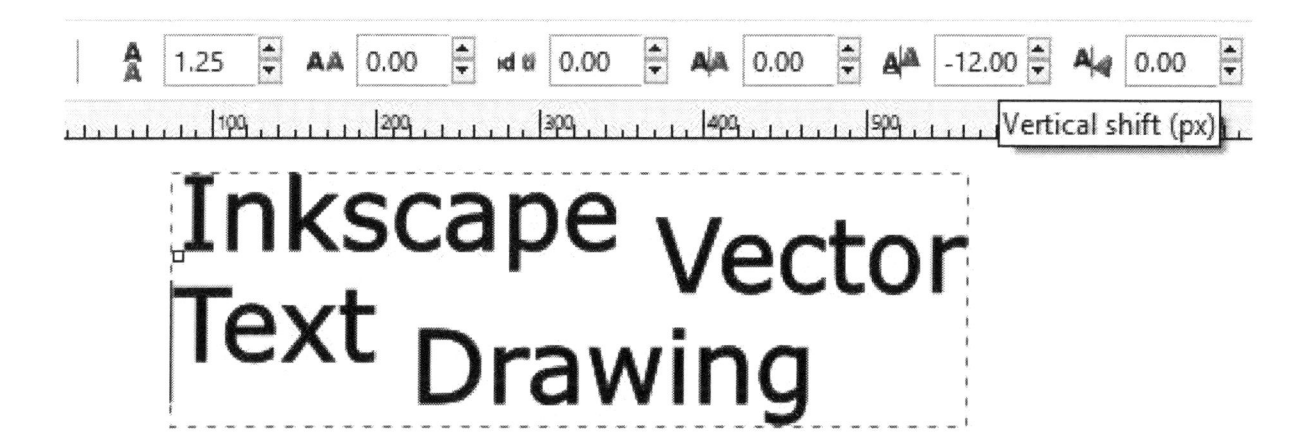

The fifth typographical control allows you to adjust the *vertical shift*. It seems to adjust the vertical shift of the entire line to the right of the insertion point. Shown above, I have adjusted the vertical positions of various words in the paragraph.

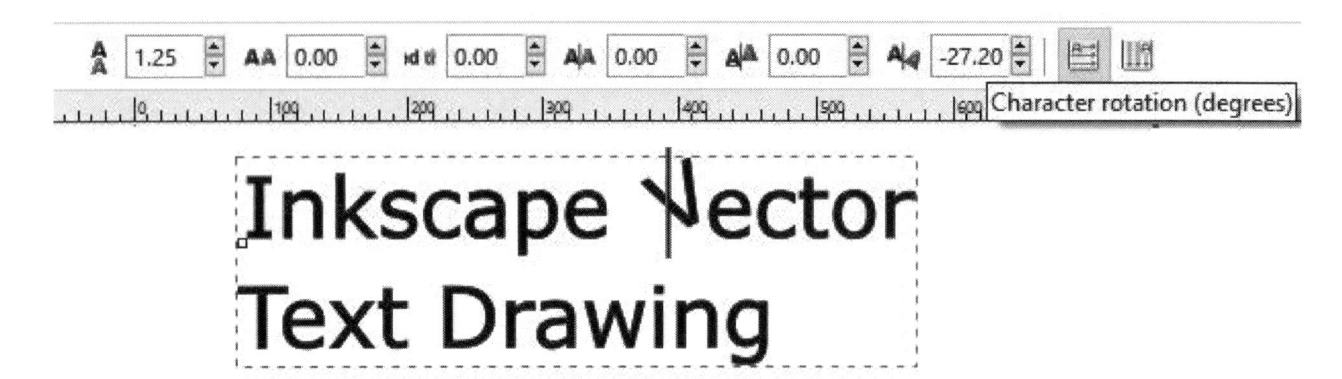

The sixth typographical control allows you to adjust the *character rotation*. It adjusts the rotation of the character at the point of the insertion point. Shown above, I have rotated the "V" in the word "Vector".

As you can see, although Inkscape might be considered a vector *drawing* application, it is also a powerful *typographical design* program.

Text on Path

CONTENTS

One of the most amazing things Inkscape can do, and one of the easiest, is to place text on a curved path.

First draw your text by clicking on the *Create and edit text objects tool*. Of course, selecting your font, font size, and text style using the *Tools Control Bar*.

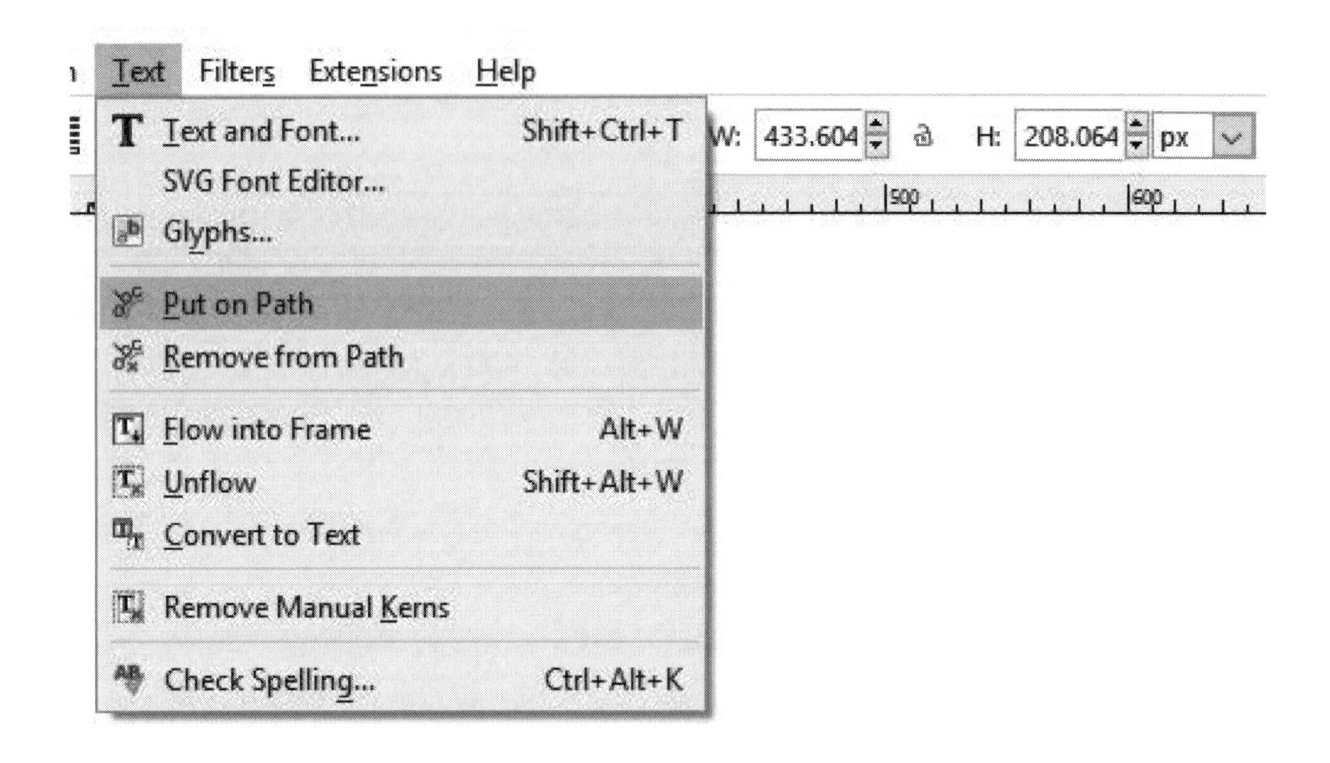

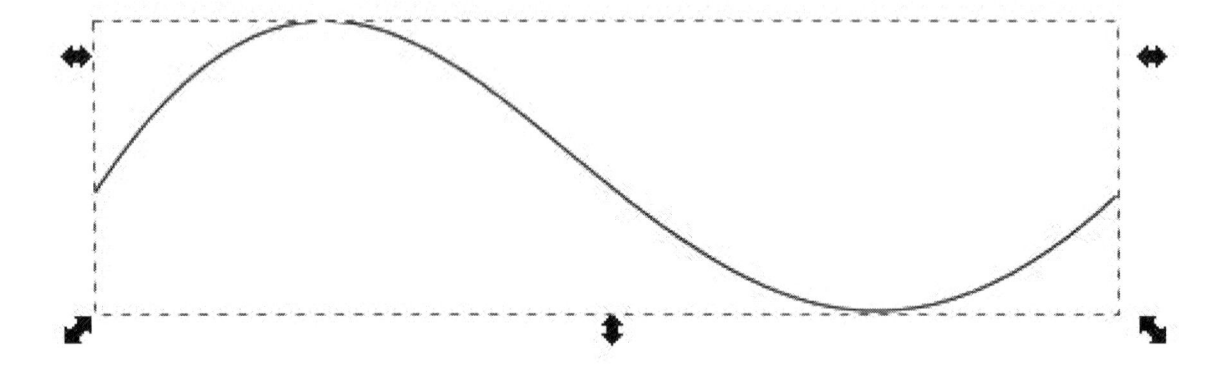

Next draw your path using the *Draw Bezier curves and straight lines* tool. You probably want to, in the *Fill and Stroke* dialog box, set your *Stroke style* Width to 0.

With the *Select and transform objects* Tool, draw a selection box around both the text and the path.

Inkscape Vector Drawing

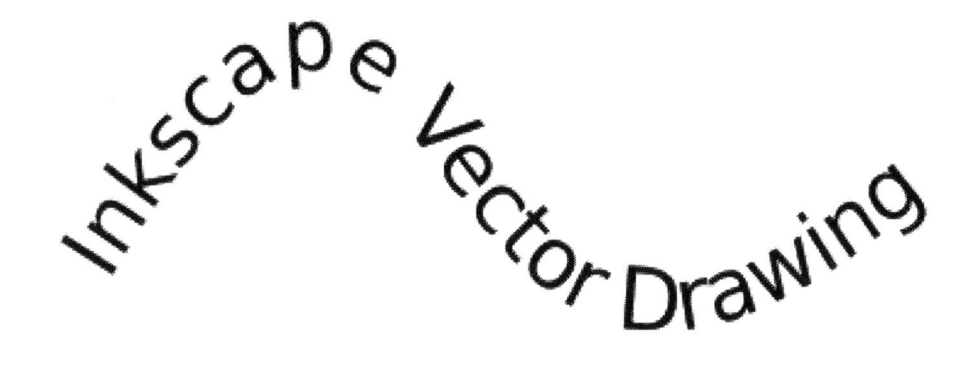

Then, in the main menu, select *Text| Put on path*. You can always adjust the shape of the path later, using the *Edit paths by nodes* tool, after you have placed the text on the path.

Inkscape Vector Drawing Inkscape Vector Drawing

How did I make the text shown above go in a circle? I just drew a circle using the *Create circles, ellipses, and arcs* tool, then used the *Text| Put on path* menu same as before, because, you see, every shape in Inkscape is actually a path.

Text in Shape

CONTENTS

Another interesting thing InkScape can do is to place text inside a shape.

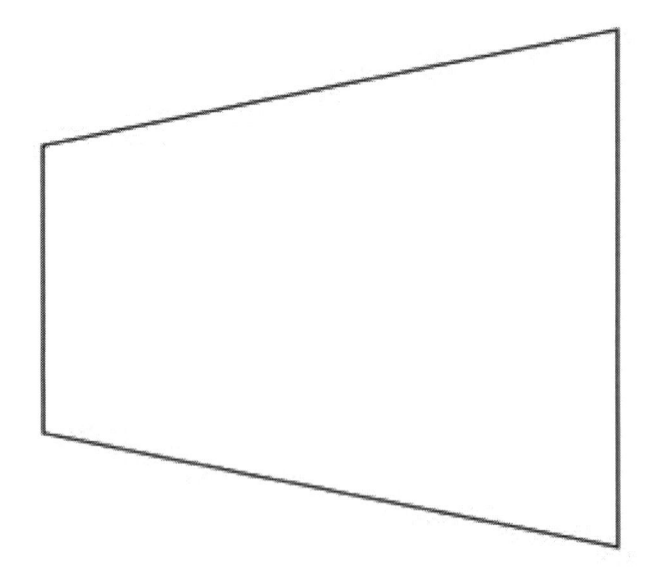

MYTEXT

First draw the shape by selecting the *Draw Bezier curves and straight lines* tool. Then draw the text by selecting the *Create and edit text objects* tool. Of course, selecting your font, font size, and text style using the Tools Control Bar.

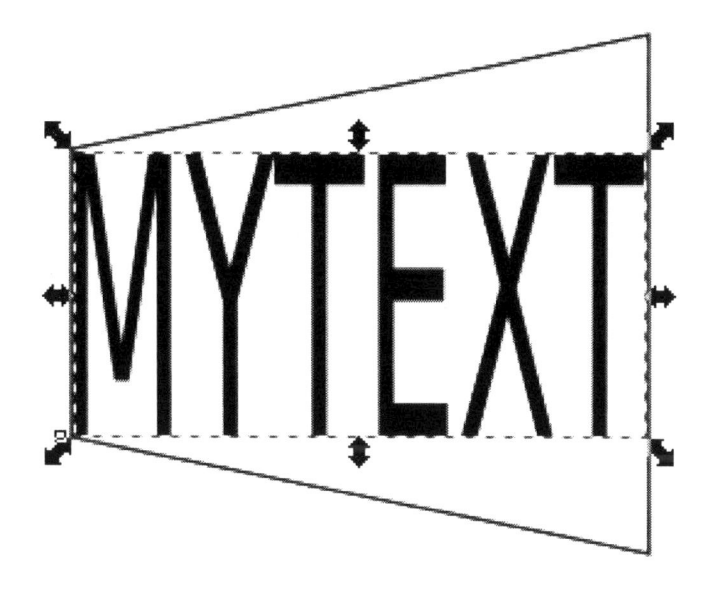

Next, using the *Select and transform objects* tool, fit the text to the shape, as shown above.

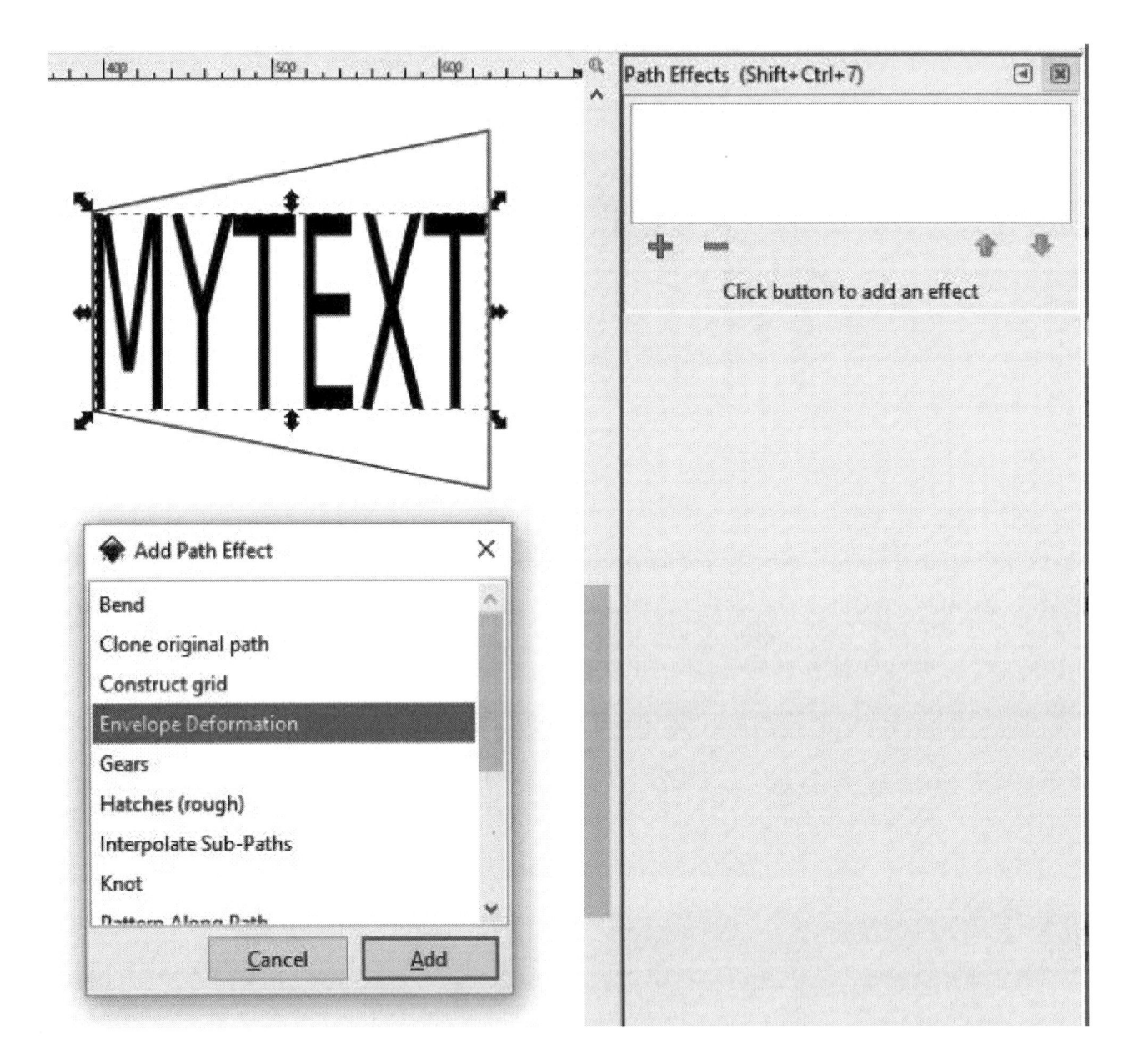

With the text selected, in the main menu select the *Path* menu. In the *Path* menu, select *Object to Path* (near the top of the menu). Then, in the *Path* menu, select *Path Effects* (near the bottom of the menu). This will open the *Path Effects* dialog box (if not already open).

In the *Path Effects* dialog box, click on the [+] icon, the *Add path Effect* dialog box will appear. In the *Add path Effect* dialog box, click on *Envelope Deformation*, then click on the [Add] button.

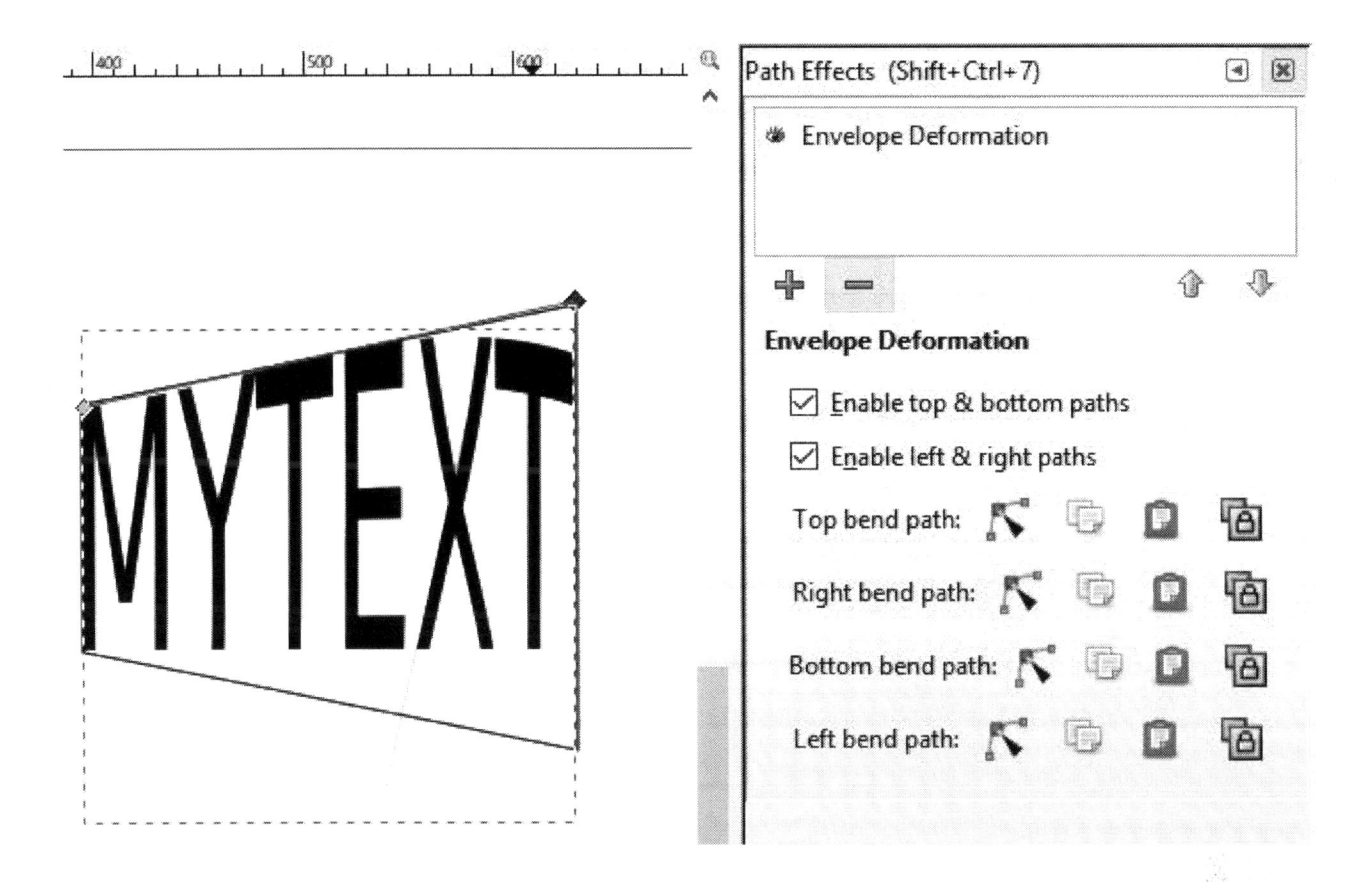

"Envelope Deformation" will appear in the *Path Effects* dialog box, and the *Path Effects* dialog box will display the *Envelope Deformation* controls. Make sure the *[x] Enable top & bottom paths* and the *[x] Enable left & right paths* check boxes are checked.

Just to the right of *Top bend path:* click on the icon (which looks similar to the Edit paths by nodes tool icon). This will place a green top path adjustment line on top of the text. The control, line has a diamond shaped handle on each end. use the right-side handle to adjust the shape of the text. Don't worry if the text doesn't distort exactly the way you had in mind, you have three more controls to use.

MYTEXT

Click on the *Right bend path:* icon and use the handles on each end to distort the text. Similarly use the *Bottom bend path:* and *Left bend path:* controls to adjust the shape of the text. Between the side distortion icons and the *Select and transform objects* tool, you should be able to fit the text inside your shape.

Also note that if you select the *Edit paths by nodes* tool you can shape the paths from which each letter is constructed, giving you complete control. After you have adjusted the paths to fit the shape to your satisfaction, you can delete the shape itself, if desired.

Place Greek Letters in Drawing

CONTENTS

Sometimes in a drawing, you need a character other than the English alphabet and numbers. For example star maps always use Greek characters to label the stars. Here is how you place Greek letters in an Inkscape Drawing (Windows operating system).

1. In the Start menu, navigate to *All Programs | Accessories | System Tools* and click on *Character Map*.

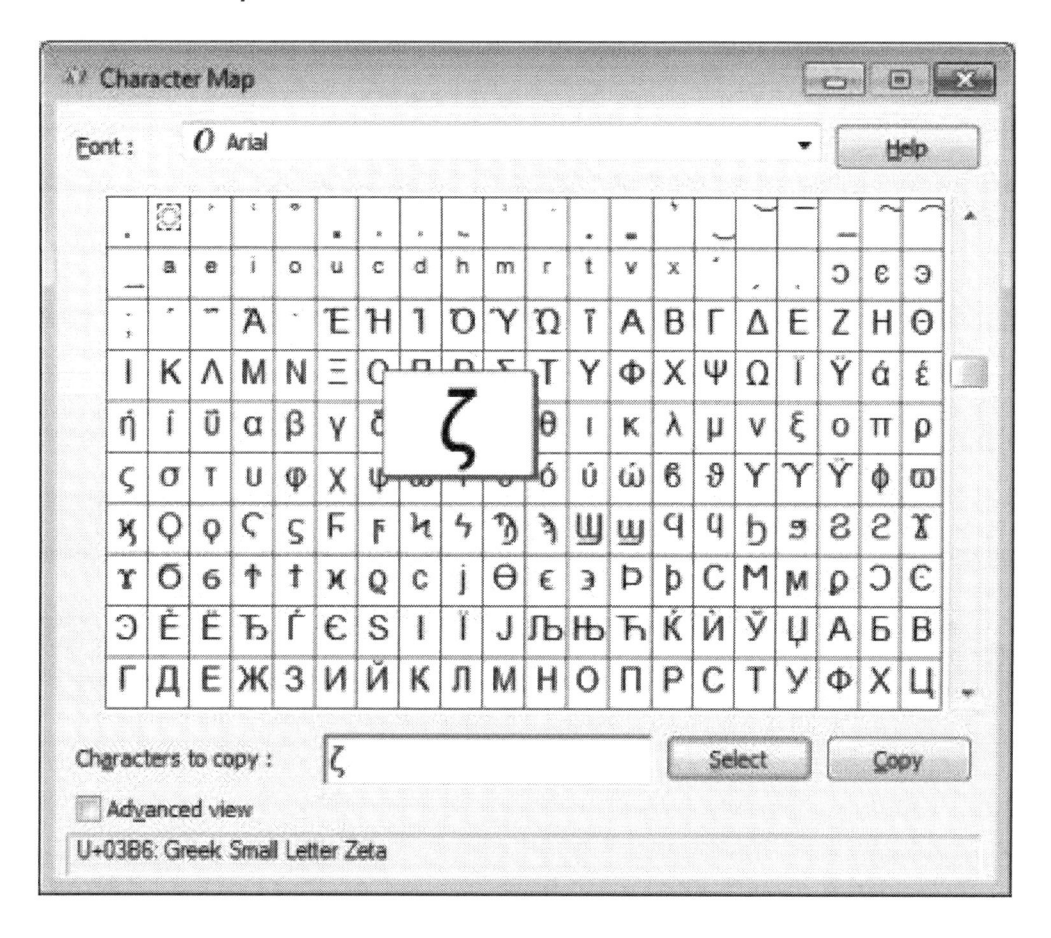

2. In the *Character Map* dialog box, scroll to and click on the character you want. Then click on the [Select] button.

The character will appear in the *Characters to copy:* text box and a description of the character will appear at the bottom of the Character Map dialog box. Note each time you click on the [Select] button another copy of the selected character will appear in the *Characters to copy:* text box, but you can easily edit the text box.

3. Click on the [Copy] button. Any character(s) in the *Characters to copy:* text box will be placed in the copy buffer.

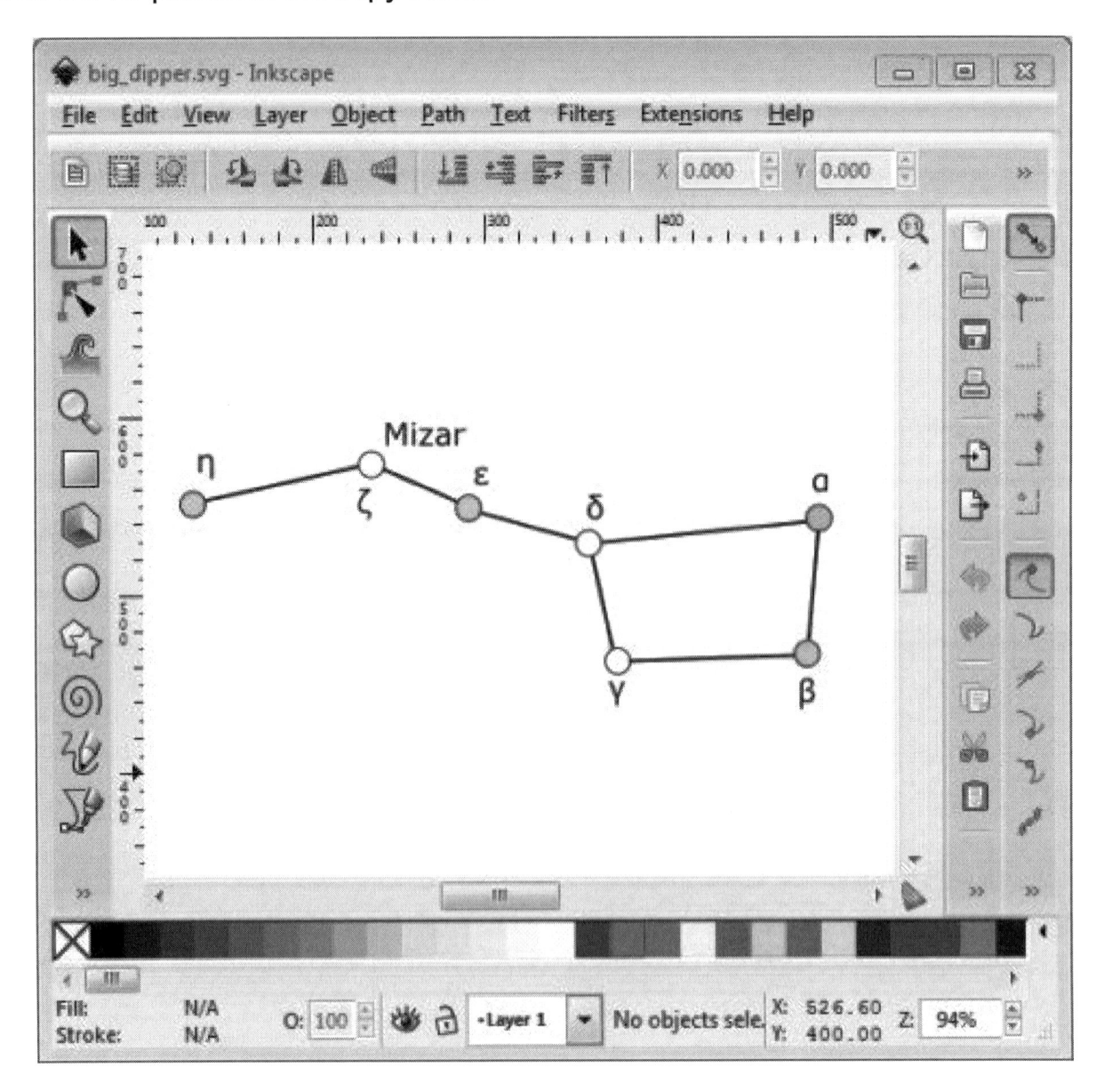

4. In Inkscape's toolbox, click on the text tool, and click in the drawing area where you want the character to appear.

5. In Inkscape's main menu, select *Edit | Paste*.

6. The character from the Character Map dialog box will appear in the drawing.

After you have pasted the character(s) you need into the drawing, you can click on the select tool (arrow) and on a character to resize or relocate the character as required.

Chapter 8: Advanced Techniques and Tools

Filters

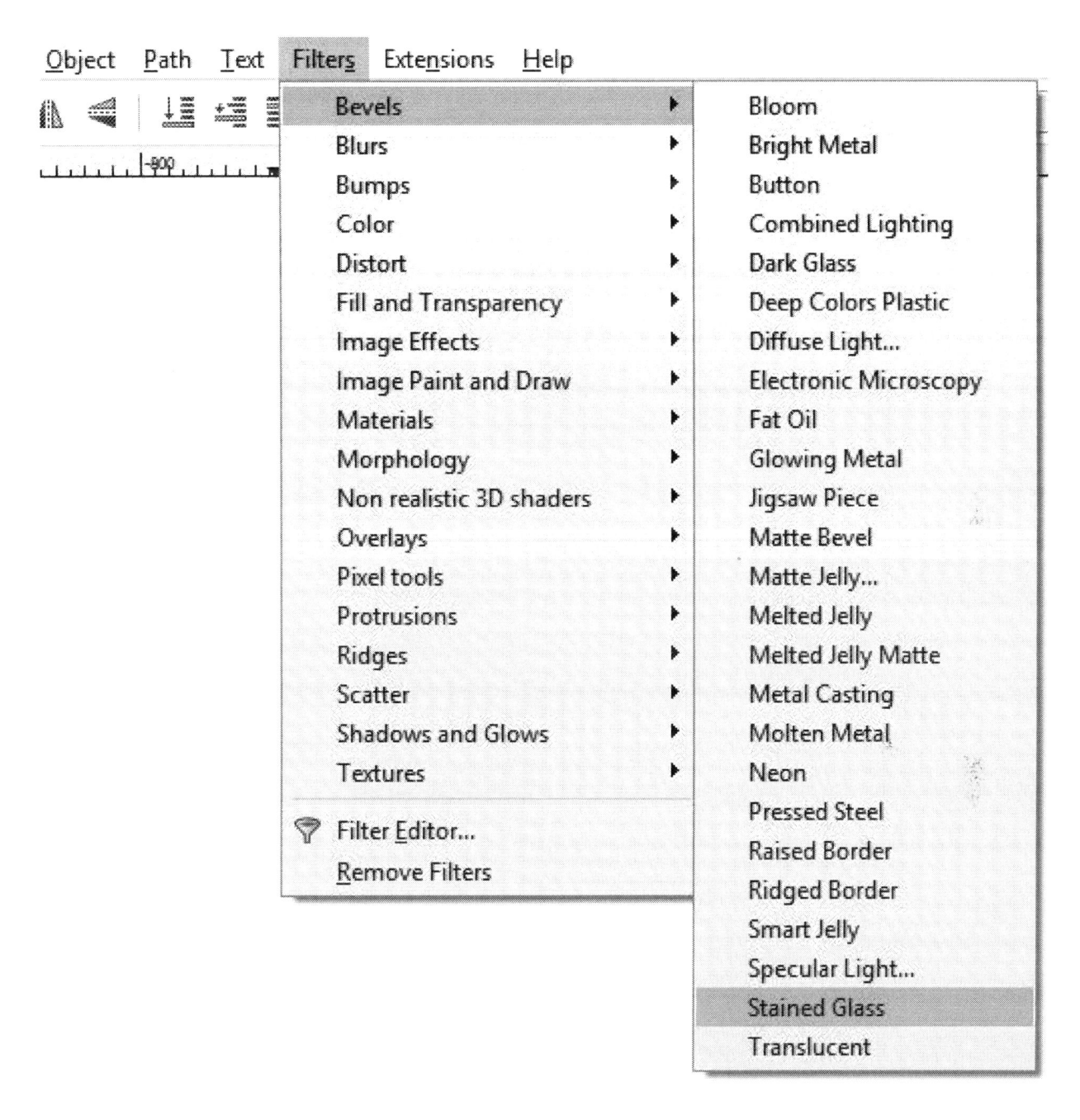

One of the most interesting things about Inkscape is that it provides hundreds of *filters*. A filter is a program algorithm that manipulates the digital data contained within an image. Filters have been around since the PC was invented, but never have so interesting filters many been provided for free. Filters have traditionally been used to perform such functions as adjusting the contrast, brightness, or sharpness of photographs. But today there are filters that produce unbelievably amazing effects. Below I describe a few of my favorite filters.

To create the above image, I used the *create rectangles and squares* tool to draw a square. I filled the square with light gray. I set the *Stroke style* Width to 0 (zero), and then applied the *Bevels | Stained Glass* filter.

I used the same method to create the above image, except this time I applied the *Distort | Torn Edges* filter.

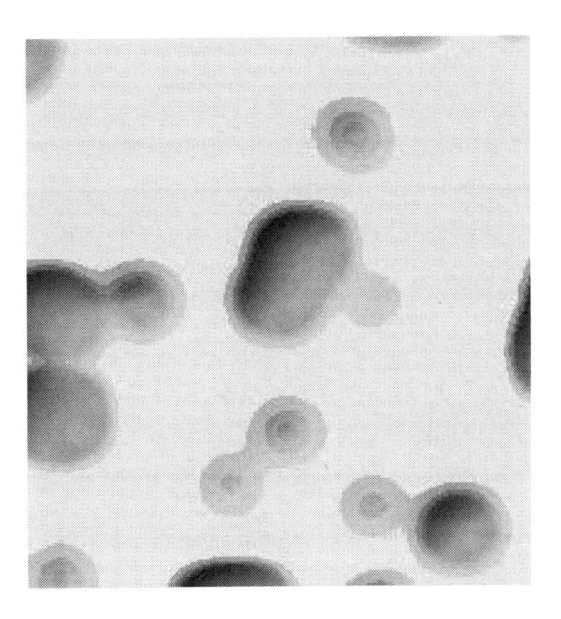

Again, same method to create the above image, except this time I applied the *Overlays | Swiss Cheese* filter.

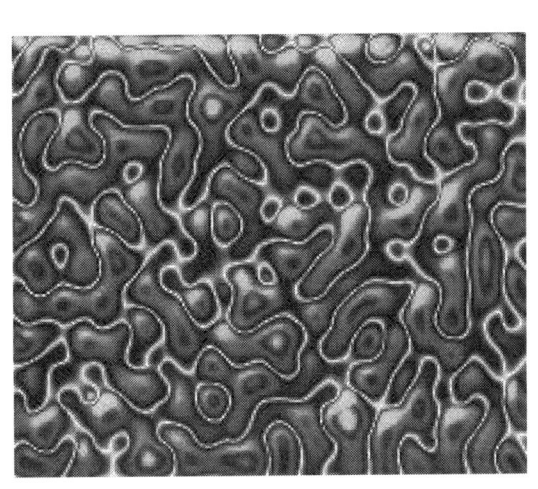

In the Materials submenu, Lizard skin creates an interesting effect that somewhat resembles lizard skin. Incidentally, after applying an effect to an area, you can still adjust its fill color, which can make a big difference in the appearance of the effect.

This is just a tiny sample of what you can do with filters. When you have time, you should play with different filters to see what they do. After you test a filter, just select the *Remove Filters* menu to clear the filter and try a different one. Filters provide a huge resource to enhance your drawings.

Filters That Create Buttons

CONTENTS

One of the most common uses of Inkscape is to create webpage elements. Although there are many ways to create 3D buttons in Inkscape, there are several filters that can be used to almost instantly create great looking web 3D buttons. First create the rectangle to which you will apply the filter to create the button.

Select the *Create rectangles and squares* tool in the toolbox. Draw a rectangle and, while it's selected, right click on it. In the popup menu that appears, select *Fill and Stroke*. In the *Fill and Stroke* dialog box that appears, on the *Stroke style* tab, set the *Width* to zero. Then on the *Fill tab* tab, set the fill color of the rectangle.

Bloom Filter

With the rectangle selected, choose *Filters | Bevels | Bloom* in the main menu. Shown above is an example of the nice button shape the Bloom filter creates.

Deep Colors Plastic Filter

With the rectangle selected, choose *Filters | Bevels | Deep Colors Plastic* in the main menu. Shown above is an example of the nice button shape the Deep Colors Plastic filter creates.

Pressed Steel Filter

Click Here

With the rectangle selected, choose *Filters | Bevels | Pressed Steel* in the main menu. Shown above is an example of the nice button shape the Pressed Steel filter creates.

Raised Boarder Filter

Click Here

With the rectangle selected, choose *Filters | Bevels | Raised Boarder* in the main menu. Shown above is an example of the nice button shape the Raised Boarder filter creates.

3D Marble Filter

Click Here

With the rectangle selected, choose *Filters | Materials | 3D Marble* in the main menu. Shown above is an example of the nice button shape the 3D Marble filter creates.

Select *Create and edit text objects* in the toolbox and create the text for your button. With your text selected, right click on it. In the popup menu that appears, select *Fill and Stroke*. In the *Fill and Stroke* dialog box that appears, on the *Fill tab* tab, set the color of the text. Then drag your text to the button and resize it to match with the size of the text.

Clipping

CONTENTS

Clipping is the process of defining a "clipping area" which might be a regular shape or a shape created with paths, and placing that clipping area over a part of the drawing. When the clip is set, everything outside the clipping area is removed (not displayed).

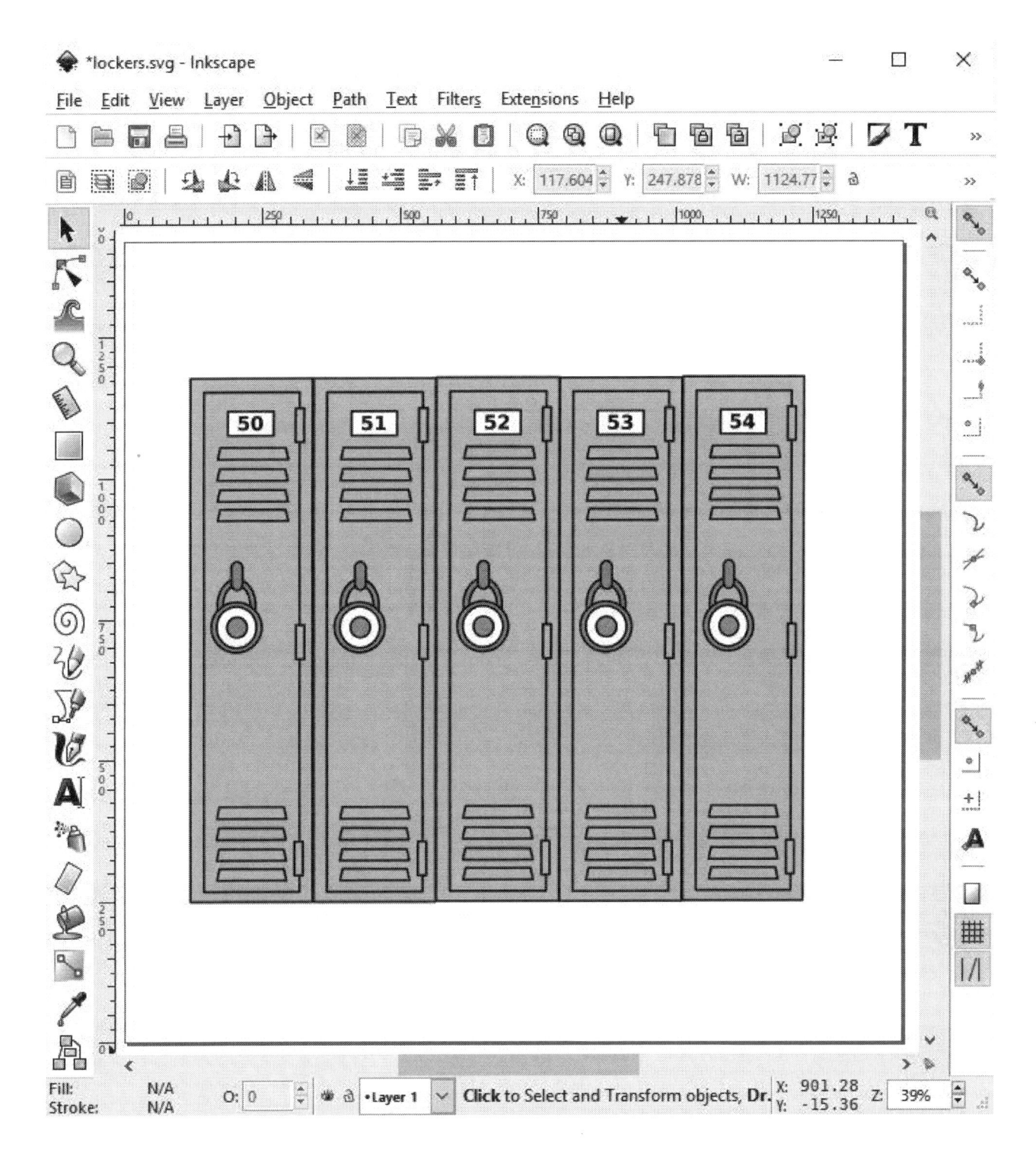

If the area to be clipped contains more than one object, the objects must be grouped. To group objects, use the *Select and transform objects* tool to draw a box around the objects, then in the main menu select *Object | Group*.

Draw the clipping area. You may draw the clipping area immediately on top of the object or group to be clipped, or next to it and then drag over the object to be clipped. In any case the clipping path must be higher in the z-order than the object to be clipped. You can use the main menu "Object | Raise to Top" selection.

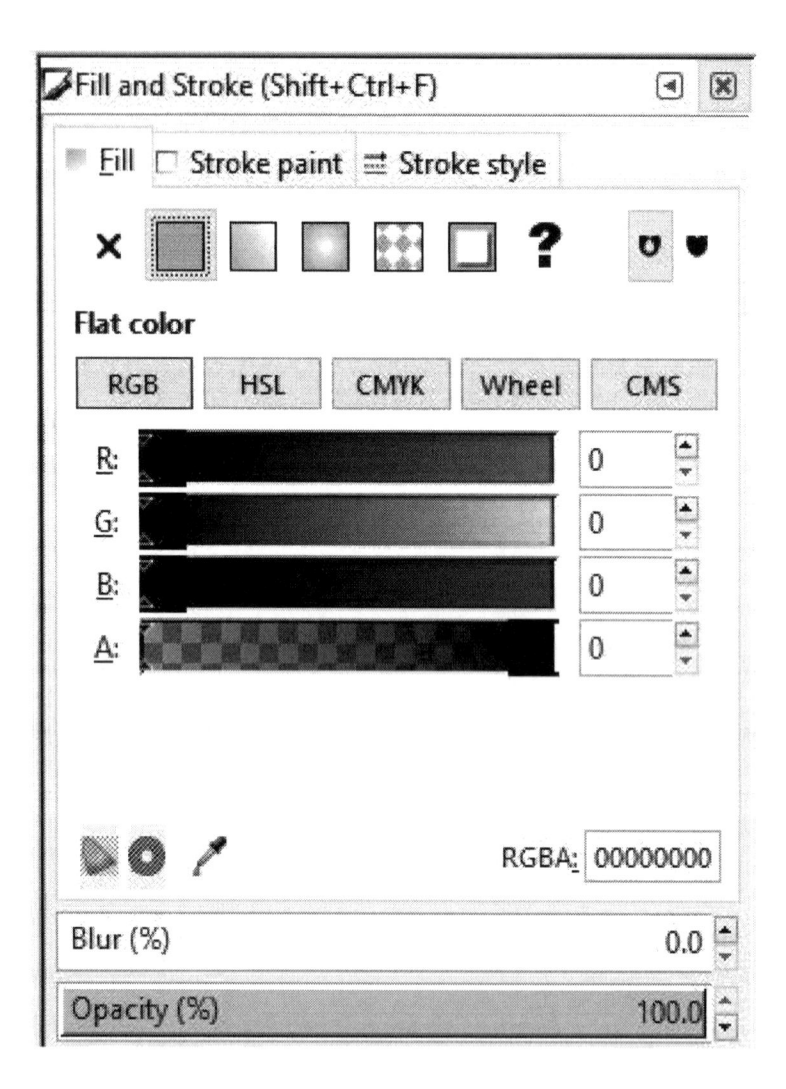

Make sure the clip area fill is has its alpha (transparency) set to zero. Shown below is a clipping area shaped like a graduation cap.

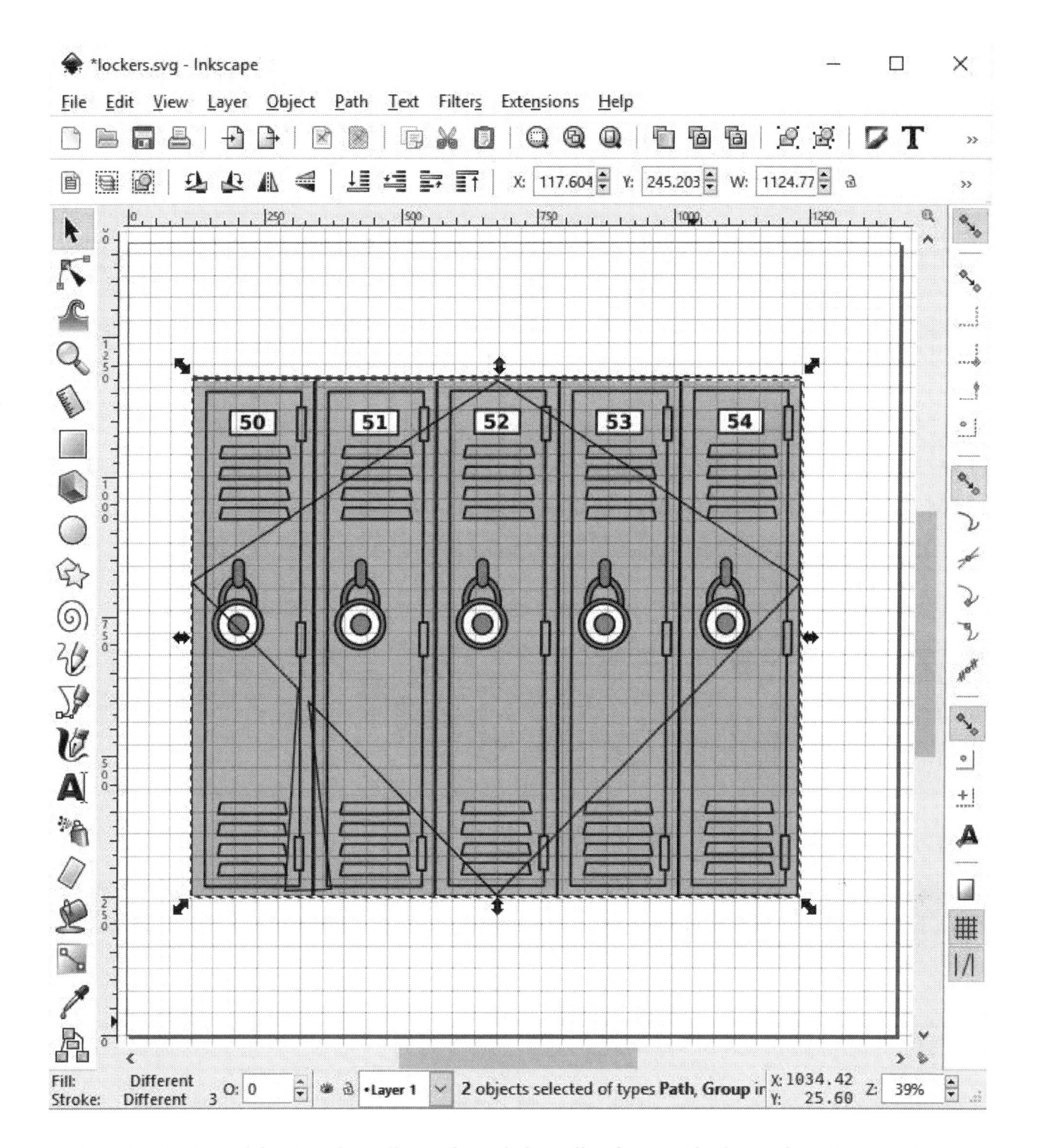

Select both the object to be clipped and the clipping path, by using the "Select and transform objects" tool to draw a box around them both. Then in the main menu "Object" menu, select "Clip | Set".

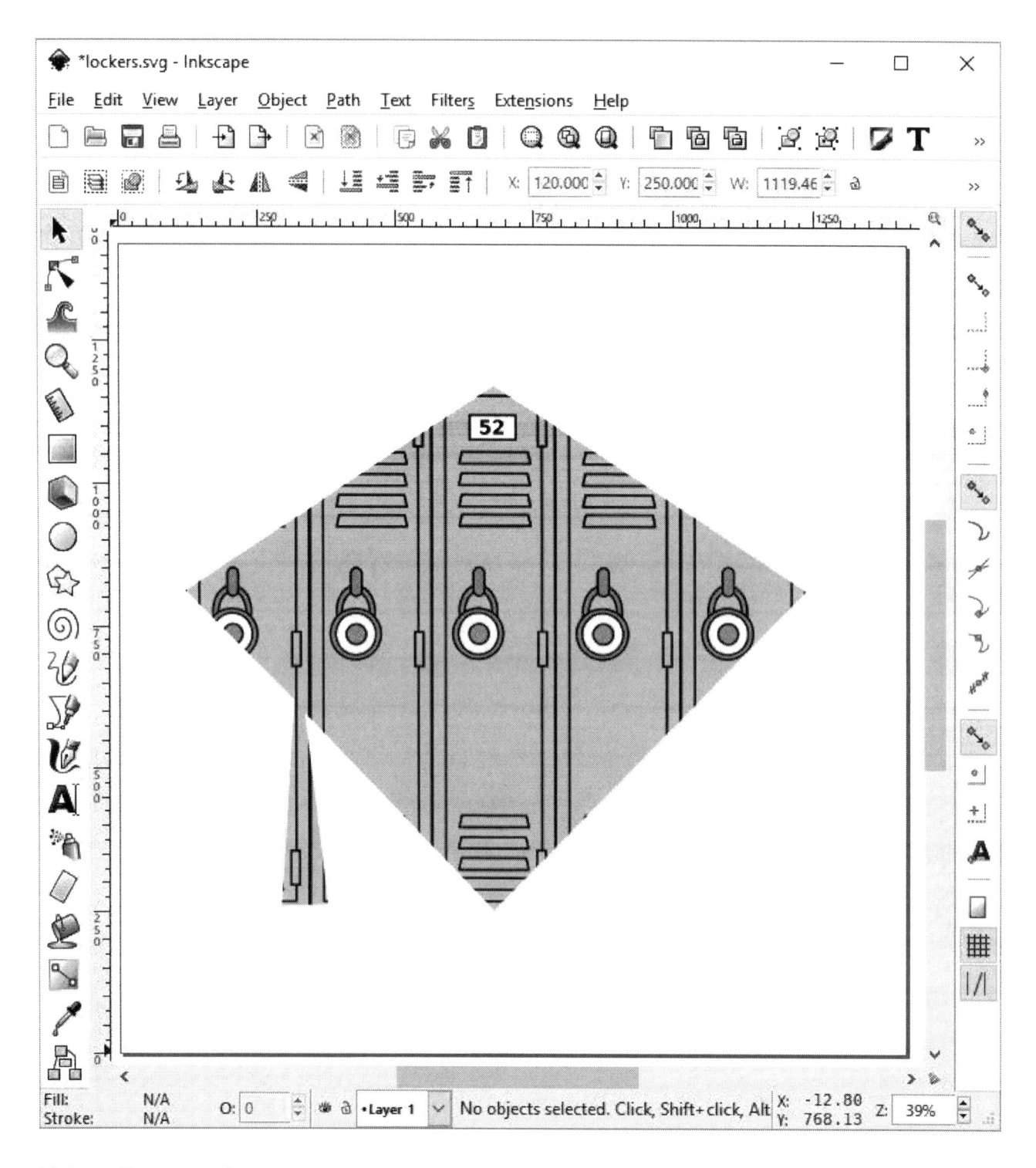

If the clip area does not appear as required, with the object selected, in the main menu "Object" menu, select "Clip | Release". Then you can adjust the shape or size of the clip arrea and try again.

Embed Drawing in Webpage

CONTENTS

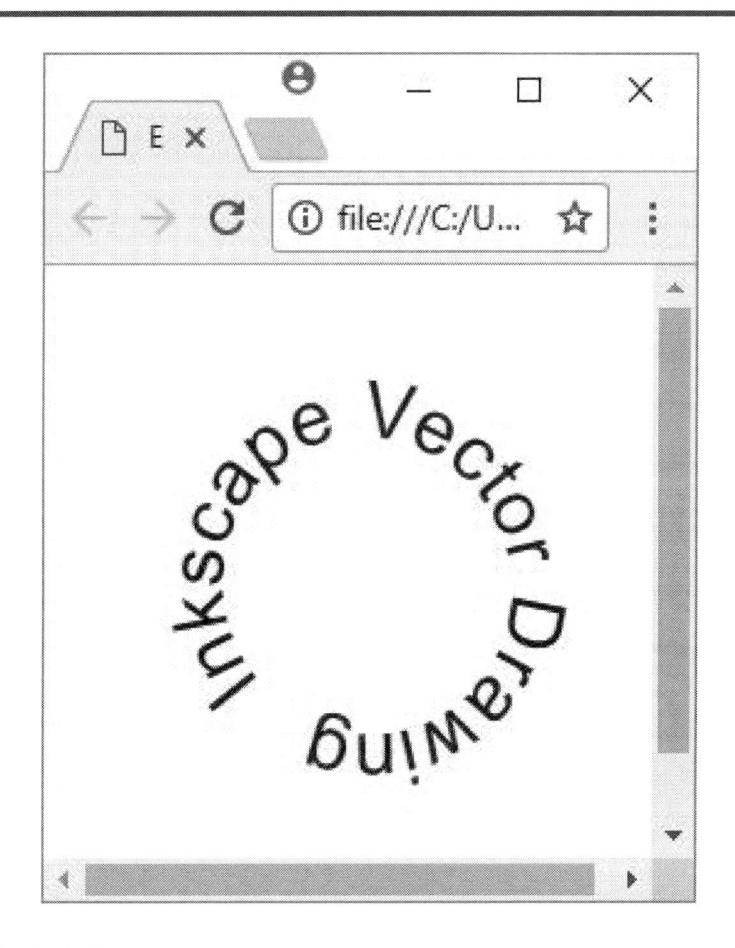

```
<!DOCTYPE html>
<html lang='en'>
<head>
<meta charset='utf-8'>
<title>Embed in Webpage</title>
</head>
<body>

<embed src="lbd.svg" width="250" height="250"></embed>

</body>
</html>
```

Being able to embed an Inkscape drawing in a webpage can be a huge advantage. Since a regular raster image consists of 128 bits or more per pixel, describing a line drawing with vectors can greatly reduce the load time of a webpage. I was once in a situation where FTP was not allowed. Fortunately I had an application on the server that let me write files to the server, and an Inkscape .svg file is actually just a text file.

Shown above is example code to embed an Inkscape file in a webpage. Use the *embed* tag. Set the *src* attribute to the path to the file. Set the *width* and *height* to the dimensions of the Inkscape document, which you can get from the *File | Document Properties* menu.

Export Inkscape Drawing as Image

CONTENTS

Although Inkscape images can be embedded in webpages, for most other applications you'll need a raster image format such as .png (public network graphic). You can export your drawing in that format by selecting *Export PNG image* in the *File menu*.

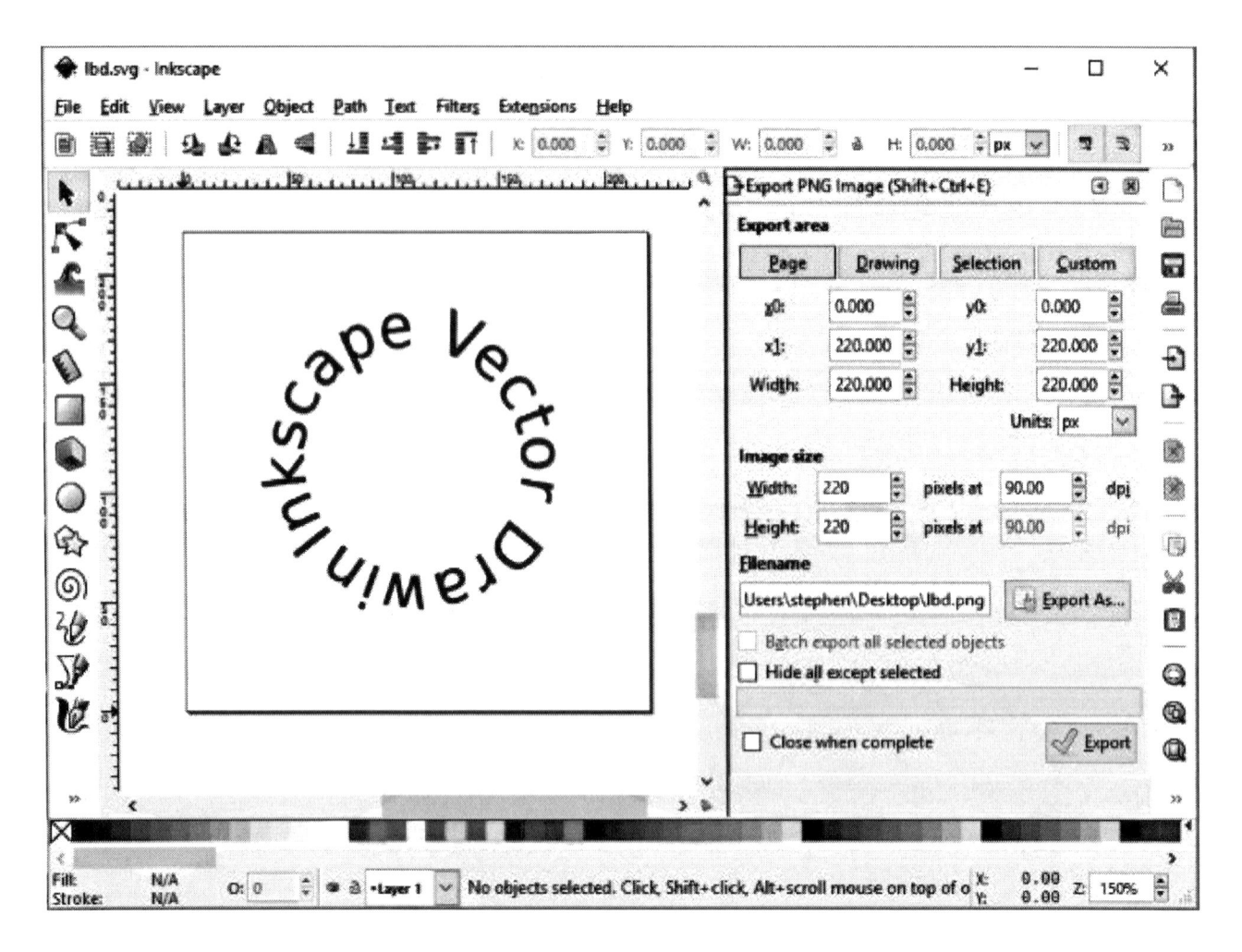

The *Export PNG image* dialog box will appear. In this dialog box you can enter the coordinates of the part of the drawing that you want to export as an image. The easiest way to export an image is export the page as an image. Click on the [Page] button, then in the *Filename* text box enter the path and filename you want the image saved to. Also make sure the *Image size* spin boxes are set to the size of the page, which you can determine by selecting *Document Properties...* in the *File* menu.

When all the information is set, click on the [Export] button. The image file will appear at the location you have specified. If .png file format is not what you want, you'll need to use a paint program to convert the file to the desired format.

Configuring Document Properties

CONTENTS

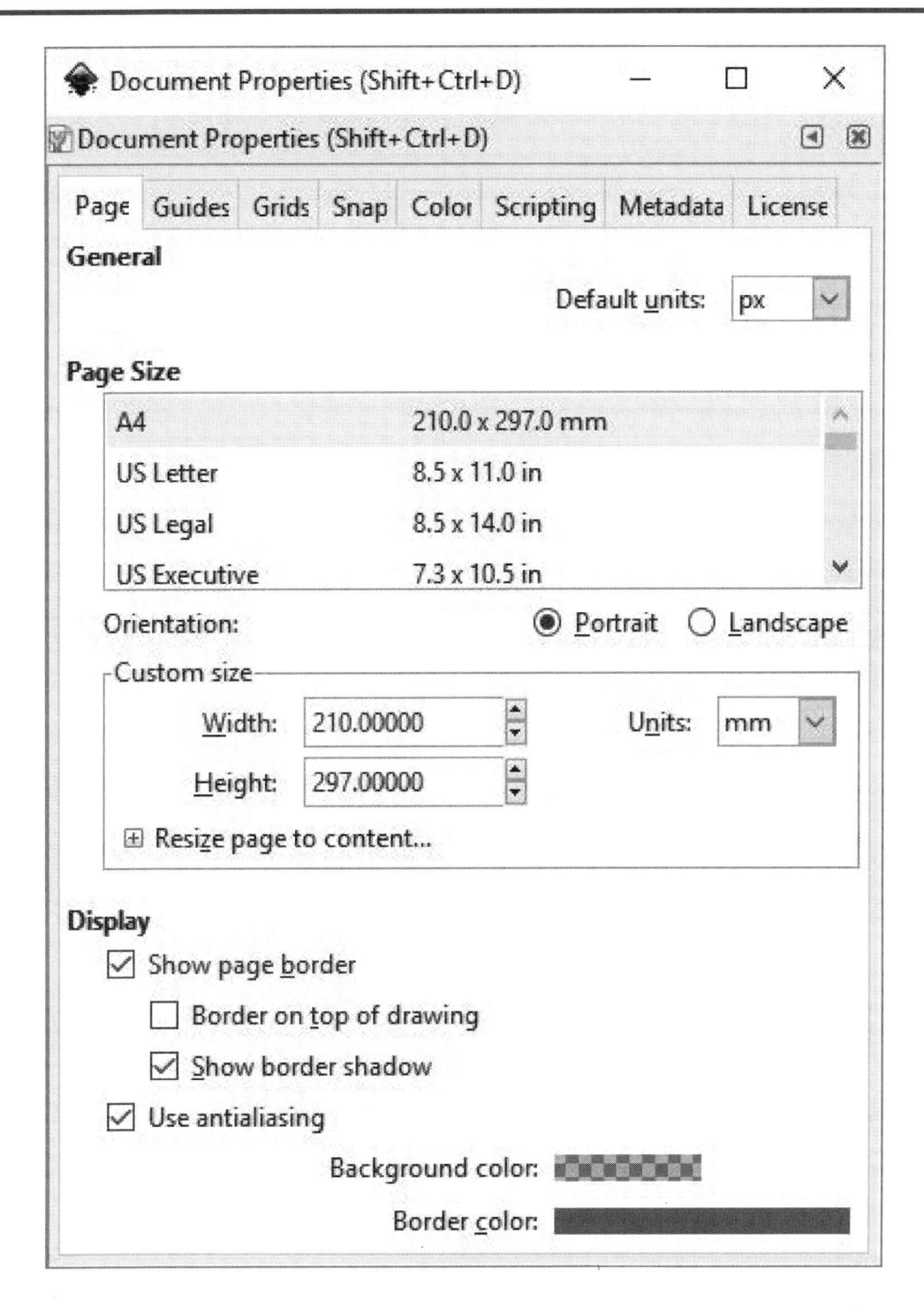

One of the first things you might do when starting a drawing is to configure the document's properties. In the main menu select *File | Document Properties...*, the Document Properties dialog box will appear.

On the *page* tab, you can set the size of the page. You might want to do this if you are printing or exporting the drawing.

Note at the bottom of the Document Properties dialog box, if you click inside the box next to *background color:* or *Border color:*, a small dialog box will appear containing color adjustment controls.

As you move the mouse pointer around the canvas you'll see tiny arrows on the rulers that move to stay horizontally and vertically aligned with the mouse pointer. Place the mouse pointer over one of these arrows, press and hold the mouse button while you drag onto the canvas, a guide will appear.

On the *Guides* tab, check the checkbox next to *Show guides*. If you click inside the box next to *Guide color:* or *Highlight color:*, a small dialog box will appear containing color adjustment controls.

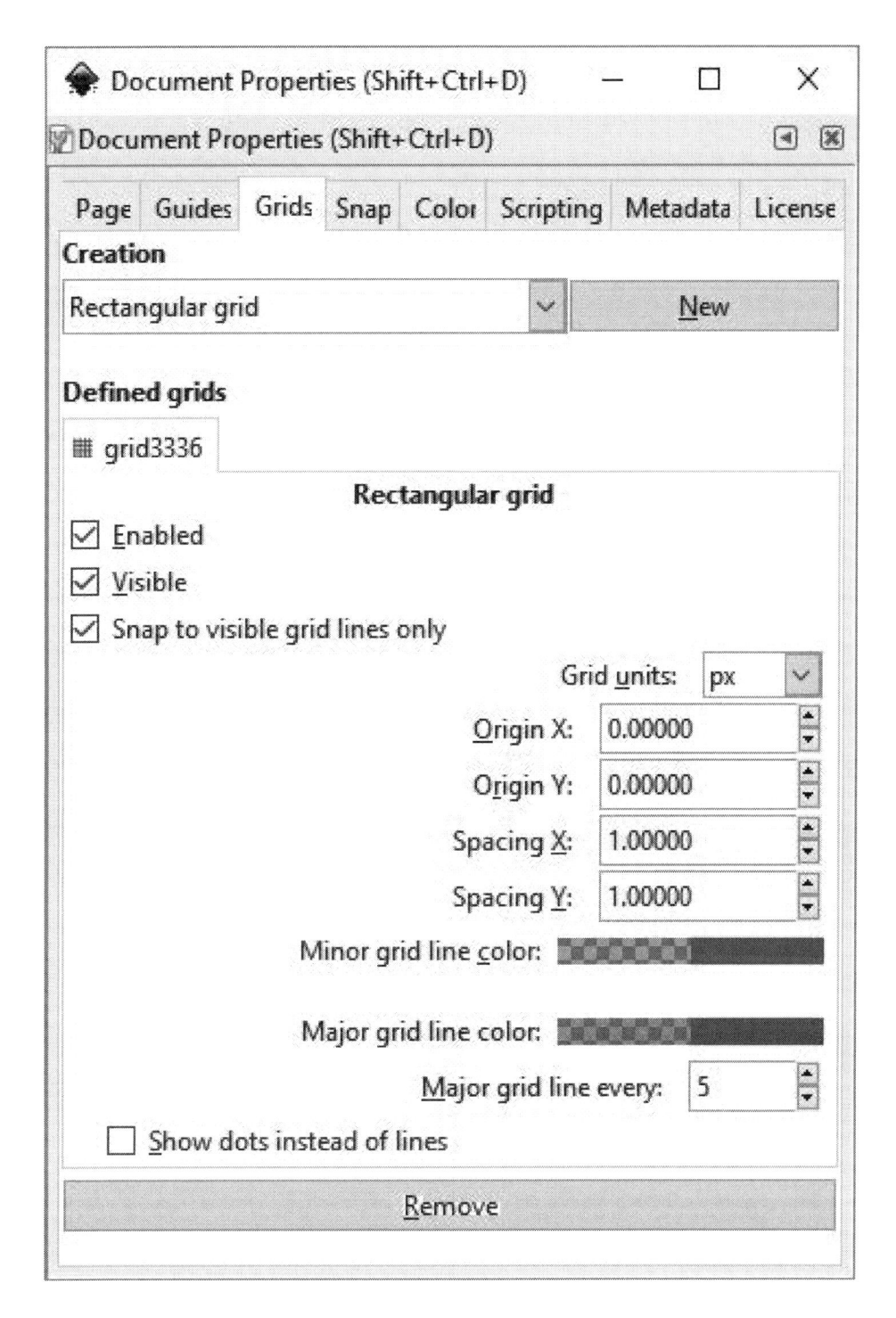

On the *Grids* tab, click on the [New] button and controls will appear that allow you to set the grid origin and spacing. A check box near the bottom of the dialog box lets you select to show dots instead of lines.

If you click inside the box next to *Minor grid line color:* or *Major grid line color:*, a small dialog box will appear containing color adjustment controls.

By clicking on the [New] button You can define multiple grids. Click on the [Remove] button at the bottom at the dialog box to delete a grid.

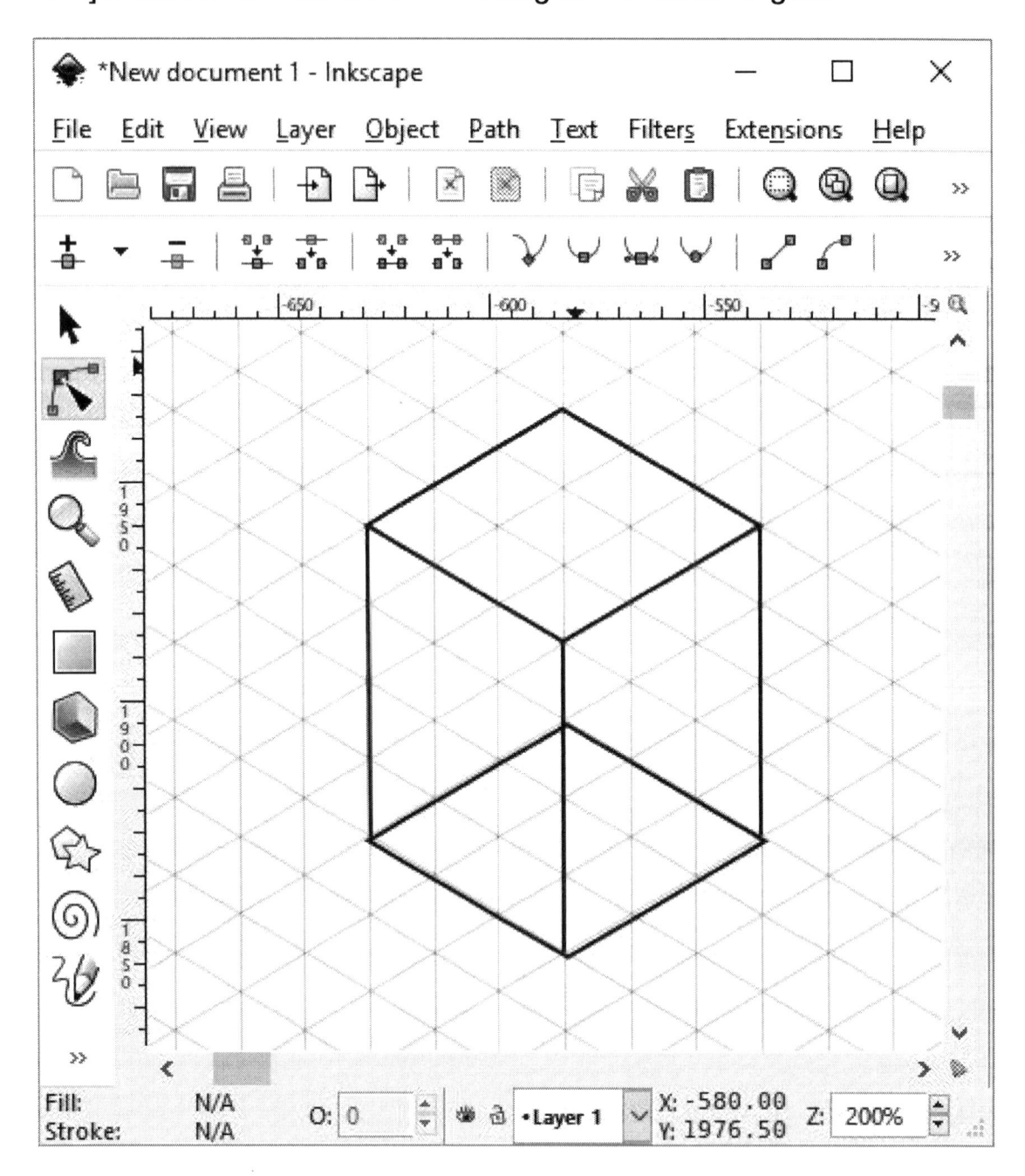

The drop-down list on the Grids tab lets you select an *Axometric* grid. The axometric is, by default, set to 30 degrees. An axometric grid makes it easier to draw with a 3D appearance. The angles of the axometric grid lines are configurable.

Snap is when you are dragging something like a node, and when you get within a certain distance of a grid or guide, the node you are dragging pops to it. On the *Snap* tab are slide controls that let you set how close you must be to cause a snap.

Many Inkscape users find snap annoying and it's not clear how to disable it. To disable it, in the main menu select *View | Show/Hide* and set a check next to *Snap Controls Bar*. Then in the Snap Controls Bar, click on the icon at the very top *Enable Snapping*.

I think you'll find that for some drawing tasks, snap is very helpful. For others it's very annoying.

Other tabs on the Document Properties dialog box let you add meta data to the document such as *Title, Date, Creator, Rights*, etc. But the main tabs you'll find useful are *Page, Grids* and *Snap*.

Configuring Inkscape Preferences

CONTENTS

Inkscape is a highly configurable application. Many of these configuration options can be set through the *Preferences* dialog box. To open the Preferences dialog box, in Inkscape's main menu choose *Edit*, and scroll down to the bottom of the menu to select *Preferences....*

There is probably a hundred things you can configure through the Preferences dialog box. Here I'll describe a couple of the most important ones.

One thing you might want to configure is how bounding boxes work. A bounding box is a rectangular border around a selected object or area. The sides of a bounding box run along the vertical and horizontal axis. A bounding box usually has little squares that you can drag to move, transform, rotate, or scale the object.

A bounding box should be the smallest size that contains the entire selected object or area. Inkscape has two kinds of bounding box. The *Visual* bounding box which includes the object including the stroke thickness, and the *Geometrical* bounding box which uses the objects nodes. This makes a more precise bounding box.

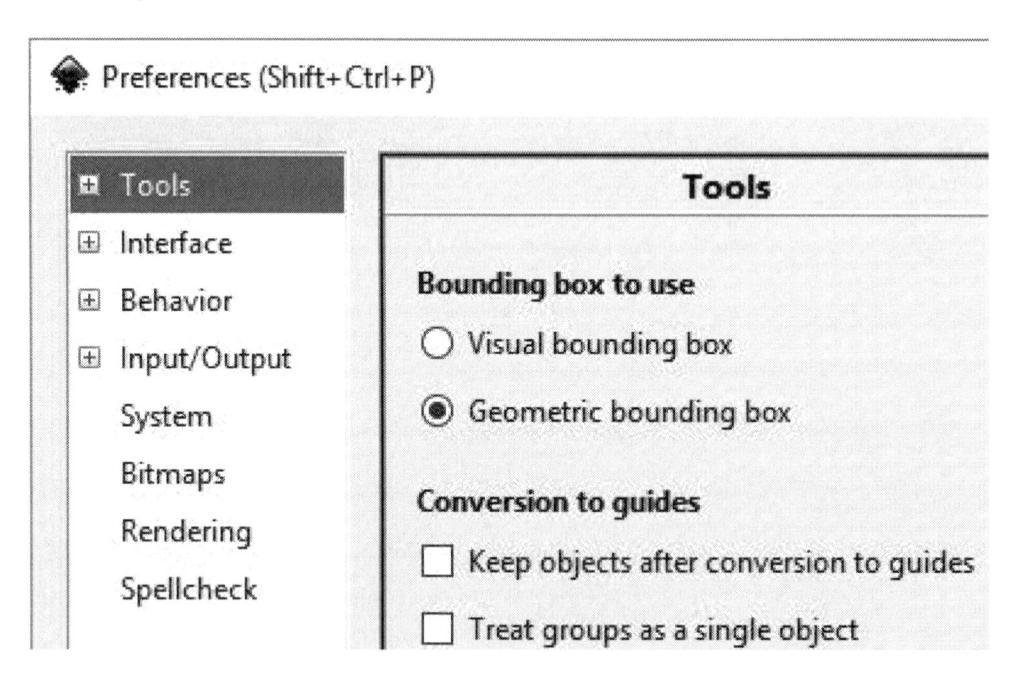

To configure the type of bounding box, expand the *Tools* branch and click on the text *Tools* to highlight it and open the *Bounding box* setting page. Here you'll find radio buttons to set the bounding box to either *Visual bounding box* or *Geometric bounding box*.

The grid is a very important aid to accurate drawing. But having the canvas so covered with lines may make it cluttered. To set grid preferences, expand the *Interface* branch and click on *Grids* to highlight it and open the *Grids* setting page.

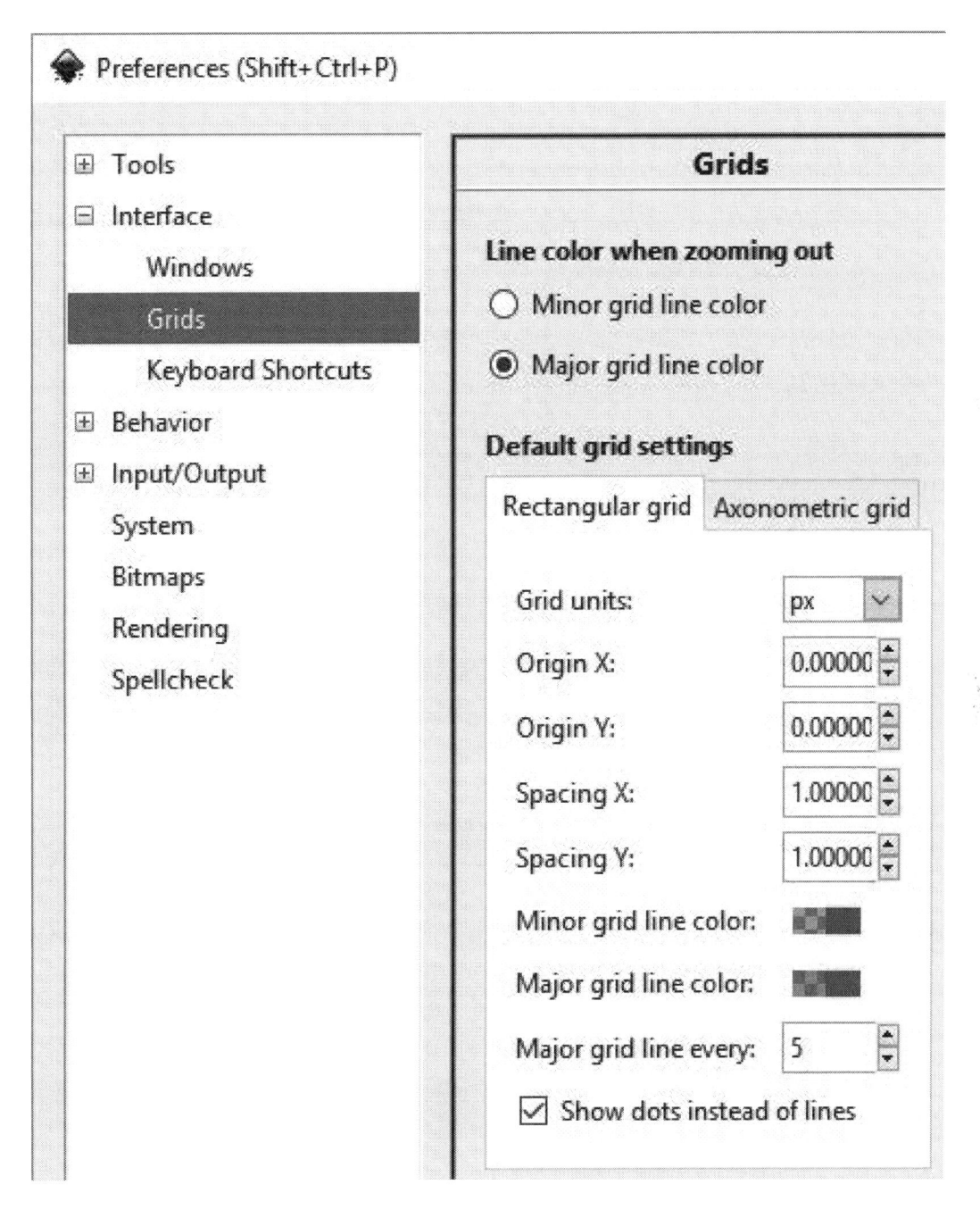

Here you'll find settings for the grid units, the grid origin, the grid spacing, and how many units apart to place grid lines. But the setting I find most interesting is the checkbox [] *Show dots instead of lines*. Set this checkbox to be able to use the grid without it being so cluttered with lines.

One of the most important actions involved in drawing is moving around (scrolling and zooming) the canvas. Zooming is easily accomplished by tapping the keyboard [+] and [-] keys. Scrolling is easily accomplished by holding down the [Ctrl] key and using the arrow keys, or using the mouse wheel. The mouse wheel pans up and down. Hold down the [Shift] key and the mouse wheel pans left and right.

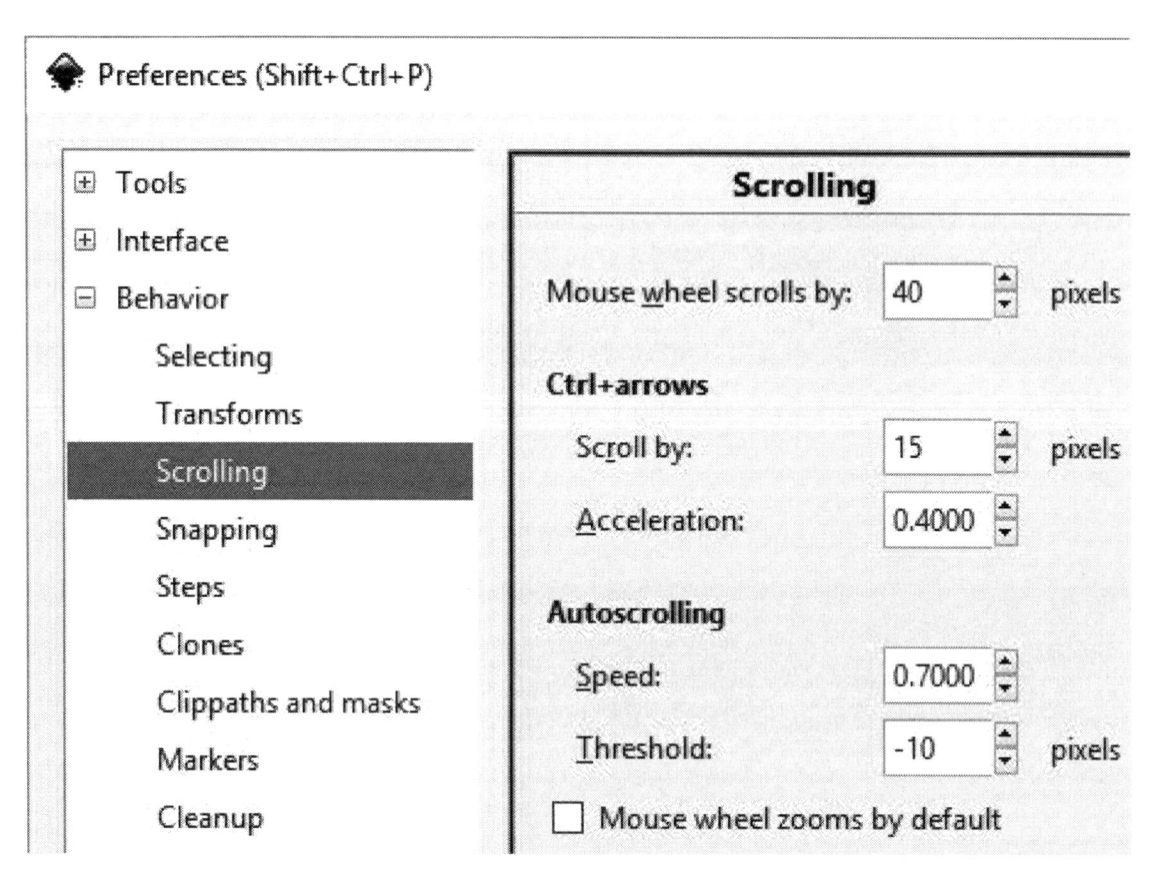

You can configure the speed of scrolling in the Preferences dialog box by expanding the *Behavior* branch and clicking on *Scrolling*. At the bottom of the Scrolling settings page is a checkbox [] Mouse wheel zooms by default. I uncheck this box because zooming is quite easy by tapping the keyboard [+] and [-] keys, however panning requires using two keys ([Ctrl] and arrow key) if you don't configure the mouse wheel for scrolling.

Exercise : Draw an Apple

CONTENTS

In this section you'll learn how to make a complete Inkscape vector drawing. If you're an experienced Inkscape user, you should skip this section. If you're new to Inkscape and vector drawing, this is a very easy beginners example. It does not demonstrate all of Inkscape's features, not by a long shot, but it will allow you to create respectable results.

1. Open Inkscape to full screen and set the zoom to 150%. To set the zoom, in the bottom-right corner of the screen, type 150 into the Z: text box and press [Enter]. If the Z: text box is not visible in the bottom-right corner of the screen, then you don't have the Statusbar enabled. To enable the Statusbar, in the *View* menu select *Show/Hide* and in the submenu set a check next to *Statusbar*.

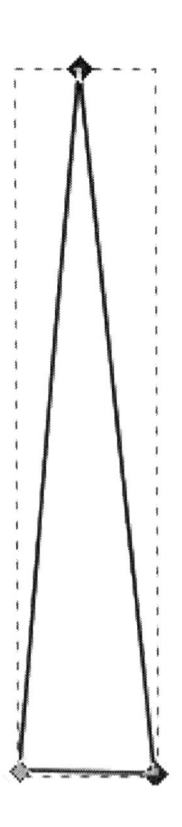

2. Draw the outline of the apple. In the toolbox on the left side of the screen, click on the *Draw Bezier curves and straight lines* tool. Then click in the drawing area and draw the triangle shown above.

To draw the paths for the triangle, move the mouse pointer to the bottom-left node of the triangle and click. Move the mouse to the top of the triangle and click again to set the node. Move the mouse pointer to the bottom-right of the triangle and click again to set that node. Then move the mouse pointer directly on top of the bottom-left node and double click. Double-clicking ends the creation of paths.

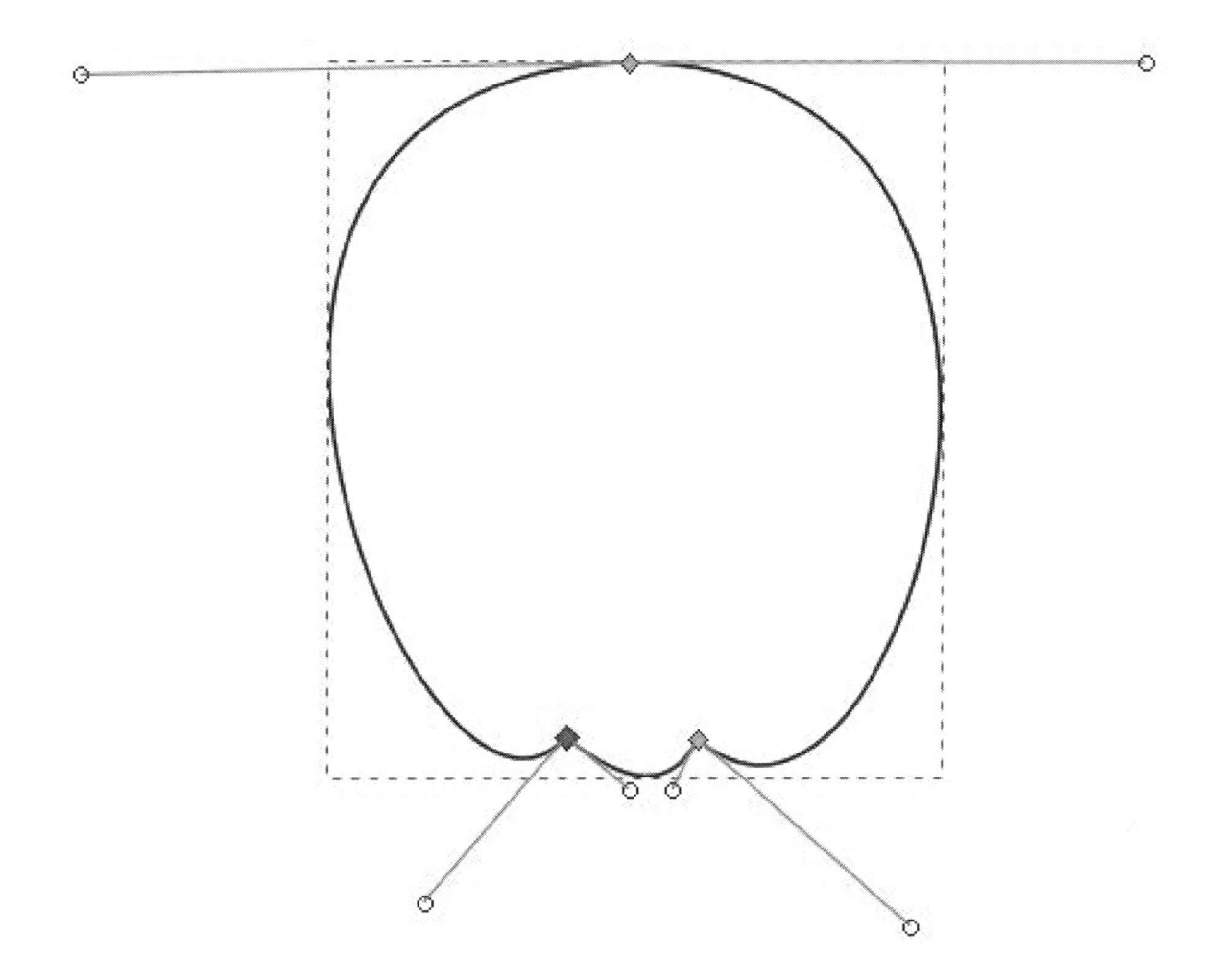

3. Set the shape of the apple. In the toolbox, select the *Edit paths by nodes* tool. Then move the mouse pointer over any one of the paths in the triangle and click. The nodes will become visible. Press and hold the mouse button and use the mouse to shape the path.

With the *Edit paths by nodes* tool selected, when you click on a node, *handles* will become visible. Press and hold the mouse button and drag the tiny circle at the end of a handle to aid in shaping the path.

You need to shape the apple exactly as shown here.

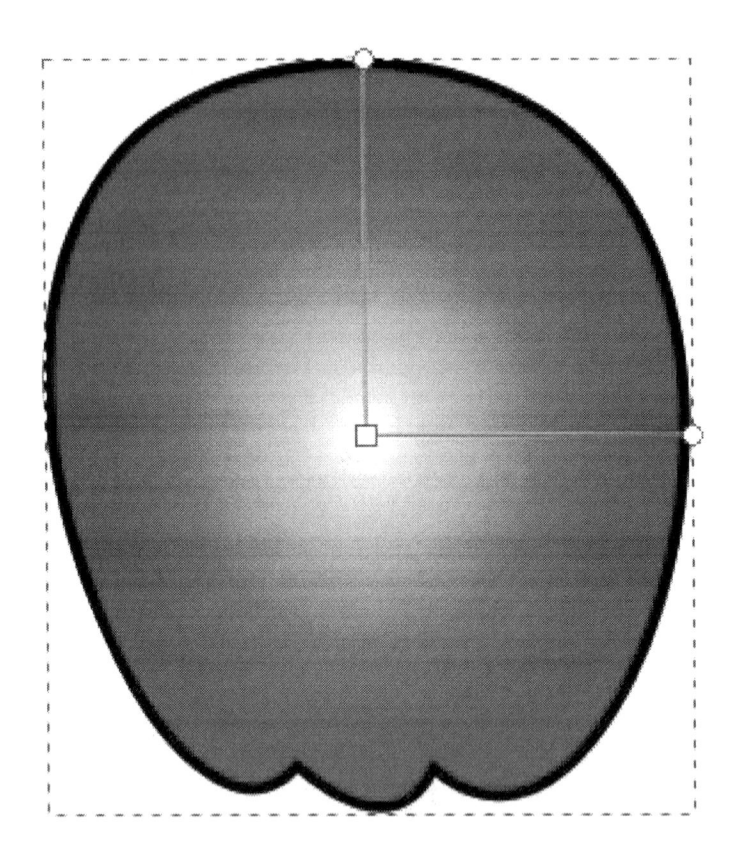

4. Set the stroke width. With the apple outline selected, right-click on one of the paths. In the popup menu that appears, select *Fill and Stroke*....

In the *Fill and Stroke* dialog box that appears, select the *Stroke Style* tab and in the *Width:* text box type 3 and press the [Enter] key. Make sure *px* (pixels) is selected in the units drop down box next to the *Width:* text box.

5. Set the fill color. In the *Fill and Stroke* dialog box, select the *Fill* tab. On the Fill tab, click on the *Flat Color* button. Below that , click on the *RGB* button. Drag the R: slide control all the way to the right (the text box should contain 255).

Drag the G: and B: slider controls all the way to the left (the text box should contain 0). The A: slide control should be all the way to the right (255).

6. Set the radial gradient. In the *Fill and Stroke* dialog box, click on the *Radial gradient* button. A radial gradient will appear on the apple. Most likely the radial gradient will be reverse what you want. To reverse the gradient, select the *Create and edit gradients* tool. Click on one of the gradient stops, then press the [Shift][R] buttons. The gradient should reverse.

Next, select the *Edit paths by nodes* and tool move the center stop of the radial gradient to the upper-left area of the apple. You can also drag the end stops to shape the radial gradient as desired. Press the [Esc] key when complete.

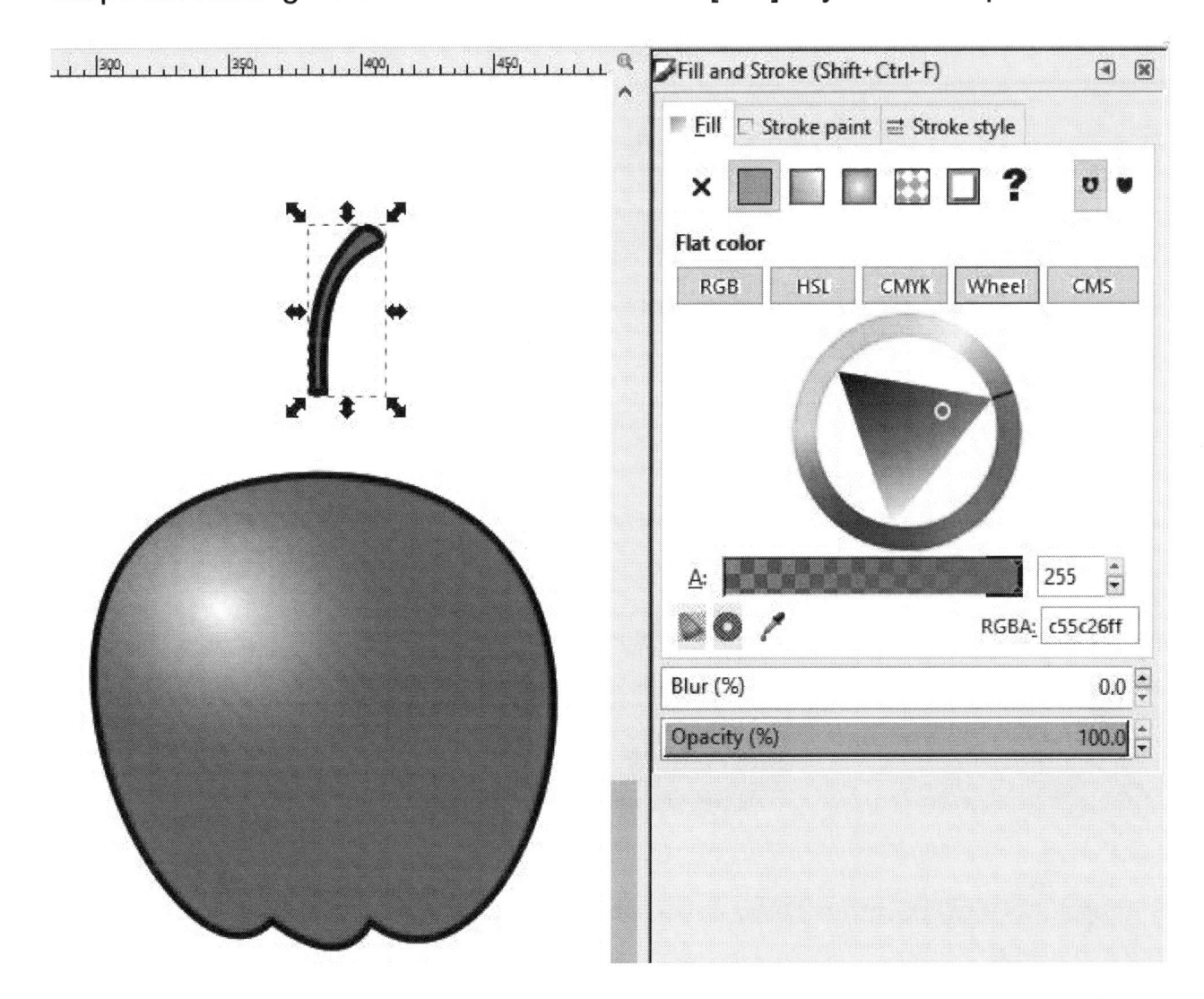

7. Draw the apples stem. Select the *Draw Bezier curves and straight lines* tool and draw the apple stem as shown above. Use the same technique to shape the stem as you did to shape the apple. If you need to zoom in to make your work easier, tap the [+] key. ([-] key to zoom out.

Set the stem's stroke width to 3 px as you did with the apple's shape. Set the stem's color to brown. With the *Fill* tab selected in the *Fill and Stroke* dialog box, click on the *Flat Color* button, then click on the [Wheel] button. In the Wheel color selector, drag the color selector to a brown color for the stem's fill color as shown above.

With the stem selected, drag it to a proper position on the apple. Note that the *crossed arrows icon* must be visible to allow dragging.

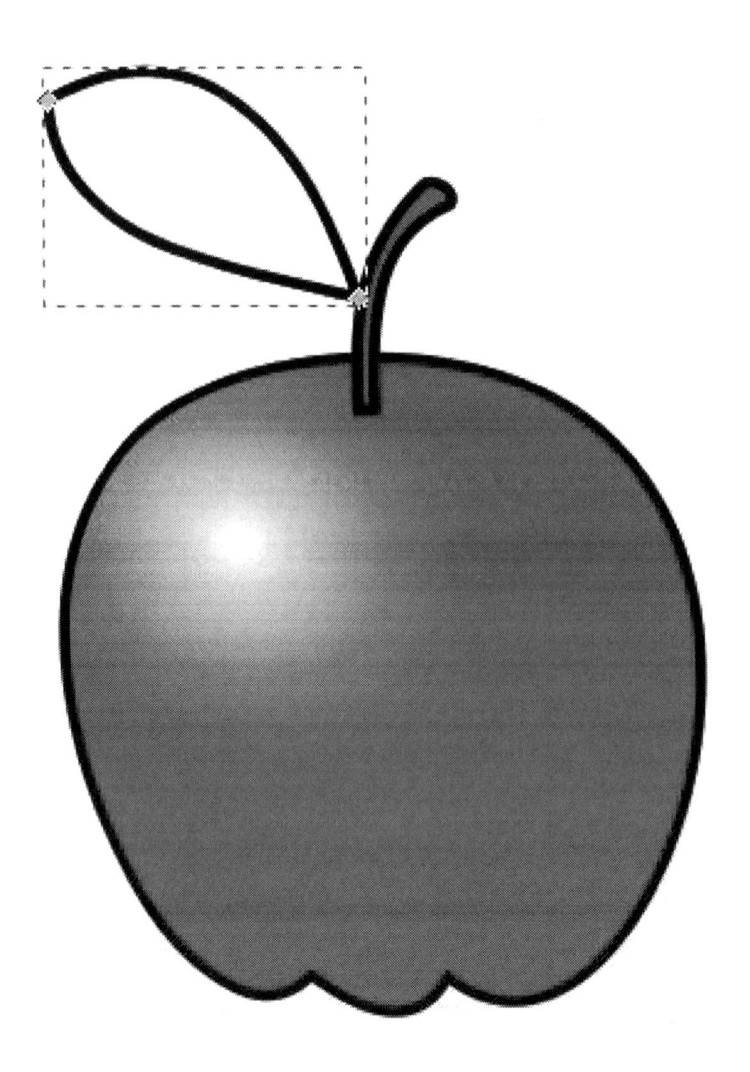

8. Draw the leaf. With the *Draw Bezier curves and straight lines* tool selected, draw a leaf next to the stem. The outline of the leaf requires only two nodes. Click to set the first node, move and click to set the second node, move back to the first node and double-click on it.

At first you'll have a straight line, but using the *Edit paths by nodes* tool you can shape the leaf. Set the *Stroke width* to 3 px.

With the leaf selected, in the *Fill and Stroke* dialog box, click on the *Fill* tab. Click on the *Flat Color* button. Click on the *RGB* button.

Drag the G: slide control half way to the right (128). Drag the R: and B: slide controls all the way to the left (0). The A: slide control should be all the way to the right (255).

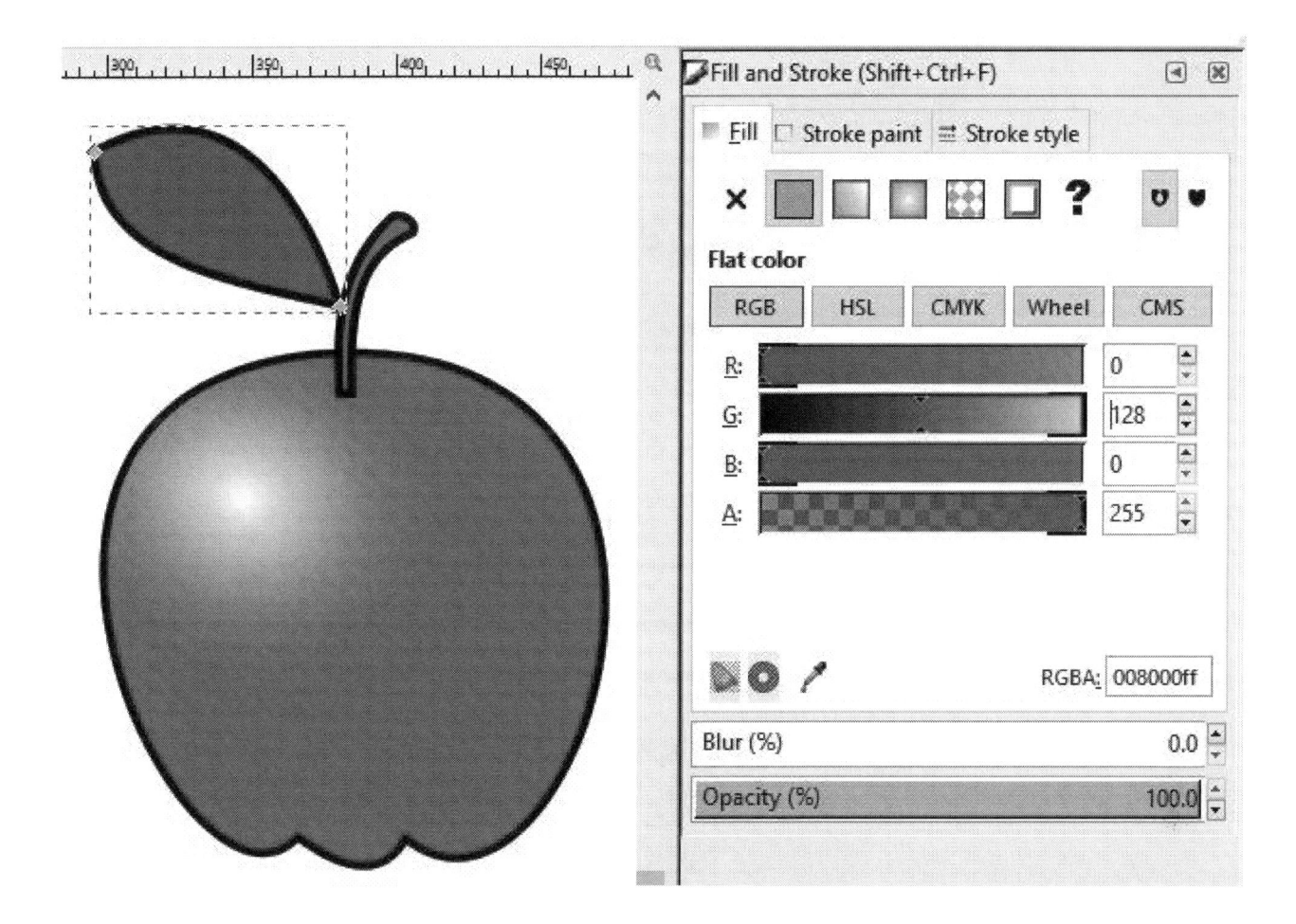

9. Draw the leaf's veins. With the *Draw Bezier curves and straight lines* tool selected, click on one side of where you want to draw a vein line. Move the mouse pointer to the other side of the vein line, then double-click.

Draw the other veins. With the *Edit paths by nodes* tool selected, shape each vein after you draw it. Also set each vein's *Stroke Width* to 2 px after you draw it.

One way to save yourself some time with this is to select the first vein you draw, then select *Edit|Copy* and *Edit|Paste* in the menu. Drag the copy of the vein to its proper position and reshape it.

That's it. Your completed apple should look similar to the one shown above.

Exercise: Draw a Rose

CONTENTS

In this section you'll learn how to make an InkScape drawing of a rose. The rose is one of the most well known flowers. It's a tradition to send roses to a loved one on Valentine's Day. Roses come in many different colors from yellow to orange. You can send any color rose, but be aware that any color, other than red, means "I value our friendship", while red roses says "I love you".

It's important to know the structure of something that you want to draw. A rose is like any other flower in that it has a pistil and stamen.

The biggest producer of roses is the Netherlands. The Dutch produce over 8 billion blooms each year, which they sell in their famous flower auctions. The Dutch harvest the roses as soon as they bloom so they can be shipped fresh. In this early stage, the rose petals are closed up around the pistil and stamen flower parts so you can't see them. All you see is the beautiful rose petals. This is what people like, and why you'll never see a picture of a fully opened rose with the pistil and stamen showing.

Shown above is picture of a rose petal. Note the bottom of the petal is curved to wrap around the lower part of the stamen, called the ovule. The top part of the petal flares out. The petals are arranged around the flower in layers with five petals to each layer. The layers grow from the inside out in a spiral like fashion. The number of layers depends upon the rose species and the specific flower, but five layers is common.

So drawing a rose from a top-down view is very easy, all we need to do is draw a petal from a top-down-view, then make the required number of copies, adjusting the size, rotation angle, and layer of each petal.

1. Open InkScape to full screen and set the zoom to 150%. To set the zoom, in the bottom-right corner of the screen, type 150 into the Z: text box and press [Enter]. If the Z: text box is not visible in the bottom-right corner of the screen, then you don't have the Statusbar enabled. To enable the Statusbar, in the View menu select Show/Hide and in the submenu set a check next to Statusbar.

2. Draw the outline of the petal. In the toolbox on the left side of the screen, click on the *Draw Bezier curves and straight lines* tool. Then click in the drawing area and draw the triangle shown below.

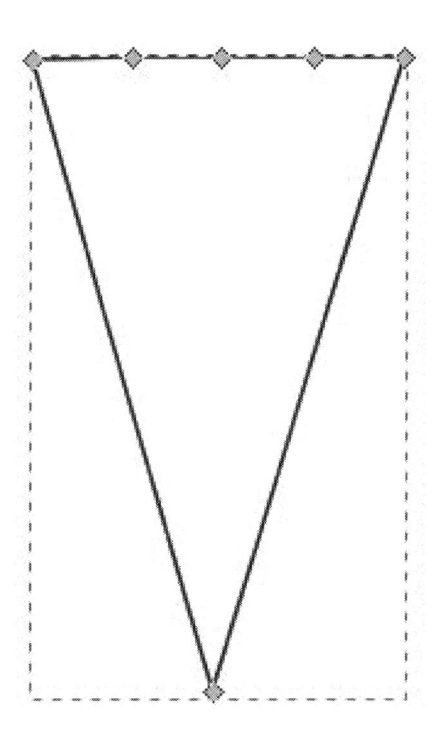

Note that the triangle has five nodes on the top side. This is so we can create the wavy structure of the top of the petal. The locations of the five nodes doesn't have to be exact.

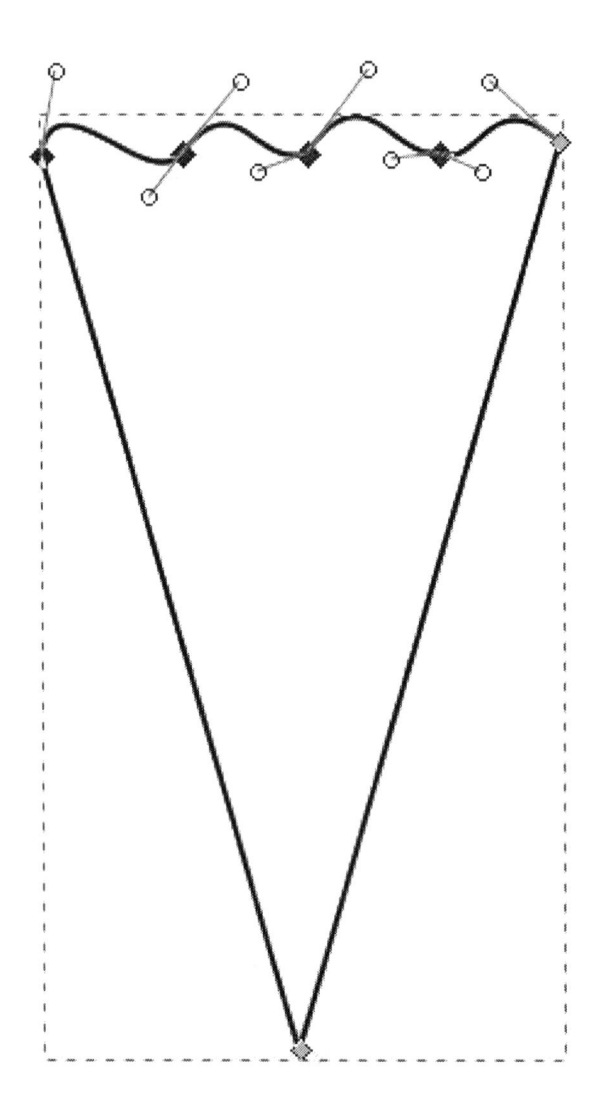

3. Shown above is how we create the wavy structure of the top of the petal. You may want to zoom in a bit to do this. You can zoom in by simply tapping the [-] key. With the *Edit paths by nodes* tool selected, place the mouse pointer over a line segment between two nodes, press the right mouse button, then drag the line segment. After you have dragged a line segment a slight distance the *handles* will appear, you can then use the mouse pointer to drag a handle to adjust the shape.

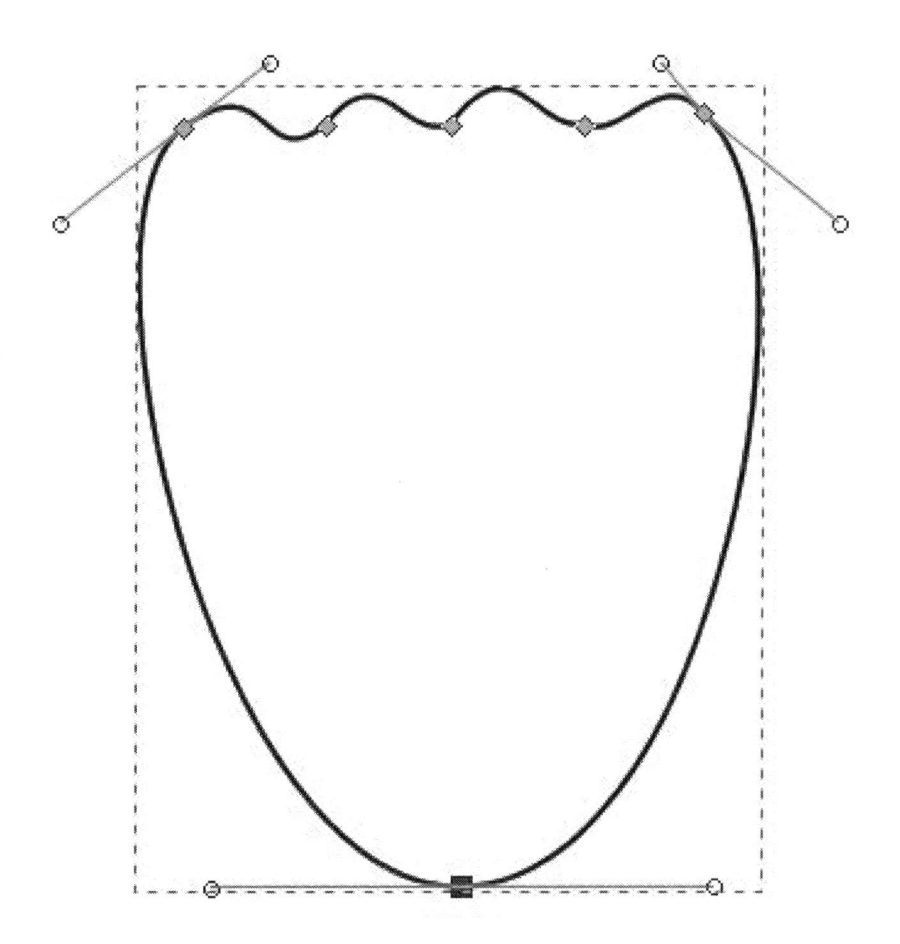

4. In a similar fashion, adjust the three corner nodes of the shape to get the appearance shown above. Remember you don't have to be exact.

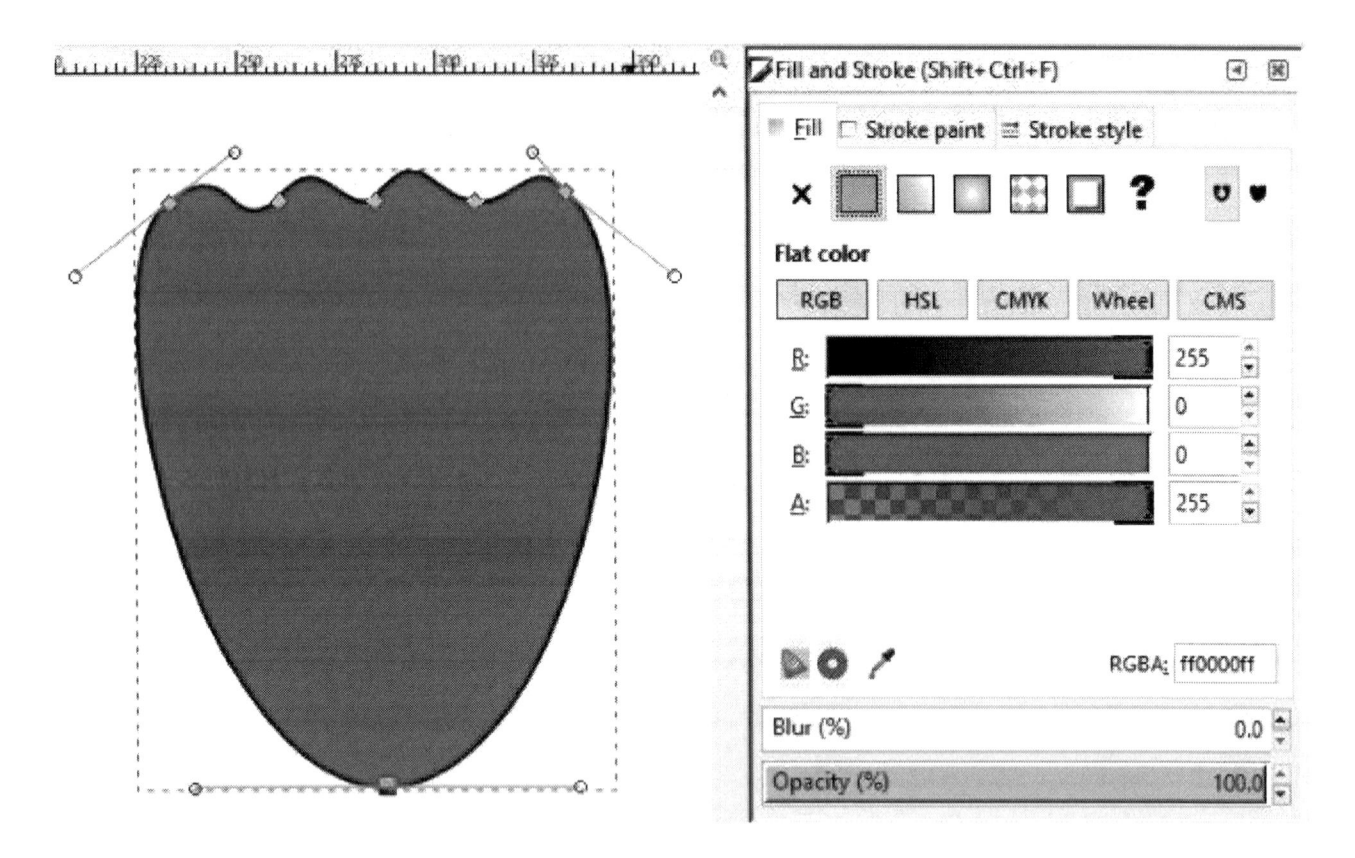

5. Next, fill the petal shape with red color. If the *Fill and Stroke* dialog box is not visible, right-click in the shape and select it in the popup menu that appears. Make sure the shape is selected and the *Fill* tab is selected in the *Fill and Stroke* dialog box.

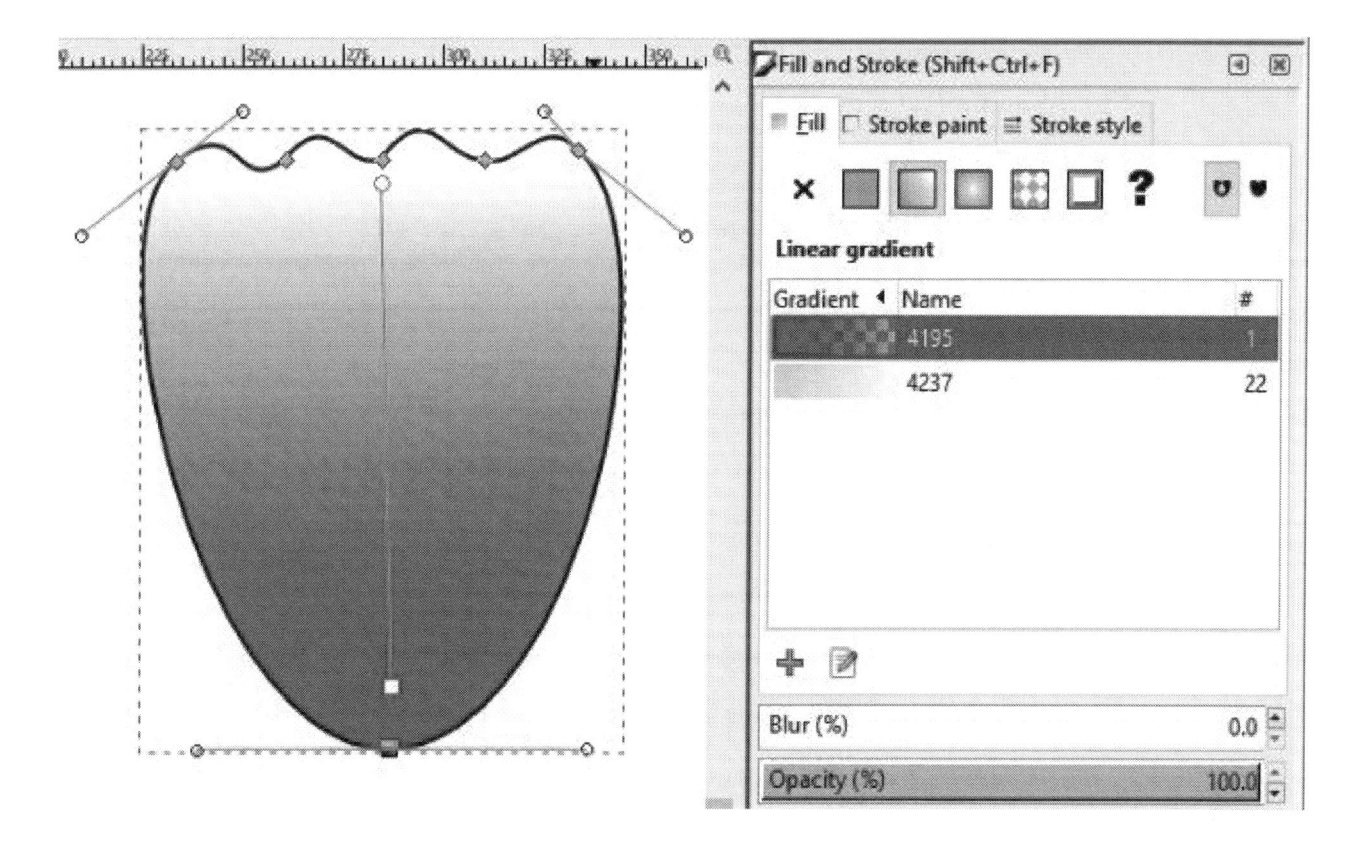

6. In the Fill and Stroke dialog box, click in the *Linear gradient* box, a line will appear with a square handle on one end, and a round handle on the other end. With your mouse pointer drag the handles to arrange the linear gradient as shown above.

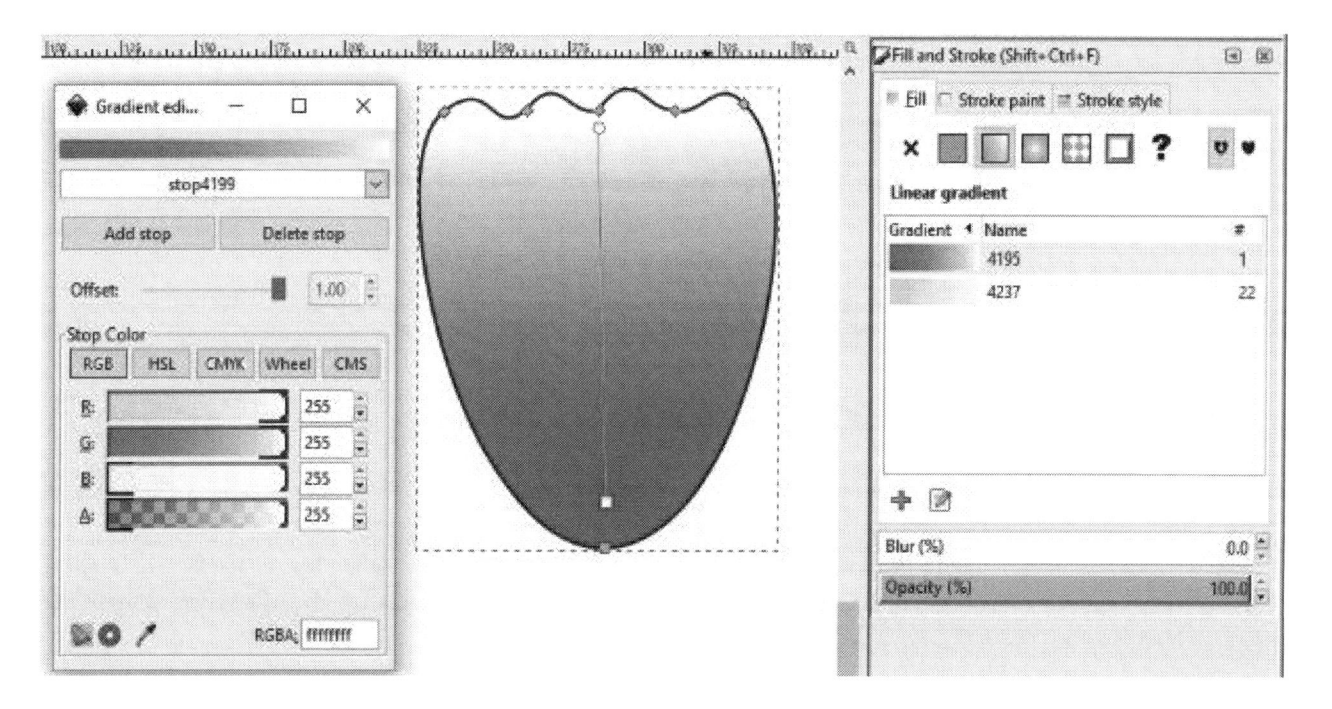

7. Unfortunately, when a gradient is first created, the white portion of it has it's opacity set to fully transparent. In this exercise, that will allow lower petals to show though. You will most likely need to edit the gradient. To edit the gradient, with the shape selected, click on the *Edit gradient* icon (note icon) near the bottom of the Fill and Stroke dialog box, the *Gradient editor* dialog box will appear. In the drop-down list, select the white color or "stop" in the gradient and move the A: slide control to the right side of the control. This sets the white color to fully opaque.

Congratulations! You've drawn your first rose petal. Now, to draw the rose flower all you need to do is make copies of the petal, adjusting the size, rotation angle, and position of each copy. You should save what you've drawn up to now (I like to save frequently).

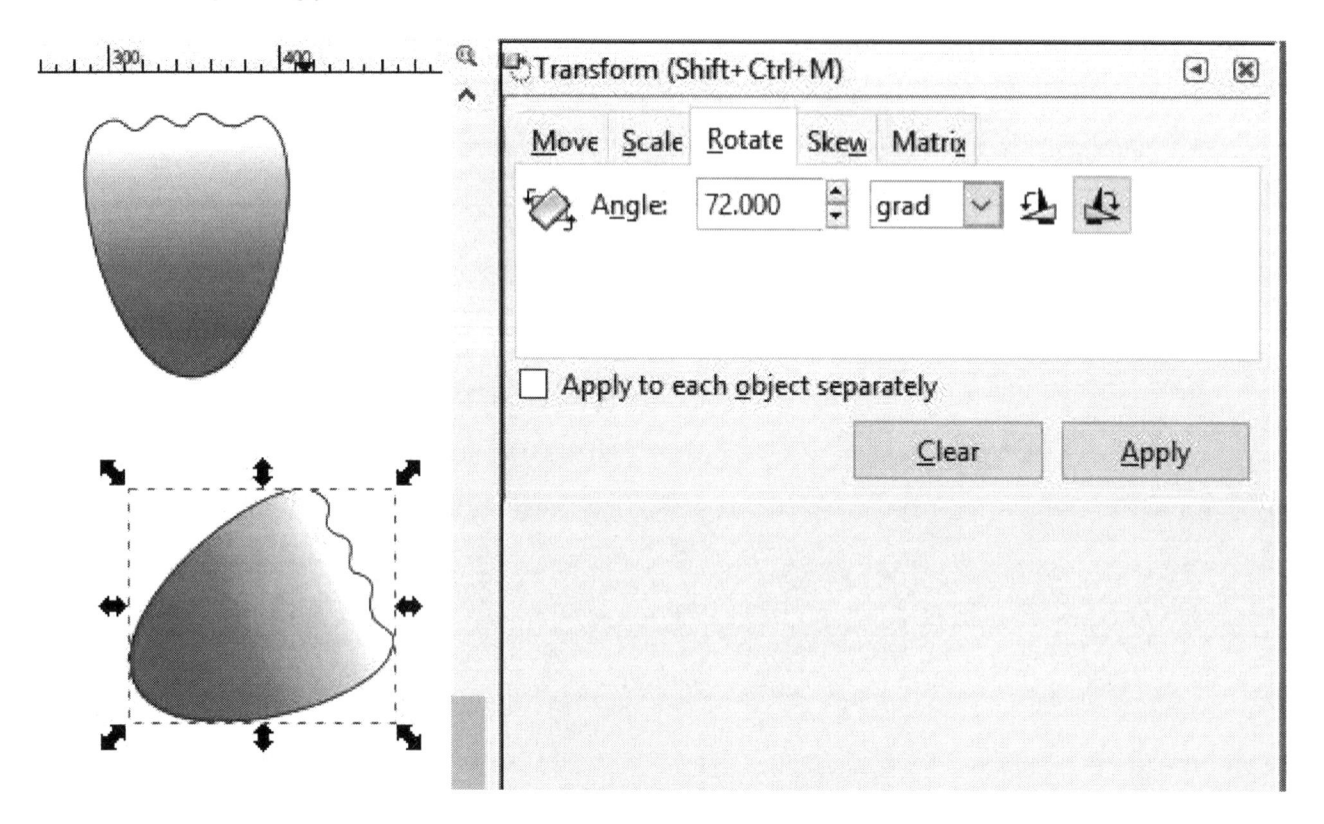

8. To make a copy of the rose petal, select the *Select and transform objects* tool. In the main menu, *Edit* menu, select *Copy*. Then In the main menu, *Edit* menu, select *Paste*. Drag the copy to a convenient location on the canvas.

With the copy selected, In the main menu, *Object* menu, select *Transform*. In the *Transform* dialog box that appears, click on the *Rotate* tab. In the *Rotate* section of the *Transform* dialog box, set the angle to 72, the system drop-down to *grad* and click on the *Rotate in clockwise direction* button. When you have the parameters set, click on the [Apply] button. The copy will rotate 72 degrees.

138

9. Make a copy of the rotated petal. With the copy selected, and the parameters in the Transform dialog box still set to 72 degrees, click on the [Apply] button. The copy will rotate another 72 degrees. You will need five copies, each rotated 72 degrees from the previous copy.

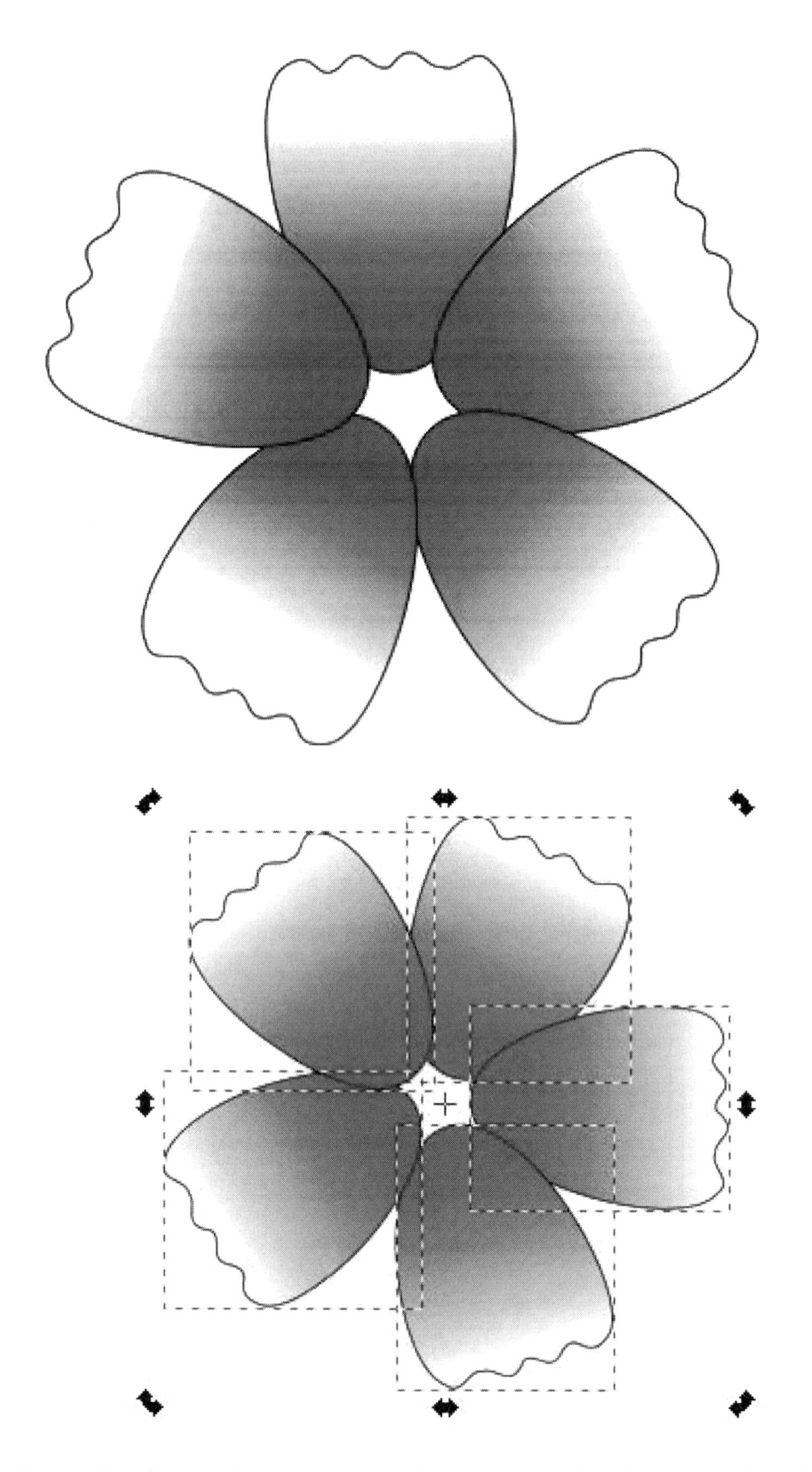

10. Select the entire flower image and make a copy of it. Reduce the size of the copy and rotate it. You select the entire flower image using the Select and

transform objects tool. With the image still selected click on it again and the resizing handles will turn into rotation handles. With the mouse pointer drag a rotation handle.

11. Select the copy and place it on top of the original flower image. Now repeat that process, making three more copies, each smaller and each rotated, stacking them all on top of the rose image. You may have noticed that I adjusted the gradient on the pedals in each layer reducing the white area, which makes the pedals look more vertical.

12. Finish off the rose by drawing a center area. I drew three red filled ellipses of successively smaller sizes staked on top of one another.

Congratulations! You've drawn your first rose. In this exercise you've learned how to shape paths, use linear gradients, select and copy objects, and move and rotate objects. Actually, This is my impression of a rose, I'm sure you can draw a much better one.

Chapter 9: Specialized Applications

Fashion Design With Inkscape

Fashion designers create original clothing, accessories, and footwear. They sketch designs, select fabrics and patterns, and give instructions on how to make the products they design. According to the U.S. Bureau of Labor Statistics, most Fashion designers work in wholesale or manufacturing establishments, apparel companies, retailers, theater or dance companies, and design firms, and their median pay (2017) is $67,420 per year.

Inkscape gives Fashion designers a huge advantage over hand drawing. Shown above is one of the templates from Christopher Hart's book "Sketchits! Faces & Fashion" (978-1942021490). You can scan this template, or one of the other more than 100 templates in the book, import it into Inkscape, and use it to design your own fashion. Of course you can scan images from other sources, but the object is to, in Inkscape, change the design to your own creation.

Above is my Inkscape drawing over the template. Of course as you can see, I didn't make any changes. I'm not really a fashion designer. My goal here is show you how Inkscape can be used to create fashion drawings.

You'll need faces for your fashion models. To get maximum re-use of your graphics, you should design all your fashion drawings so that they can use either a *front view, side view*, or what Christopher Hart calls the *3/4 view*. He provides an example of each in his book. Shown above is my Inkscape 3/4 view of a face. I copied and pasted this drawing from one Inkscape window to another window where I imported the template. Note that I had to shrink it down quite a bit to use it, which is real easy in Inkscape.

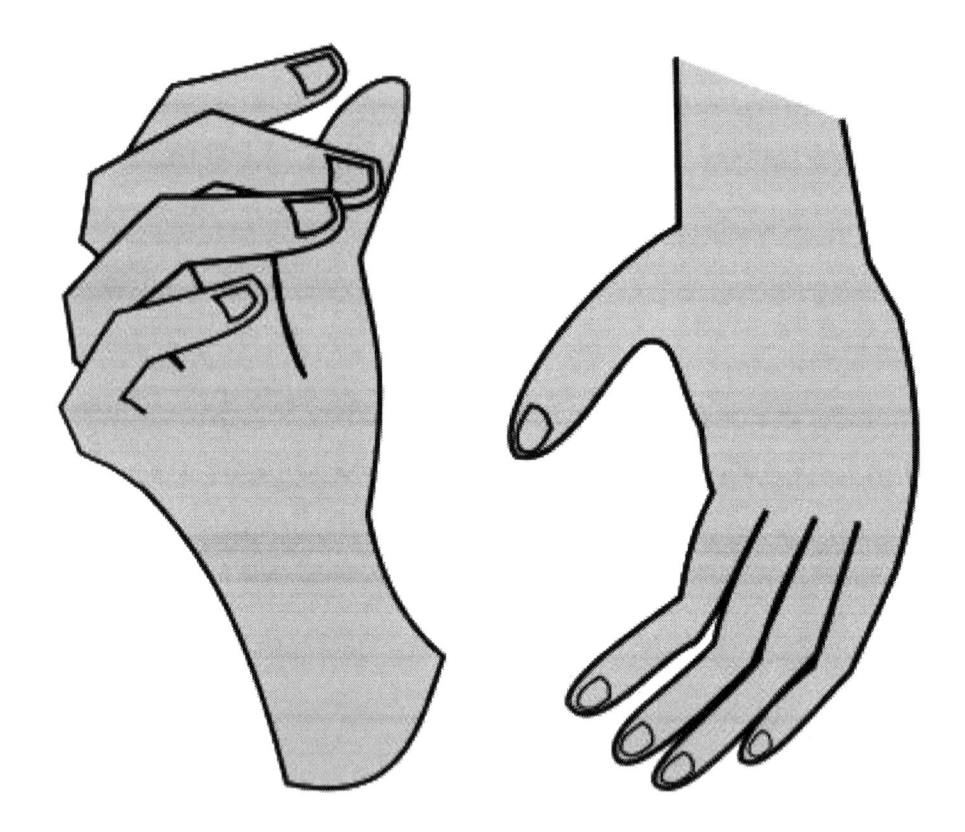

You'll also need hands for your fashion models. To get maximum re-use of your graphics, you should design all your fashion drawings with the arms positioned so that they use one of a limited collection of hands. Shown above is my Inkscape drawing of hands. I copied and pasted these drawings from one Inkscape window to another window where I imported the template. Again I had to shrink them down quite a bit to use them.

Even the most authoritative sources on fashion today instruct designers how to draw by hand. There's nothing wrong with drawing by hand, but productivity requires reusability. With Inkscape you can create a library of reusable clothing and accessory shapes, and reusable fashion model parts.

Create 3D Boxes Tool

CONTENTS

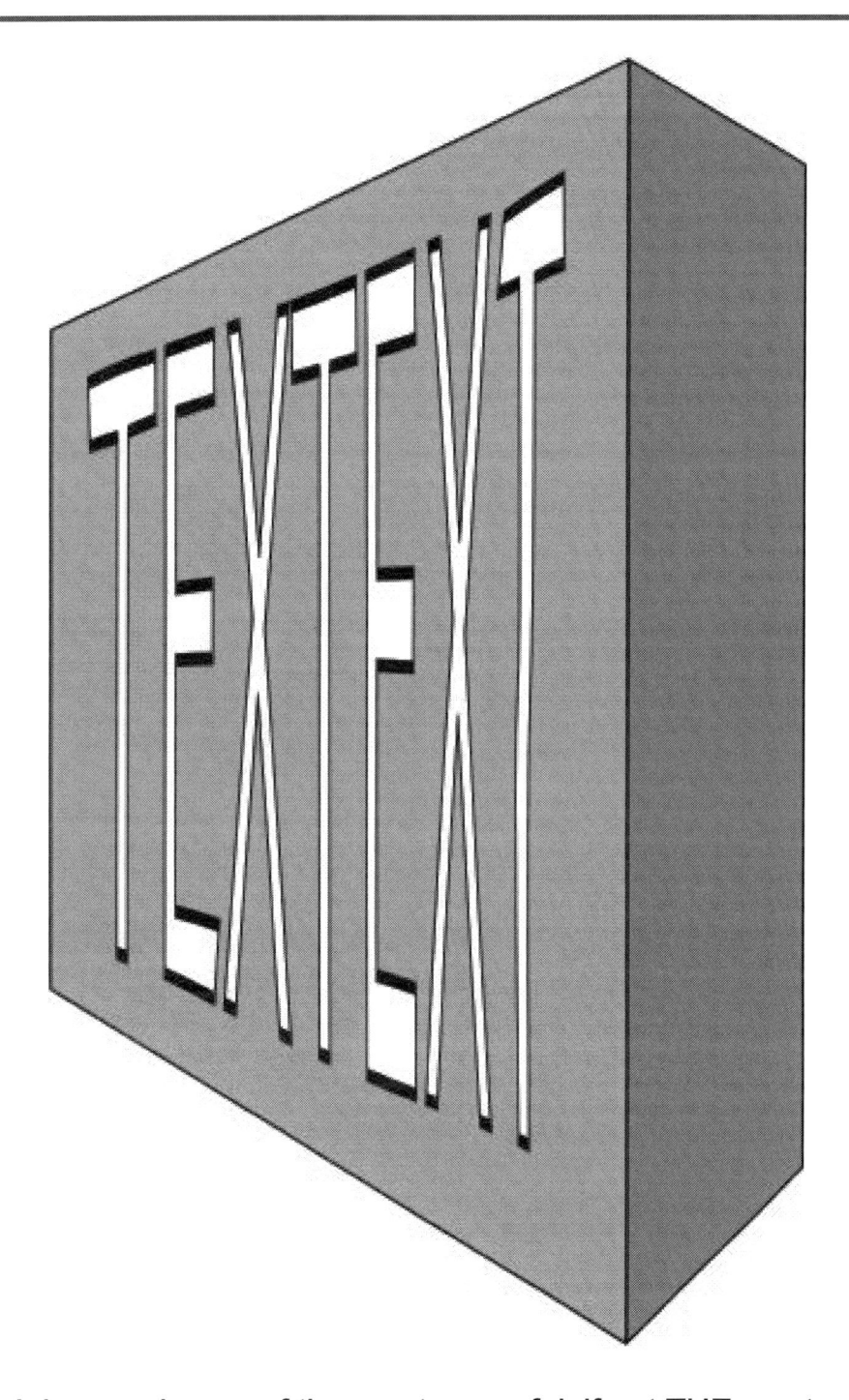

Look, I think Inkscape is one of the most powerful, if not THE most powerful 2D vector drawing tool. A 3D drawing tool it is not. But it does have a neat tool to help you draw one of the most common 3D items drawn, a product box. For example if you sell a digital download, it's a great idea to have a picture of a product box, even though your download doesn't come with and doesn't need a box.

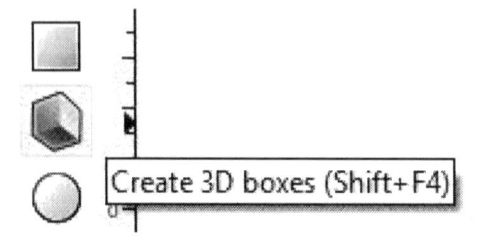

Click on the *Create 3D boxes* tool in the toolbox. In the drawing area move the mouse pointer to where you would like one corner of the 3D box to appear, with the mouse button pressed, drag the mouse to where you would like the opposite corner of the 3D box to appear.

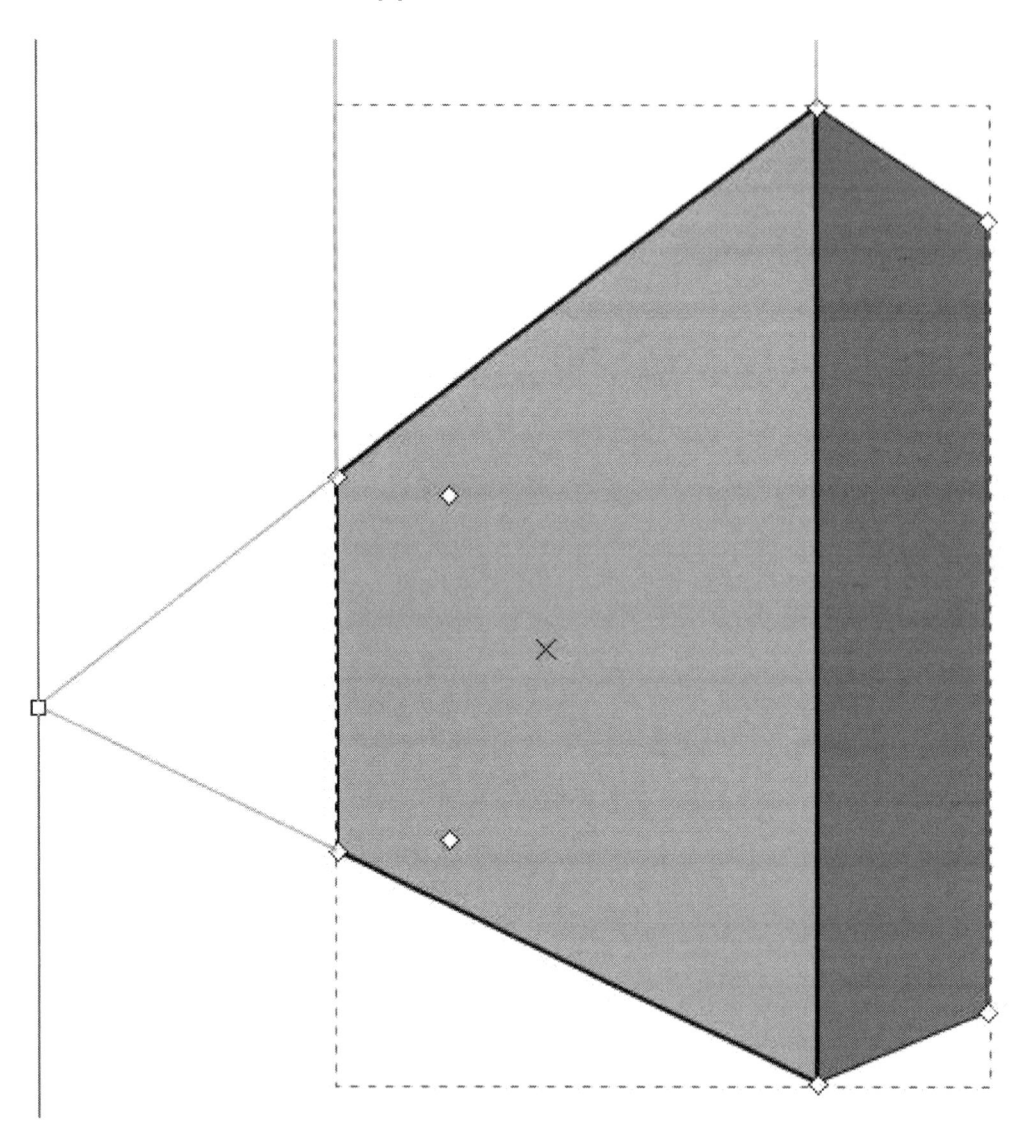

This will create a shaded 3D box. The box is drawn with perspective, in other words the sides of the box are defined by vanishing points. When you first draw the box, the corners of the sides will be marked square nodes. The vanishing points will be marked by lines, red for the x-axis vanishing point, blue for the y-axis vanishing point, and yellow for the z-axis vanishing point.

The shape of the box is determined by the location of the vanishing points. The vanishing points are visible and movable only while the "Create 3D boxes" tool is selected.

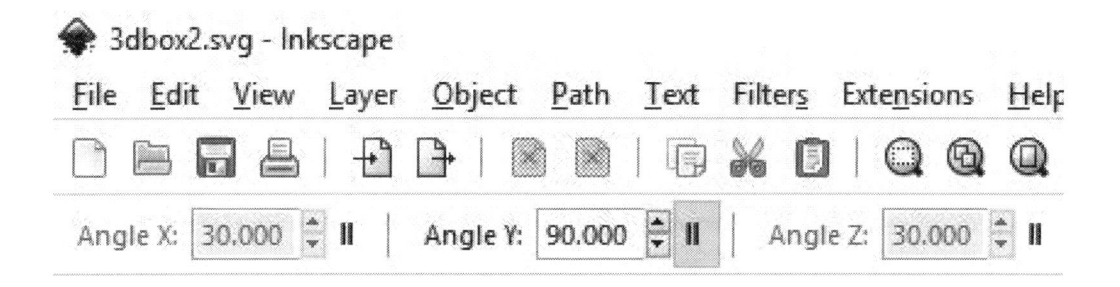

Note that the top (y-axis vanishing point) goes off-screen. This is not a bug in the program. There are two types of vanishing points, *finite*, and *infinite*, by default the y-axis vanishing point is set to infinite. Notice on the *Tool Control Bar* boxes that display the angles of the vanishing points. To the right of each box is a button that allows you to toggle that vanishing point between finite and infinite.

For the purpose of creating a product box, you probably want to leave the vanishing points where they're initially set, x 30 degrees finite, y 90 degrees infinite, and z 30 degrees finite.

By default the box is colored shades of blue. To change the color of a side of the box, press and hold the [Ctrl] button and click on the side. That will select the side so that you can use the *Fill and Stroke* dialog box to choose a new color.

Note: as I said earlier, a 3D drawing tool Inkscape is not. If you want to add text and details to the sides of the box, they will not inherit the prospective of the box. You'll need to use the method described in the *Text in Shape* section.

Auto Trace an Image

CONTENTS

As mentioned earlier, there are two main types of images; bitmaps which is a matrix, or array, of data that define the color of each pixel in the image, and vector graphics which defines the starting point and ending point of lines (also a mathematical formula describing the shape of the line). Inkscape is vector drawing application, but one of the most amazing things it can do is trace an image, thus changing it from a bitmap to a vector graphic.

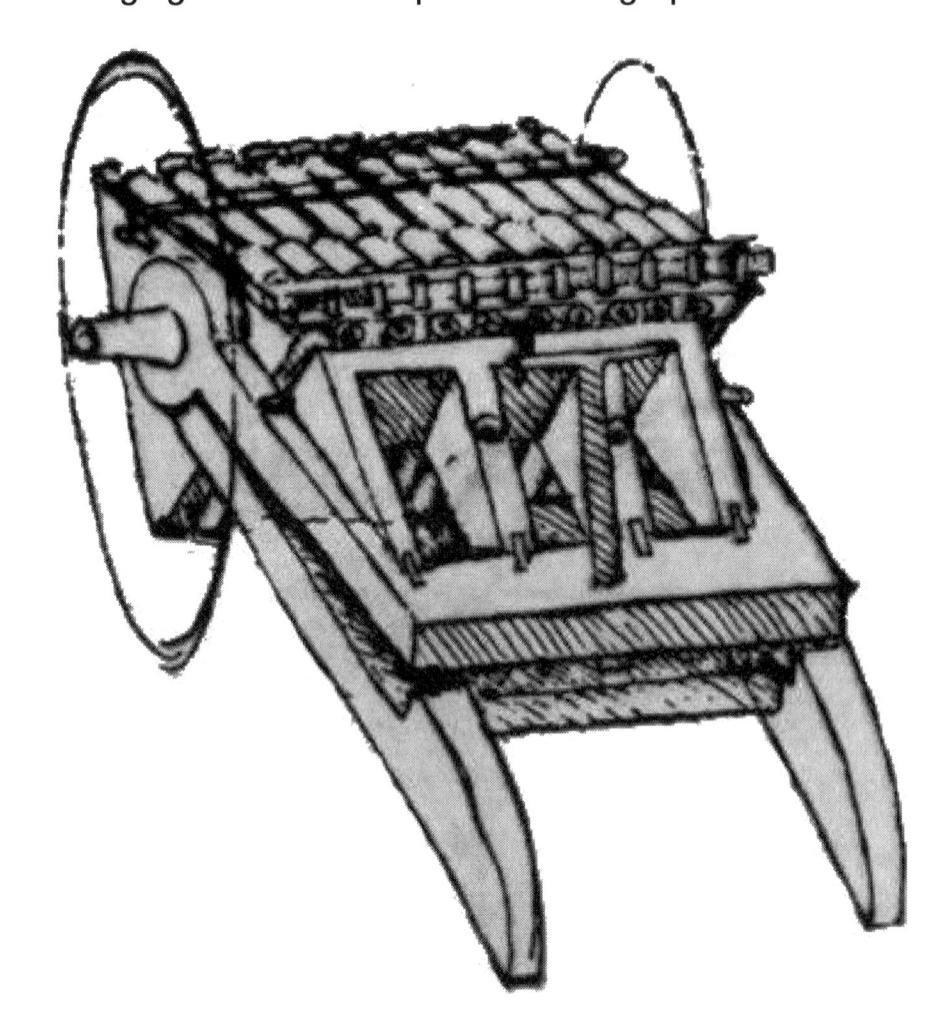

For this example, I'll trace the image shown above.

1. In the *File* menu, select *Import...*, and in the *Select file to import* dialog box, navigate to, and click on, the file name of the image that you want to trace. Click on the [Open] button.

2. In the *bitmap image import* dialog box that appears, make sure the *Embed* radio button is set. Click on the [OK] button. The image will appear on the canvas.

3. Make sure the image is selected when, in the *path* menu, you select *Trace Bitmap...*.

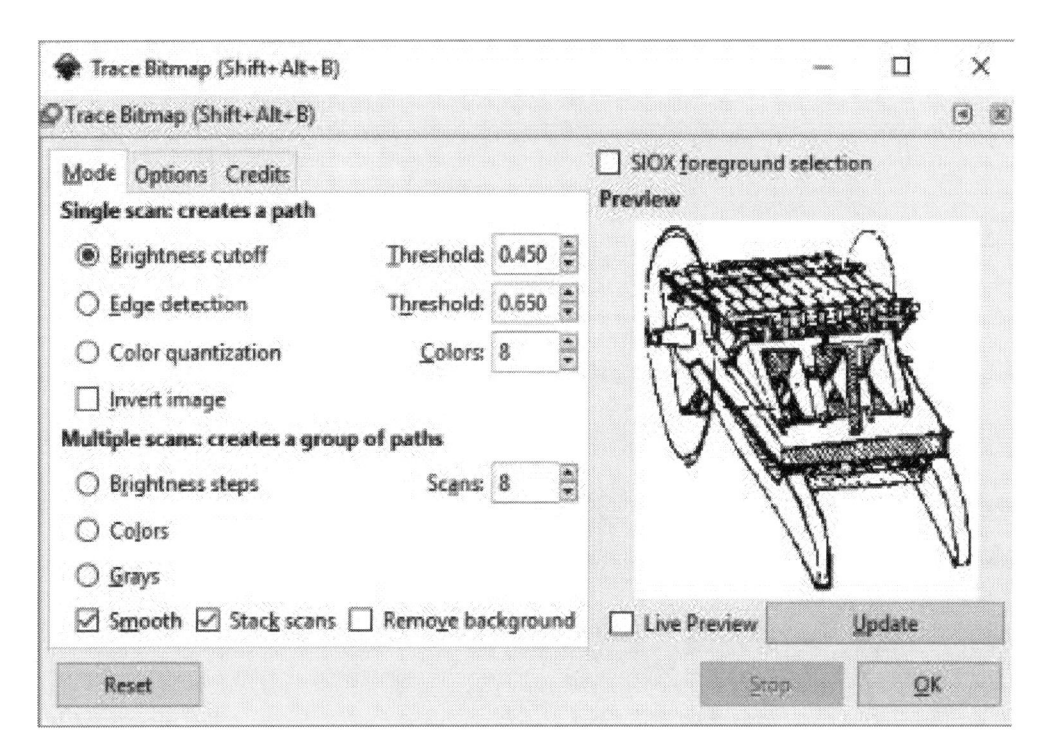

4. In the *Trace Bitmap* dialog box that appears, make sure the *Brightness cutoff* radio button is selected. A preview of the traced image should appear in the dialog box. Click on the [OK] button, and close the *Trace Bitmap* dialog box.

5. The image trace will not be visible in the main window. That's because it's directly on top of the original image. Use your mouse pointer to drag it to another location.

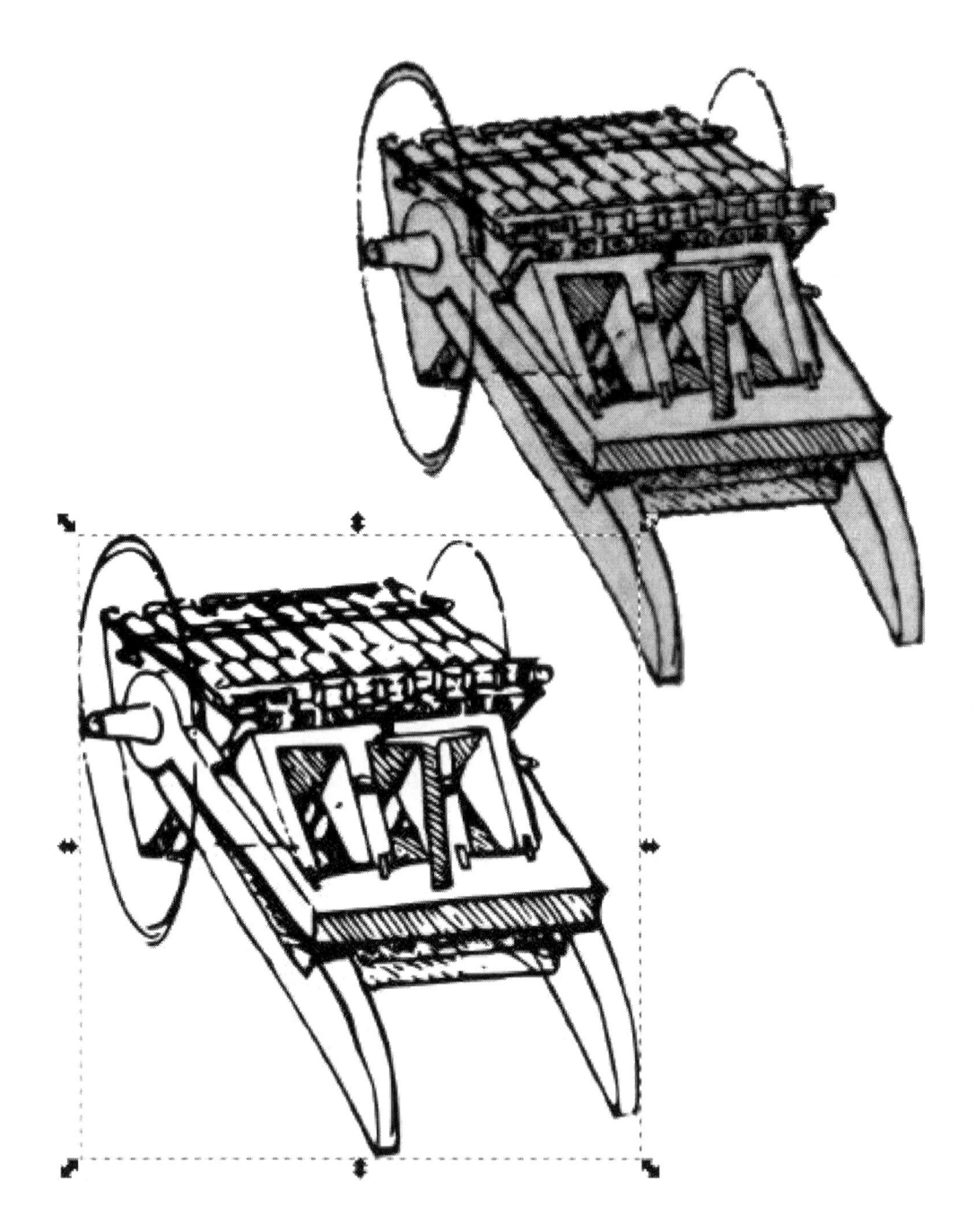

One of the problems with Inkscape's *Trace Bitmap* function is that it creates too many nodes. You can observe this by, with the trace selected, clicking on the *Edit paths by nodes* tool. This is a far greater number of nodes than you would you would create if you traced the image yourself using the *Draw Bezier curves and straight lines* tool.

You can try to remedy this by selecting, in the *Path* menu, the *Simplify* item, but the result will be a much less sharp image. You can also try to reduce the number of nodes by adjusting the *Brightness cutoff* thresholds in the *Trace Bitmap* dialog box.

The excessive number of node in a bitmap trace will make the file larger and the image more difficult to edit, but other than that, the larger file size may not be a problem for you.

By the way, the image used for this example is Leonardo da Vinci's invention of the machine gun taken from his notebook. If using a computer application to trace an image drawn in the last half of the 15th century by the smartest, most talented man that ever lived doesn't give you awe, then nothing nothing ever will.

Hand Trace an Image

CONTENTS

Having the ability to auto-trace an image, why would you want to hand trace one? One of the problems with Inkscape's Trace Bitmap function is that it creates too many nodes. The excessive number of nodes will make the image more difficult to edit, and the file size will be large. You can toy with the Path menu's Simplify item, or try to reduce the number of nodes by adjusting the

Brightness cutoff thresholds in the Trace Bitmap dialog box, but the results are rarely optimal.

There are three possible reasons why you would want to trace an image:

1. To change the file format from bitmap to vector to reduce the file size.
2. To simplify the image by leaving out much of the fine detail, for example for educational purposes.
3. To make one or more changes in a drawing to make it yours.

In either of these cases, tracing the image yourself using the Draw Bezier curves and straight lines tool will give you better results than auto-tracing.

As an example, I want to trace the cute angel image shown above. My goal is to give the angel hands, and a bit bigger wings. Change the angels skirt design and her dress color, and the angel is mine. Don't get me wrong, the image is in the public domain, so I'm free to change it as I please.

The first step is to use the *File* menu *Import...* item to open the *Select file to import* dialog box to navigate to and import the drawing to the Inkscape canvas. Next examine the drawing to determine what the layers are. It looks like the wings are on the lowest layer. Next is the body. The head and it's features are on the highest level. You draw the parts of the image from the lowest layers to the top. If you get this wrong, just use the *Object* menu's *Rise* or *Lower* selections to change a component's layer.

Shown above, I have drawn larger wings right over the imported image.

Next I draw the angel's dress.

Next I draw the angel's hands. Note that there isn't a huge difference in the shape of the hands and the shoes. so you may as well draw them at the same time.

Next I draw the angel's head. Shown above, I have dragged the imported image off to the side. You can still trace features of the angel and drag them over to your tracing.

So here's my completed angel tracing. I have achieved my goals to give the angel hands, and a bit bigger wings. I also change the angels skirt design to pink with red hearts. For the hair I used the *Create spirals* tool. To color the hair, I cheated a bit by saving the image as a bitmap (.jpg) and using Paint.Net's fill. Of course I then ended up with a bitmap, but that's what I wanted.

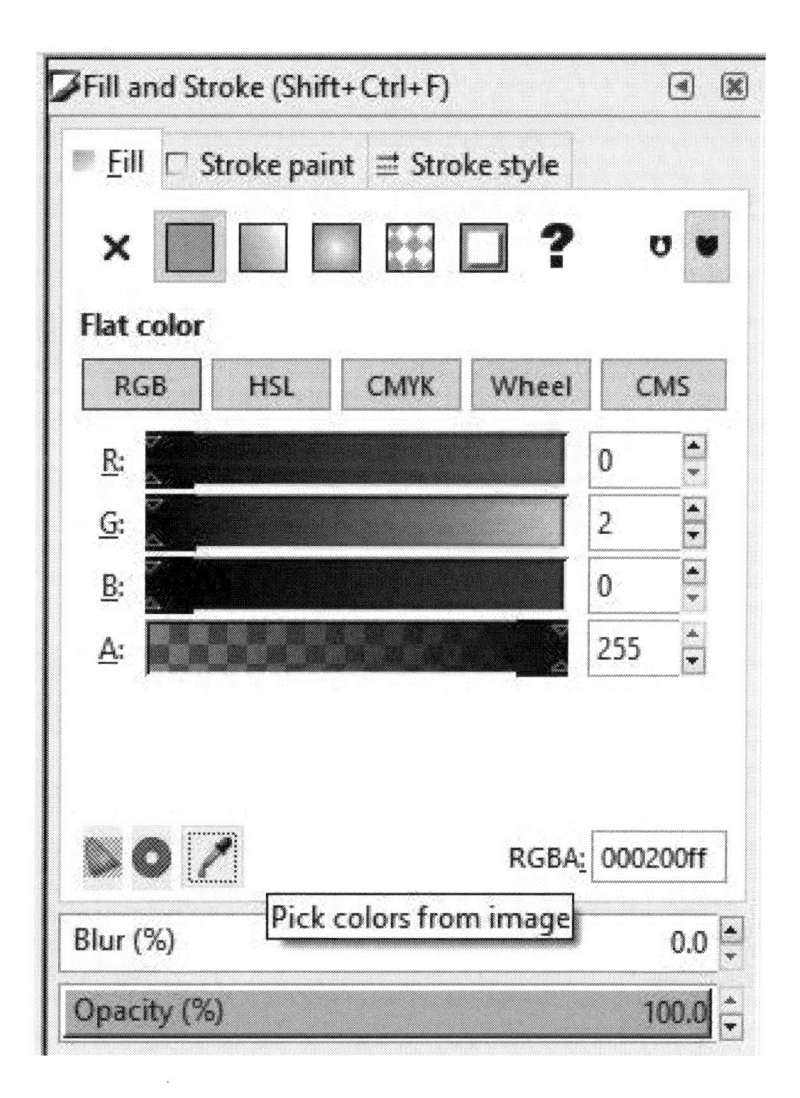

One last tip: If you're interested in copying the exact colors from the image that you're tracing, you can get the color using the *Pick colors from image tool* (the eyedropper icon near the bottom of the Fill and Stroke dialog box).

Hand Code SVG

CONTENTS

As I mentioned earlier, Inkscape uses the Scalable Vector Graphics (SVG) file format, and you can embed your Inkscape drawing in a webpage. Even neater is that you can type our own SVG code into your webpage. You probably already know that web pages are created primarily with html (Hypertext Markup Language) tags, and that you can create a webpage by typing into any basic text editor and saving the page with the *.htm* file extension. Well, SVG also is just text that you can type into a webpage. In this section I explain how to code the basic shapes; rectangles, rounded rectangles, circles, ellipses, and polygons.

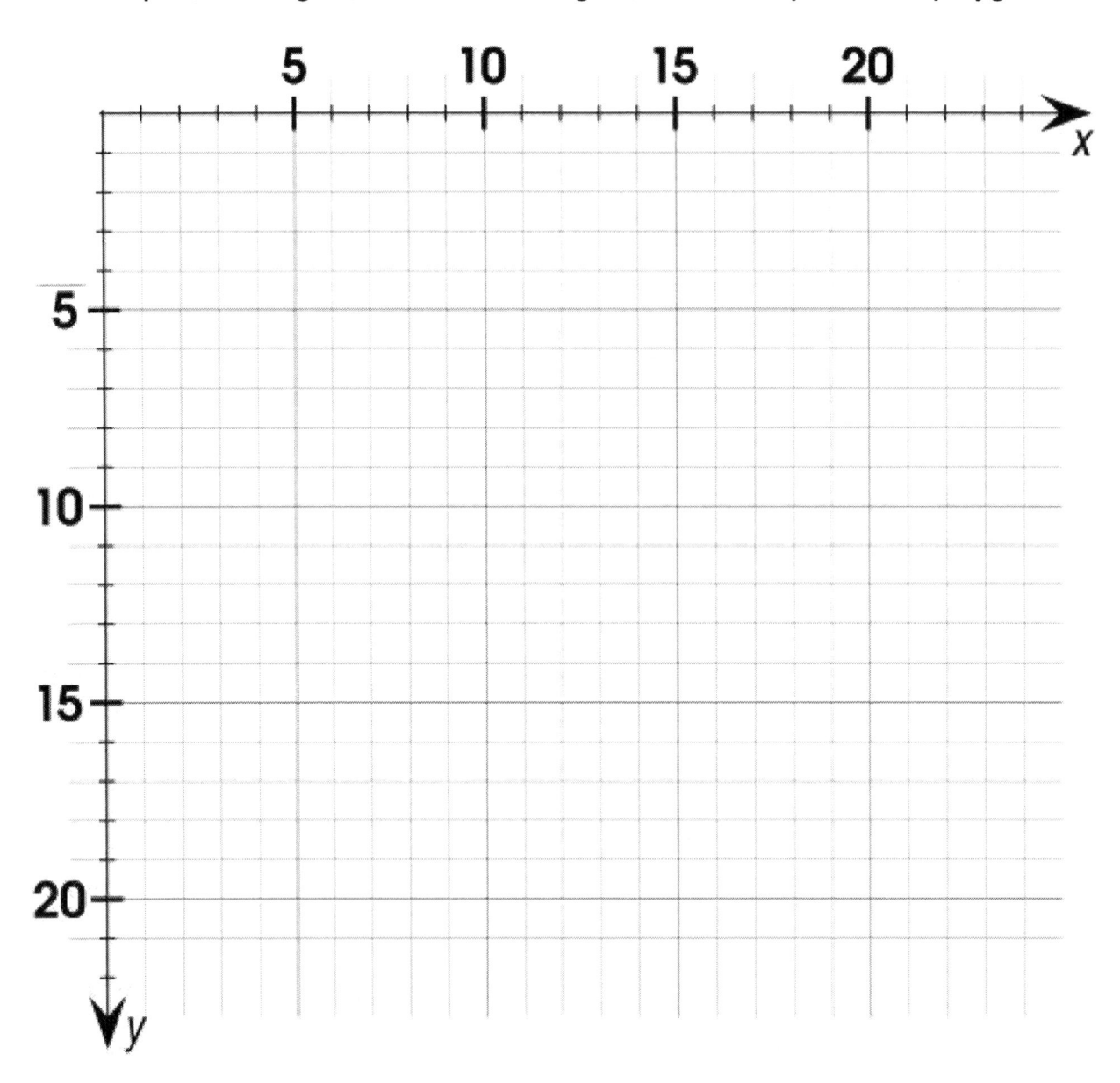

To type your own SVG code you must understand the 2D coordinate system. It's actually very simple. The location of any point is defined by its X (horizontal location from left to right), and Y (vertical location from top to bottom) coordinates.

Rectangle

```
<svg width="220" height="220" version="1.1" xmlns="http://www.w3.org/2000/svg">
  <rect x="10" y="10" width="200" height="200" stroke="black" stroke-width="4" fill="white"/>
</svg>
```

Rectangle Syntax

<rect x y width height stroke stroke-width fill>

Attribute	Description
x	x-axis coordinate of the left side of the rectangle
y	y-axis coordinate of the left side of the rectangle
width	The width of the rectangle. Zero or a negative value is an error
height	The height of the rectangle. Zero or a negative value is an error
stroke	The stroke color. rgba (transparency)
stroke-width	The stroke thickness
fill	(color) rgba (transparency)

Rounded Rectangle

```
<svg width="220" height="220" version="1.1" xmlns="http://www.w3.org/2000/svg">
  <rect x="10" y="10" rx="10" ry="10" width="200" height="200" stroke="black" stroke-width="4" fill="white" />
</svg>
```

Rounded Rectangle Syntax

<rect x y width height rx ry stroke stroke-width fill>

Attribute	Description
rx	For rounded rectangles, the x-axis radius of the ellipse used to round off the corners of the rectangle. A negative value is an error
ry	For rounded rectangles, the y-axis radius of the ellipse used to round off the corners of the rectangle. A negative value is an error

Circle

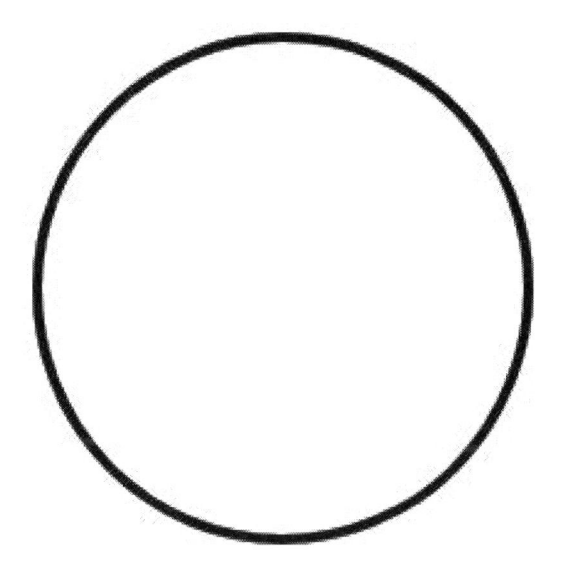

```
<svg width="240" height="240" version="1.1" xmlns="http://www.w3.org/2000/svg">
  <circle cx="120" cy="120" r="100" stroke="black" stroke-width="4" fill="white">
</svg>
```

Circle Syntax

<circle cx cy r stroke stroke-width fill">

Attribute	Description
cx	x-axis coordinate of the center of the circle
cy	y-axis coordinate of the center of the circle
r	the radius of the circle

<u>Ellipse</u>

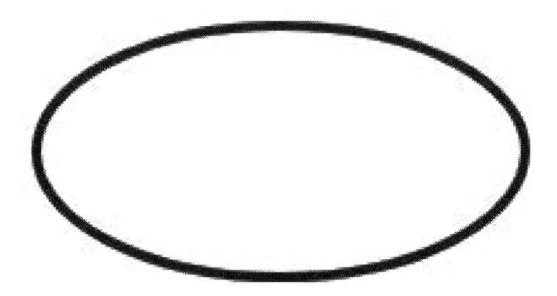

```
<svg width="240" height="200" version="1.1" xmlns="http://www.w3.org/2000/svg">
  <ellipse cx="120" cy="120" rx="100" ry="50" stroke="black" stroke-width="4" fill="white"/>
</svg>
```

Ellipse Syntax

<ellipse cx cy rx ry stroke stroke-widt fill/>

Attribute	Description
cx	x-axis coordinate of the center of the ellipse
cy	y-axis coordinate of the center of the ellipse
rx	the horizontal radius
ry	the vertical radius

Polygon

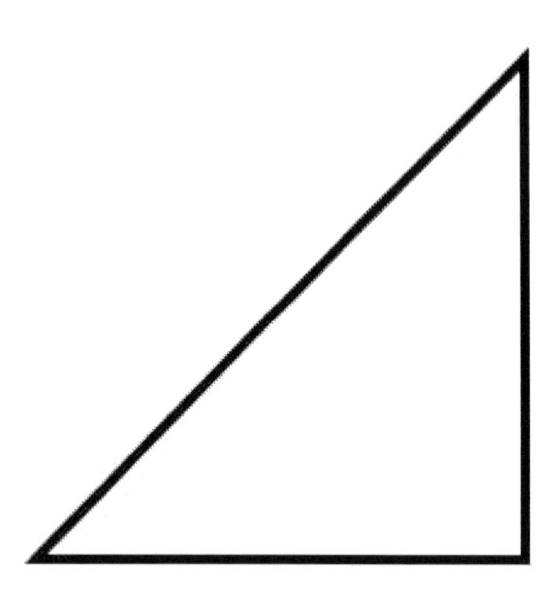

```
<svg width="220" height="220" version="1.1" xmlns="http://www.w3.org/2000/svg">
  <polygon points="10,210 210,10 210,210" stroke="black" stroke-width="4" fill="white"/>
</svg>
```

Polygon Syntax

points are pairs of (x, y) coordinates of a polygon vertexes.

Path

As you know a line or curve in Inkscape is called a *path*. Shown below is the syntax for a path tag. The *d* attribute is were we define the *path data*.

<path d="M x,y C x1,y1 x2,y2 x3,y3" />

One of the most interesting and most useful paths is the *cubic bezier curve*. The syntax for a cubic bezier curve path is shown above. The M in the path data stands for *moveto* which is followed by the starting coordinate of the curve. C is followed by the coordinates of two control points, the start control point and the end control point. The last coordinate is the end point of the curve.

```
<!DOCTYPE html>
<html lang="en">
<head>
<meta charset="utf-8">
</head>
<body>

<svg width="600" height="300">
  <path d="M 100,200 C 100,100 400,100 200,200"
    fill="none" stroke="black" stroke-width="2px" />
</svg>

</body>
</html>
```

The above shows code which you would type into a basic text editor like Windows Notepad. Maybe you remember, form the section Embed Inkscape Drawing in Webpage, the tags that define a webpage. Within those tags you have the opening and closing SVG tags. The opening SVG tag defines the size of your canvas. Withing the opening and closing SVG tags is the path tag for the cubic bezier curve.

The path starts by moving to the coordinate point 100,200 from there is draws a line to the last coordinate point 200,200 where the line ends. The curve is shaped by the control point coordinates 100,100 and 400,100. Note that further attributes are required to define the *fill, stroke*, and *stroke-width*.

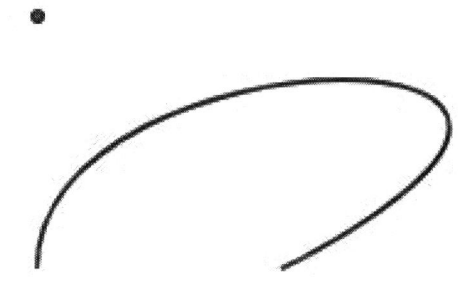

When you save your text file with the *.htm* file extension, and open it in your web browser, you should see the curve shown above. Note that in my file I added code to draw dots at the coordinates of the two control points. As you can see, the control points act like magnets pulling on the line. You should experiment with the code by editing the coordinates of the control points.

Inkscape's Built-in XML Editor

CONTENTS

Now that you understand that SVG is a vocabulary of XML and you have done a little hand-coding, it's time to introduce Inkscape's built-in XML Editor. The XML Editor is the SVG code that creates the image visible on the canvas. The XML Editor allows you to modify this code and immediately see the results. There are many reasons why you might want to inspect or modify the code Inkscape generates.

1. Exploring: You want to see how Inscape does things behind the scenes.
2. Debugging: You can't get Inkscape to do what you want and you want to know why.
3. Forcing: You can't figure out how to do what you want through the graphical interface, so you go into the code directly.
4. Adding Precision: Using the mouse or arrow keys, you can't put a node exactly where you want it, so you enter the precise coordinate in the code directly.
5. Reducing Precision: Inkscape defines coordinates to an accuracy of five digits to the right of the decimal point. You want to reduce this to zero digits to the right of the decimal point to create a light-weight file.

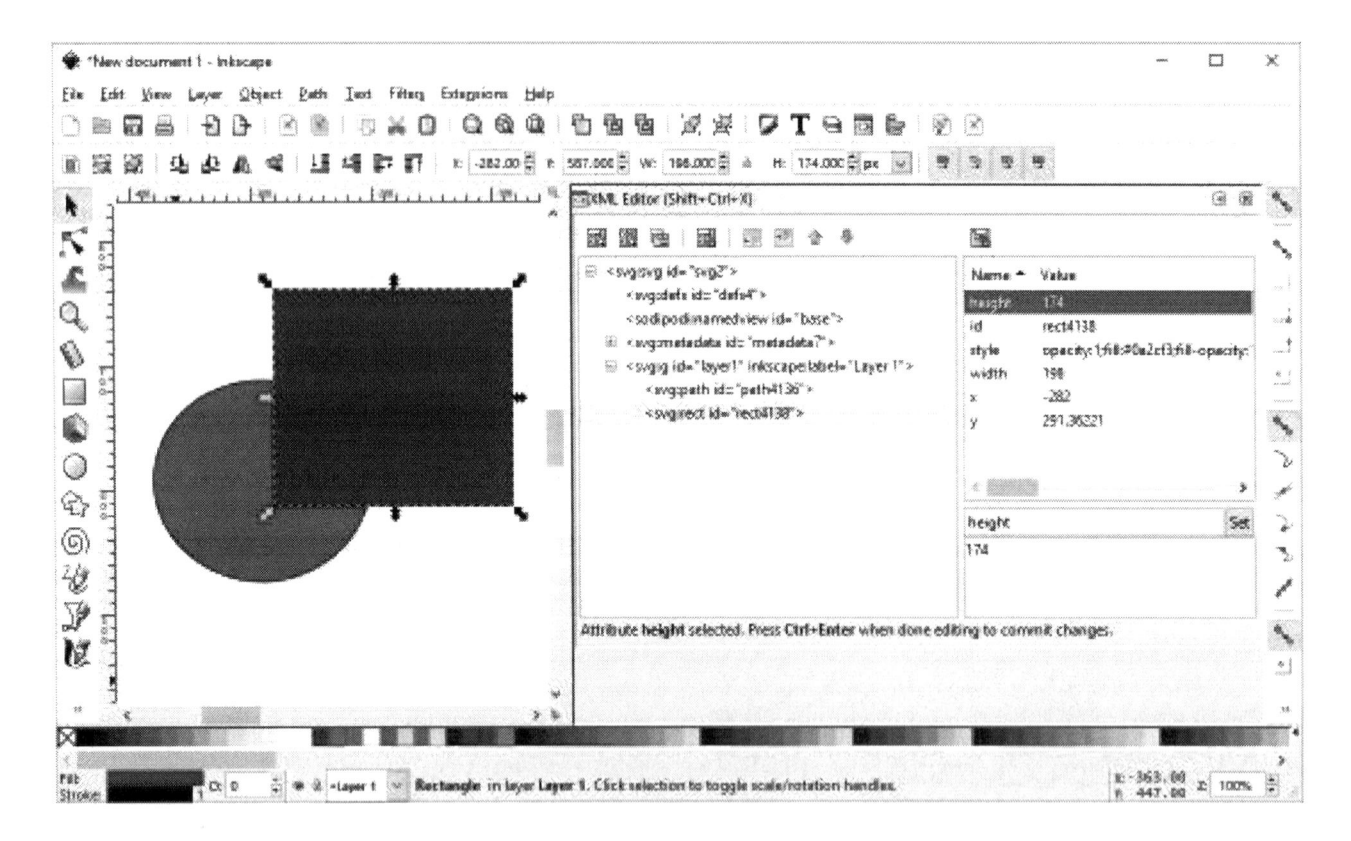

To access the XML Editor, in Inkscape's main menu select *Edit* and scroll down to the bottom of the menu to select *XML Editor*.... The *XML Editor* dialog box will open.

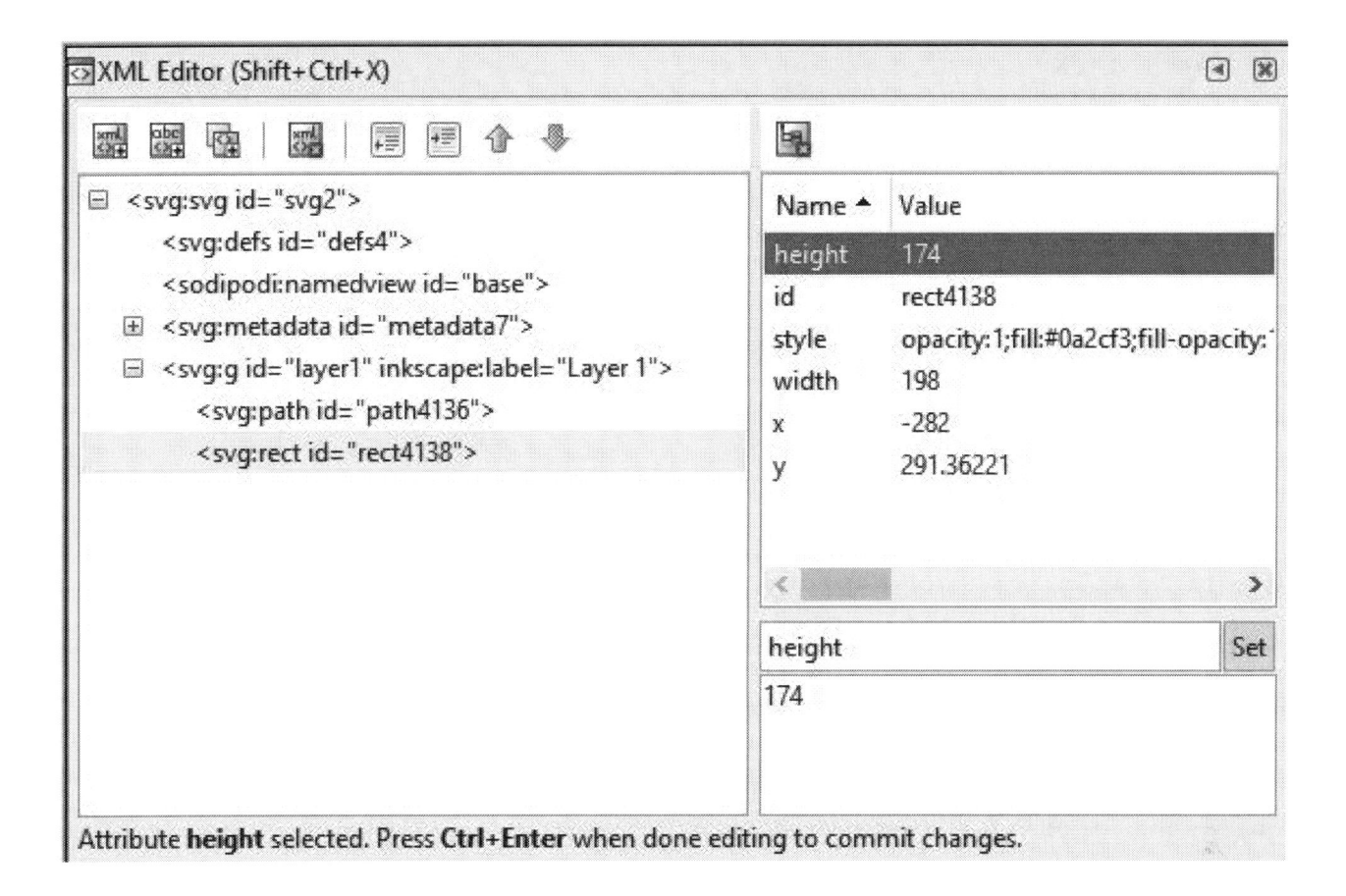

The left pane of the XML Editor dialog box display's the branches of the XML document tree. Click on a tiny box containing an "x" to expand a branch. Click on an object in the expanded branch, and it's attributes and their values will appear in the right pane of the XML Editor dialog box. Click on one of the attributes and the attribute's name and value will appear in the lower right pane of the XML Editor dialog box.

Click on the value and you can edit it. To actually edit the attribute's value on the canvas, click on the [Set] button on the right side of the attribute's name text box. Any change will immediately appear on the canvas.

Chapter 10: Integrating with Other Software

Paint.Net

Throughout this book I have pontificated about the advantages of vector drawing applications over paint programs. However, there are a few things that a paint program can do that a vector drawing progam can't do:

- Convert between graphic file formats
- Image processing
- Additional Filter effects

For this reason, you'll want to keep a paint program in your artists toolkit. If you have around $100.00 to burn, you could use Photoshop(R). But you can achieve the same results with GIMP, the free open-source raster graphics editor. In fact, if you're not using Microsoft Windows operating system, I recommend GIMP because it's a cross-platform image editor available for Linux and Mac OS X, as well as Windows. GIMP is an extremely powerful application but, as always, along with power comes complexity. GIMP is has a steep learning curve.

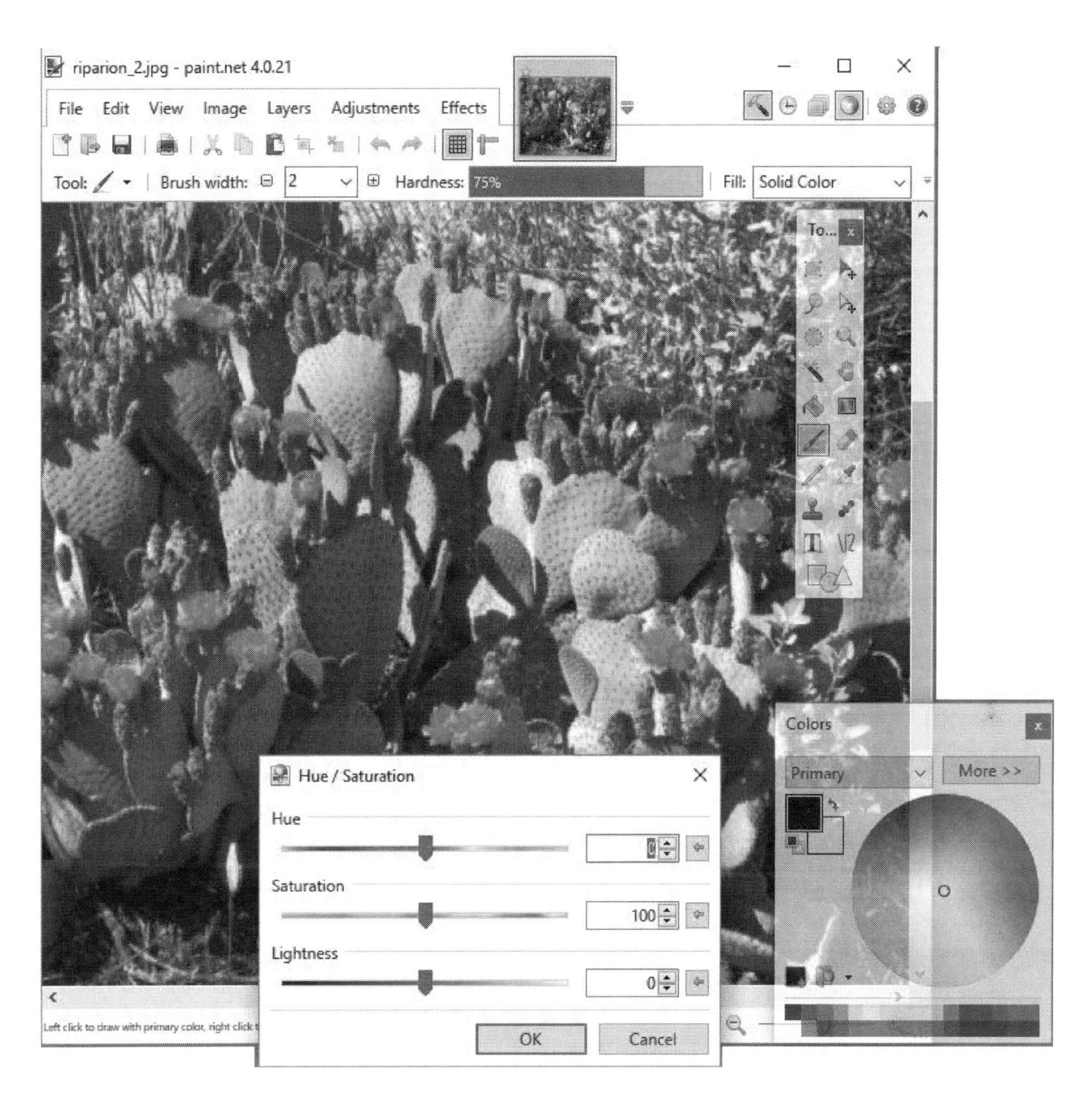

If you're a Windows user, I recommend the free *Paint.Net* graphics editing and image processing application. What I like most about Paint.Net is its ease-of-use to power ratio. Very easy to use, lots of power. It can be downloaded from www.getpaint.net. When downloading Paint.NET be alert to click on the proper download link and not some huge banner ad button that downloads spamware along with Paint.NET.

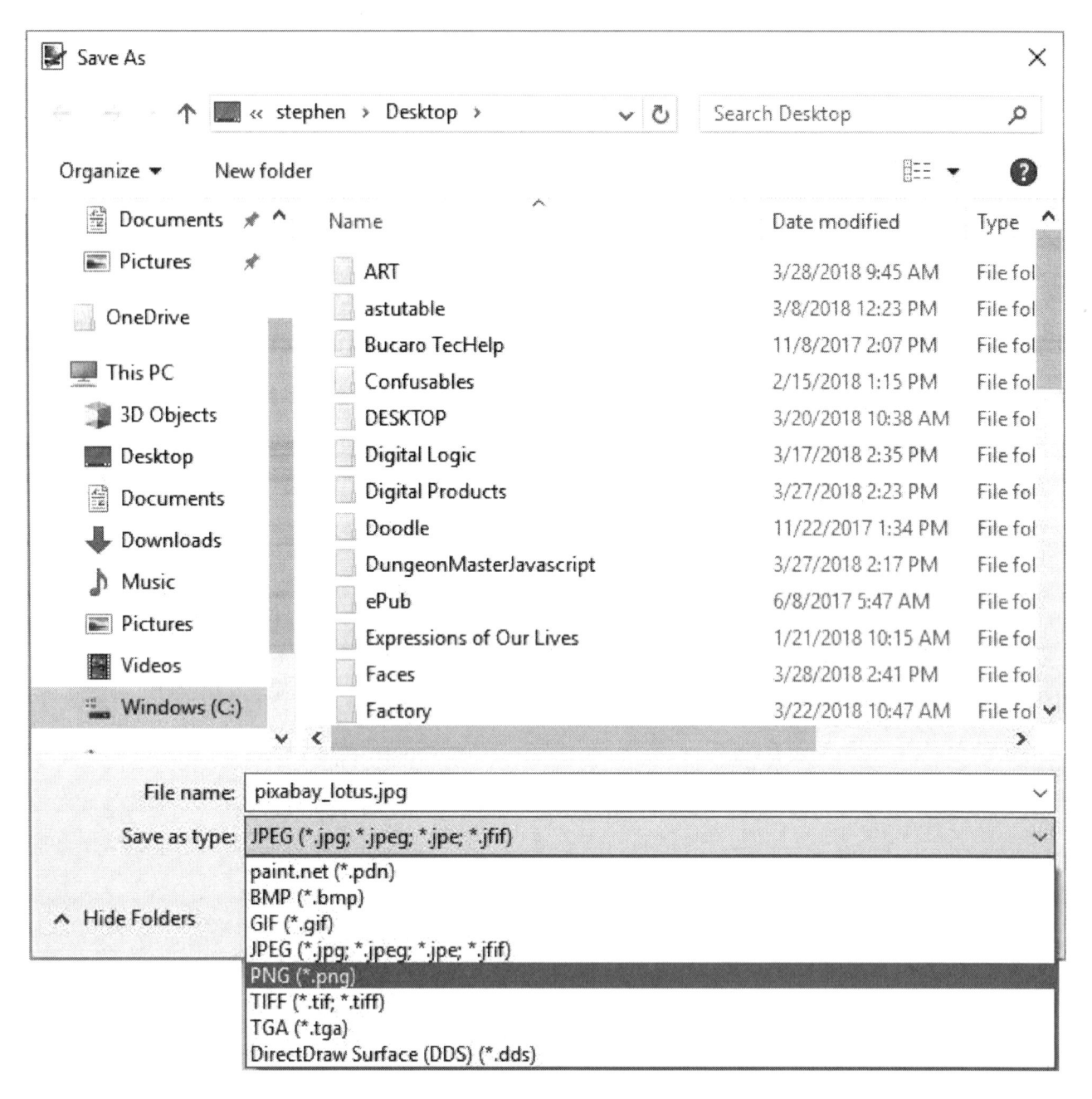

Sometimes you need to convert between image file formats. For example Inkscape exports drawings in .png format, but if you're creating a cover for your Kindle ebook, amazon requires your image to be in .jpg or .tiff format, which amazon needs for their catalog image. The easiest way to make a simple animation is to use .gif format files. Paint.Net lets you convert between file formats by saving the file in a different format then it was loaded. If the save format has the choice to set transparency, when you go to save the file, the *Save As...* dialog box will have controls to do so.

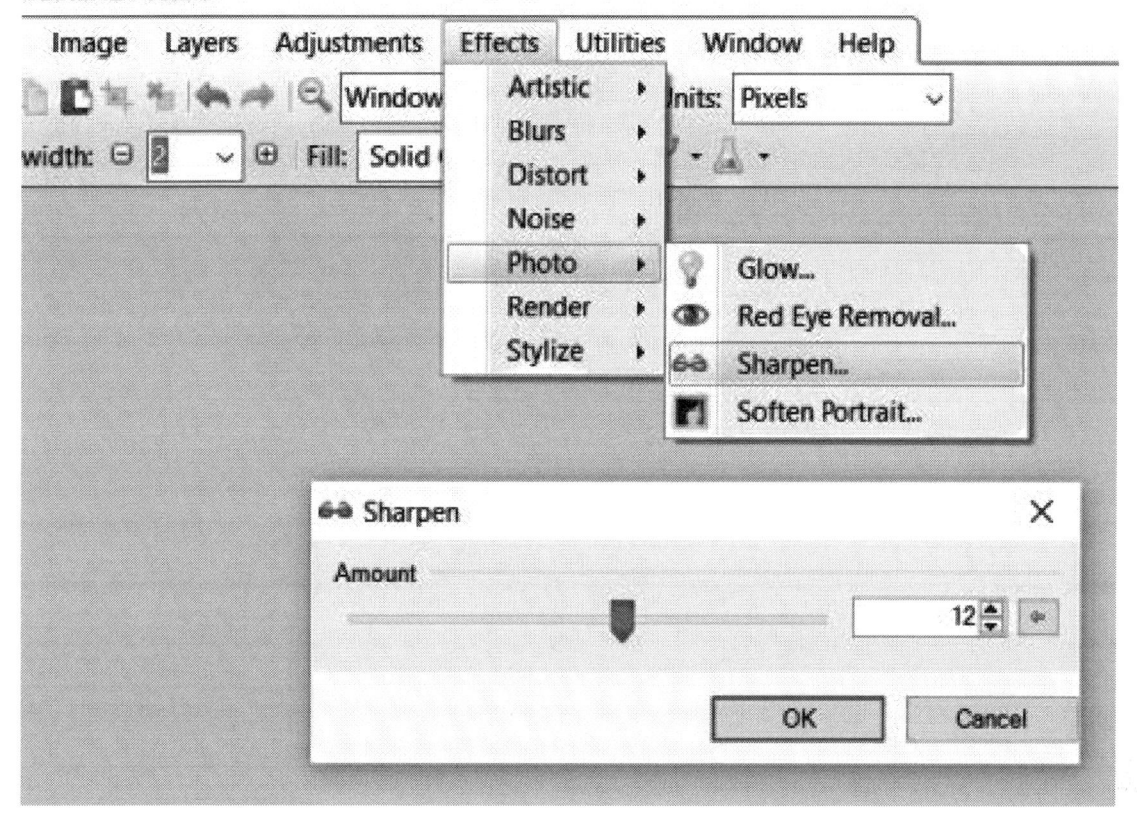

Paint.Net Provides many image processing controls: brightness, contrast, color curve, hue, saturation, histograms, and so on, which you'll find in the *Adjustments* menu. Paint.Net Provides about 35 different filters, which you'll find in the *Effects* menu.

If you select *Artistic* in Paint.NET's *Effects* menu, you'll see three items that apply very interesting and useful effects. Let's apply the *Ink Sketch* effect to the image shown above.

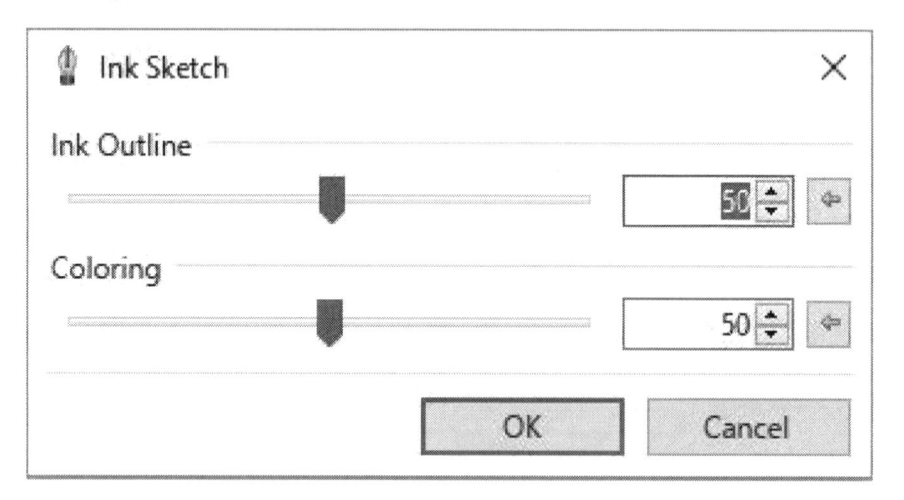

When you select the *Ink Sketch* effect, the slider control dialog box shown above appears, allowing you to set the amount of ink and the amount of color used for the effect.

Shown above is the result of the *Ink Sketch* effect. Very professional looking, and I didn't even have to change the default settings.

Now, on the same original image, lets try the *Oil Painting* effect. The result is shown above. When you select the *Oil Painting* effect, a slider control dialog box appears allowing you to set the *Brush size* and the *Coarseness* used for the effect.

I think the *Pencil Sketch* effect is the same as the *Ink Sketch* effect, except using a gray, rather than black color for the lines. The *Pencil Sketch* effect does not create stunning results on some images. But then I applied it to the lotus flower image shown above, it created the result shown below.

When you select the *Pencil Sketch* effect, a slider control dialog box allowing you to set the *Pencil tip size* and the *Range* used for the effect. The *Pencil tip size* slider controls the width of the lines. The *Range* slider controls the amount of shading. Now there's a stunning effect.

As a computer graphics artist, you'll be using the Inkscape vector graphics application for the majority of your work. But on occasion you'll find use for a paint program. The free cross-platform open-source GIMP is a powerful graphics editor and image processor. But if you're a Windows user, you'll have the opportunity to use the free powerful but easy-to-use Paint.NET application.

X3D

CONTENTS

Inkscape is a 2D vector drawing application. With the use of gradients, many talented computer graphics artists have been able to simulate 3D in their drawings. One feature of Inkscape that adds realism to a drawing is *bitmap fill*. But bitmap fill has limitations in its ability to create prospective and curved textured surfaces. For example, it would be very difficult to create a textured cone in Inkscape.

To get a prospective or curved bitmap texture in Inkscape, you need to create it in a 3D graphics application, give it a transparent background, import it into your drawing, and then use it as a bitmap fill. Unfortunately, I have been unable to find an easy-to-use 3D graphics design application. But if you've come this far in this book, then you know how to hand code SVG and embed it in a webpage. There is another graphics standard called X3D (Extensible 3D) that you can easily hand code and display in a webpage.

The Web3D Consortium (web3d.org) develops the standards for X3D. X3D is an open platform-independent file format to represent 3D scenes and objects. To use x3d you must link to x3dom.js, a JavaScript library, on your webpage. Shown below is the code required to link to x3dom.js, which you place in the head section of your webpage.

```
<script src="http://www.x3dom.org/x3dom/release/x3dom.js"></script>
```

As I've already stated in the section on hand-coding SVG, to create a webpage all you need to do is type text into a basic ASCII text editor like Windows Notepad, and save the file with the extension *.htm*. Shown below is the basic template for an HTML 5 webpage.

```
<!DOCTYPE html>
<html>
<head><meta http-equiv="Content-Type" content="text/html;charset=utf-8"></meta>
<script src="https://www.x3dom.org/download/x3dom.js"></script>
</head>
<body>


</body>
</html>
```

Note that, in the code above I have included the link to x3dom.js, which would not be part of a generic HTML 5 template, but is part of the template you will use to design 3D objects.

Basic Blue Cylinder

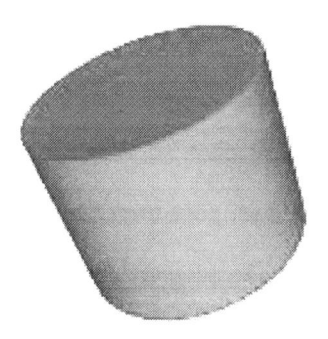

Shown above is a basic blue cylinder created with hand-codded X3D. Shown below is the code to create this object which you place in the body section of the HTML 5 webpage template.

```
<x3d width="300px" height="200px">
<scene>
<Transform rotation="1 1 1 0.78">
  <shape>
    <Appearance>
      <Material diffuseColor="0 1 1" />
    </Appearance>
    <cylinder height="3.0" radius="2.0" top="true"/>
  </shape>
</Transform>

</scene>
</x3d>
```

For our purposes there is no need to go into great detail about the code, but as a basic description: All the objects in a 3D *scene* are placed within the <scene> </scene> tags. Similar to SVG, you can define *Transform*s to rotate and / or move the scene. Within the <Transform> </Transform> tags are the <shape> </shape> tags. Here you can define one or more shapes to be in the scene. Within each *shape* section is an *appearance* section in which you define the surface appearance of the shape. Below the *appearance* section, is the tag that defines the shape, in this case a *cylinder* 3 units high with ends 2 units in radius.

Now, in reality, this image would not be difficult to produce in Inkscape. However, the image shown below would be much more difficult.

Textured Cylinder

This cylinder has a texture applied to its surface. The code for the above image is shown below.

```
<x3d width="300px" height="200px">
<scene>
<Transform rotation="1 1 1 0.78">
  <shape>
    <Appearance>
      <ImageTexture url="data:image/png;base64,iVBORw0KGgoAA . . . AAElFTkSuQmCC">
      </ImageTexture>
    </Appearance>
    <cylinder height="3.0" radius="2.0" top="true" />
  </shape>
</Transform>

</scene>
</x3d>
```

Note in this code that the texture is defined within the opening <ImageTexturegt; tag, and that the tag's *url* attribute points to the location of the texture image. Unfortunately, X3D is very particular about the location of the texture. It must be in the same domain as the X3D code file. So if you can place your file online, you can use the name of the image to use as a texture (it must be .png image format). That will not work if you are experimenting on your local computer. In that case, the *url* attribute must be a *base64 data string*.

A base64 data string is an encoding scheme that converts binary data into ASCII text. The binary data for even a tiny image would be huge. Even if converted to hexadecimal code it would still be huge because hexadecimal uses only the first six letters of the alphabet. Base64 is the most compressed form to represent image data. Even in base64 format, the code is quite large. Note in the example that I used three dots (. . .) to represent a huge chunk of the code.

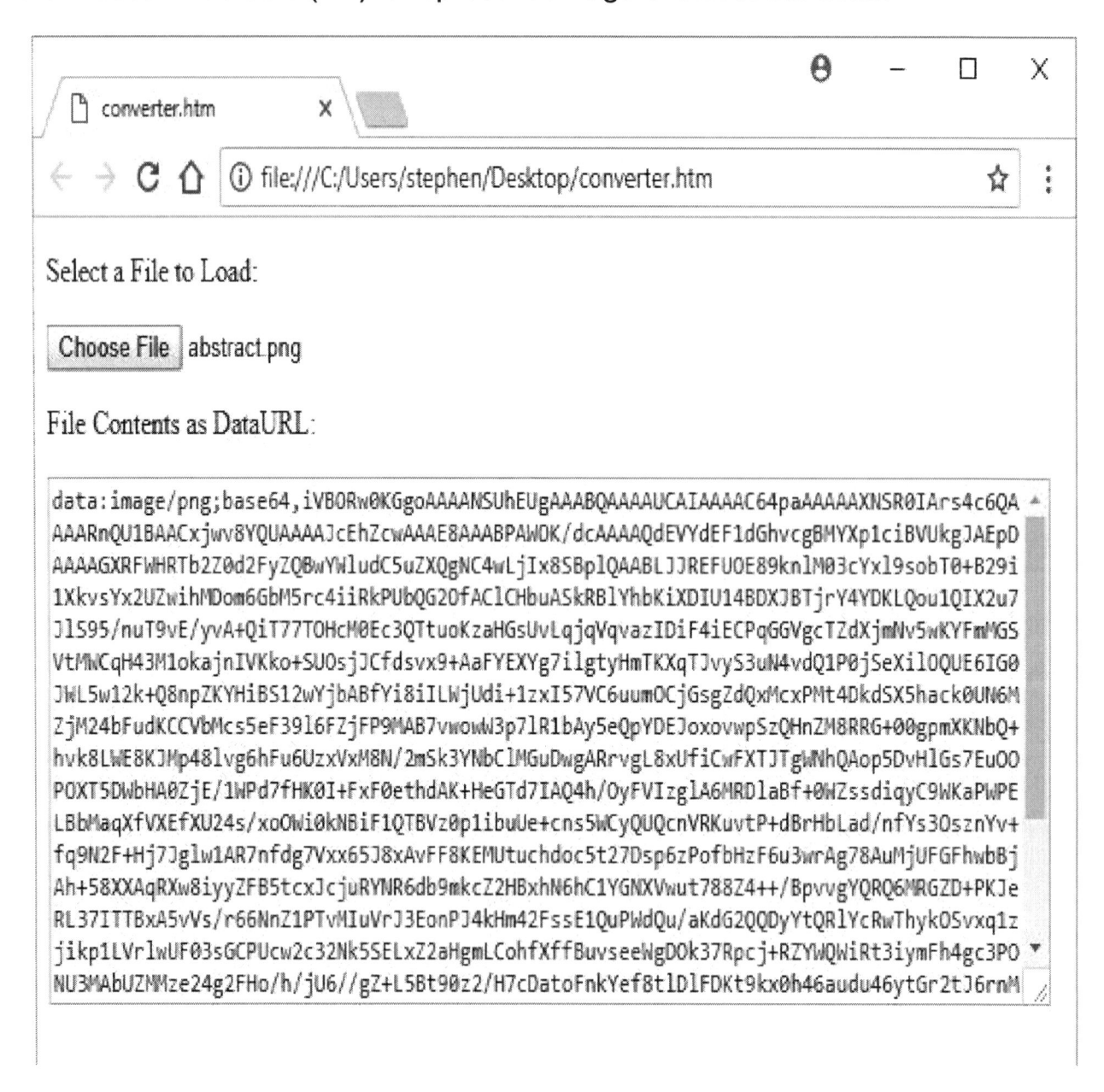

Now, if you're thinking "this is way too complicated for me", I would like to point out two things: 1. You are in the advanced section of this book, and 2. You can forget about the above explanation because I provide you with a tiny JavaScript utility that will automatically convert the code for an image on your computer to base64. All you have to do is cut and paste the data.

• Recall, that the object here is to use X3D to create a surface that would be difficult or impossible to do in Inkscape, and then import that surface into Inkscape to apply as a bitmap fill.

Basic Yellow Cone

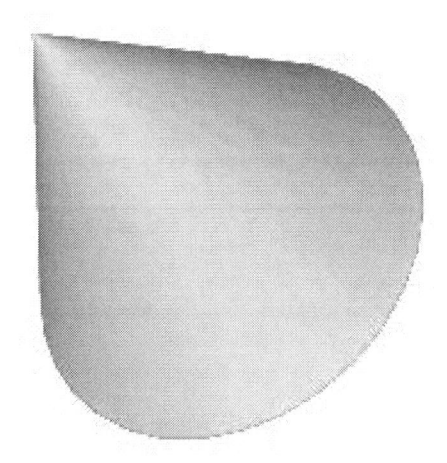

Gradient configuration for the cone shown above might be more difficult to create in Inkscape. Shown below is the X3D code for this yellow cone.

```
<x3d width="500px" height="400px">
<scene>
<Transform translation="-3 2 0" rotation="1 1 1 1.5">
  <shape>
  <Appearance>
    <Material diffuseColor="1.0 1.0 0" />
  </Appearance>
  <cone bottomRadius="2.0" height="3.0" />
  </shape>
</Transform>
</scene>
</x3d>
```

As you can see in the code above, X3D can perform *translation* and *rotation* transforms similar to SVG, except in three dimensions. The *rotation* transform in X3D has 4 numbers. The first three define the x, y and z rotation vector (the vector to rotate about), and the 4th dimension is the rotation angle in radians. Using these, you can rotate the object to present the surface you need.

Textured Cone

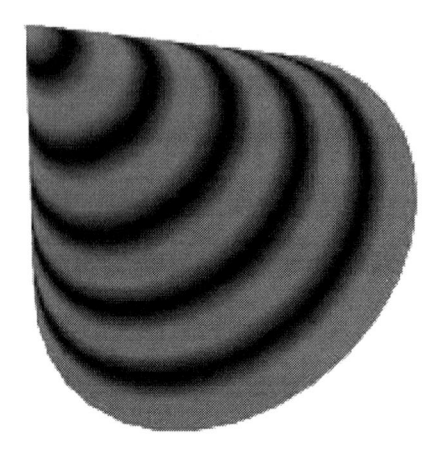

Show above is the same cone with a texture applied, the code for which is shown below (again with most of the base64 data missing).

```
<x3d width="500px" height="400px">
<scene>
<Transform translation="-3 2 0" rotation="1 1 1 1.5">
  <shape>
  <Appearance>
    <ImageTexture url="data:image/png;base64,iVBORw0KGgoAA...AASUVORK5CYII=">
    </ImageTexture>
  </Appearance>
  <cone bottomRadius="2.0" height="3.0"/>
  </shape>
</Transformv
</scenev
</x3d>
```

Textured Sphere

Show above is a sphere with a texture applied, the code for which is shown below.

```
<x3d width="300px" height="200px">
<scene>
<shape>
    <Appearance>
       <ImageTexture url="
data:image/png;base64,iVBORw0KGgoAAAANSUhEUgAAA...AAASUVORK5CYII=">
       </ImageTexture>
    </Appearance>
    <Sphere radius="3.0" />
</shape>
</scene>
</x3d>
```

3D Building

Show above are 3 textured boxes where I used the translation transform to stacked on top of one another to look like a building. The code for this is shown below.

```
<x3d width="500px" height="400px">
<scene>
    <ransform translation="-3 -2 0" rotation="0 1 0 0.5">
     <hape>
     <ppearance>
     <mageTexture url="
data:image/png;base64,iVBORw0KGgoAA...AABJRU5ErkJggg==">
     <ImageTexture>
     <appearance>
     <box> <box>
     </shape>
     </Transform>

     <Transform translation="-3 0 0" rotation="0 1 0 0.5">
     <shape>
     <appearance>
     <ImageTexture url="
data:image/png;base64,iVBORw0KGgoAA...AABJRU5ErkJggg==">
     </ImageTexture>
     </appearance>
     <box> </box>
     </shape>
     </Transform>

     <Transform translation="-3 2 0" rotation="0 1 0 0.5">
     <shape>
     <appearance>
     <ImageTexture url="
data:image/png;base64,iVBORw0KGgoAA...AABJRU5ErkJggg==">
     </ImageTexture>
     </appearance>
     <box> </box>
     </shape>
    </Transform>
</scene>
</x3d>
```

This section is only a basic introduction to X3D. X3D is amazing and powerful. with it you can display 3D objects and even whole 3D worlds in your web browser with no plugins. But, of course this book is about 2D graphics so it would be out of scope to go too deeply into X3D. Here I've shown you how to create prospective and curved textured surfaces that you can use as bitmap fill's in your Inkscape drawings.

Chapter 11: Professional Insights

What Does a Graphic Designer Do?

Graphic designers communicate ideas, it's that simple. Sometimes they do this using text. They select the font, font size, font color, and line length of text and headings. But a graphic designer's primary job is to communicate ideas using images. These images may be photographs, drawings, diagrams, animation, video, or abstract graphics that creates an emotional response.

Actually graphic designers usually use images and text together. Their job is to design a layout. To design a layout they must decide how images and text will go together on a printed page or webpage. How much space will images have? How much space will text have? What will be the visual relationship between the images and text?

Some graphic designers work by hand. Some use computer software. Most work both by hand and use computer software, taking advantage of the best aspects of both.

What Graphic Designers Design

- advertising materials
- branding
- brochures
- book illustrations and covers
- exhibition materials
- labels
- layout of newspapers, magazines, corporate reports, and other publications
- logos
- manuals
- packaging
- posters
- signage
- television advertising spots
- tradeshow signage and floor designs
- video

Today corporations are highly involved with reaching people through social media. In many positions, graphic designers are expected to keep up with the latest public buzz, consumer trends, and understand shifting consumer tastes.

In some organizations graphic designers are expected to:

- assist in the development of advertising campaigns
- assist in the production social media content
- assist with social media marketing and video projects

Where do Graphic Designers Work?

Many graphic designers have full time jobs at small to very large organizations. However, many graphic designers are freelancers. By its nature being a graphic designer requires an individual to have a great deal of creativity. Many super creative people don't have the stomach for the politics and structure of a corporate environment. They work as a freelancer consultants work for a clients.

They determine exactly what the client needs. They determine the client's target audience and the message the client wants to send with your design. The graphic designer then creates a mock-up or sketches that they present to their client for approval. After the design is approved, graphic designers check the final production before it goes to the final stage of completion.

Graphic Designers Salary and Opportunity to Advance

When you first start out, you'll probably receive on-the-job training and you'll probably need a few years of such training before you can move on to a better position within the company. Such entry-level positions usually offer a salary about $40,000-$50,000 annually, depending on your experience and skill level.

What Type of Knowledge Must a Graphic Designer Have?

A Graphic Designer must be knowledgeable in;

- Typography, layout, composition, color theory and information design
- Photo manipulation; resize, crop, add and remove objects, color correction
- CMYK printing processes and production
- Knowledge of HTML5, CSS3, and JavaScript

Today most companies expect a graphic designer to be internet savy. They are expected to:

- maintain company websites
- design User Interfaces (UI) and User Experiences (UX)
- develop video wireframes and storyboards
- develop email campaigns, website, and landing pages
- develop landing pages
- design web banners

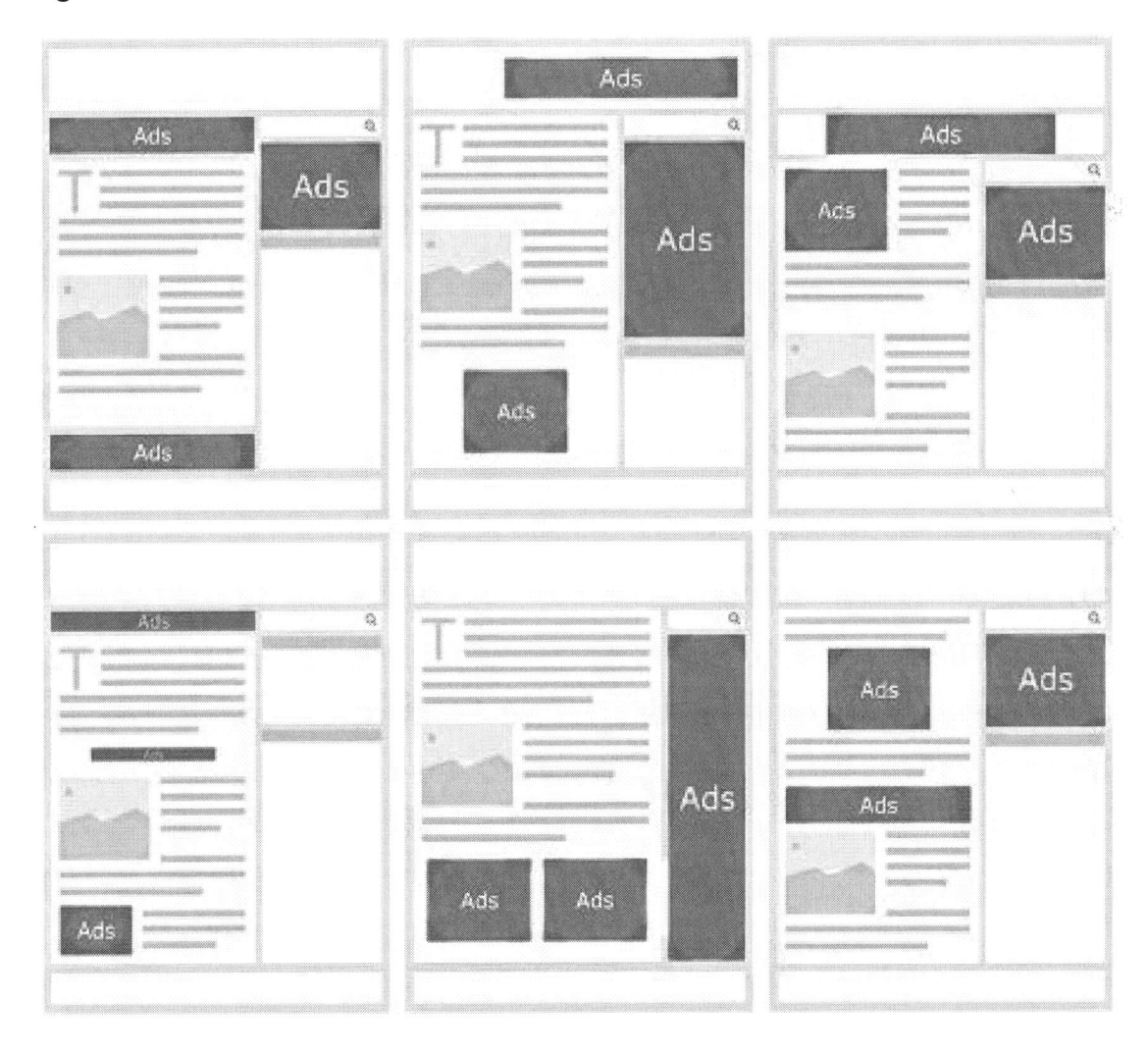

Computer Applications a Graphic Designer Must be Proficient in.

Microsoft office:

- Word
- PowerPoint
- Excel
- Outlook

Adobe:

- Creative Cloud
- Creative Suite
- InDesign
- Photoshop
- Illustrator
- Acrobat
- Dreamweaver

Many shops use Apple computers with Adobe applications, but some use Microsoft Computers with Office applications. Some shops use both. A Graphic Designer with the ability to work with both PC and Apple computers, and has knowledge of WordPress has an advantage.

What Education and Training Do You Need?

Graphic designer jobs usually require a bachelor's or less-often an associate degree in graphic design. Many colleges and universities across the country offer bachelor's degree or associate degree programs in graphic design. The curriculum for such programs usually involve courses in principles of design, commercial graphics production, printing techniques, computerized design, and website design.

An internship can provide you with invaluable on-the-job training and experience, and contacts in the industry.

The Importance of the Graphic Designer's Portfolio

A graphic designer must keep a portfolio of their best work to show to possible employers and clients. When competing for a job against someone with a similar resume, a good portfolio is what will get you the job.

Chapter 12: Keyboard shortcuts in Inkscape

Windows

Main UI Hotkeys

F1, s	Selector
Space	Selector (temporary)
Space switches to the Selector tool temporarily; another Space switches back.	
F2, n	Node tool
F3, z	Zoom tool
F4, r	Rectangle tool
F5, e	Ellipse/arc tool
F6, p	Freehand (Pencil) tool
Shift+F6, b	Bezier (Pen) tool
Ctrl+F6, c	Calligraphic tool
Ctrl+F1, g	Gradient tool
F7, d	Dropper tool
F8, t	Text tool
F9, i	Spiral tool
Shift+F9, *	Star tool
Ctrl+F2, o	Connector tool
Double click on the tool buttons opens the Preferences dialog showing the page of the corresponding tool.	

Dialogs

Shift+Ctrl+F	Fill and Stroke
Shift+Ctrl+W	Swatches
Shift+Ctrl+T	Text and Font
Shift+Ctrl+M	Transform
Shift+Ctrl+L	Layers

Shift+Ctrl+A	Align and Distribute
Shift+Ctrl+O	Object Properties
Shift+Ctrl+H	Undo history
Shift+Ctrl+X	XML Editor
Shift+Ctrl+D	Document Preferences
Shift+Ctrl+P	Inkscape Preferences
Shift+Ctrl+E	Export to PNG
Ctrl+F	Find
Shift+Alt+B	Trace bitmap

These open a new dialog window if it wasn't open yet, otherwise the corresponding dialog gets focus.

Toggle visibility

F12	toggle dialogs

This temporarily hides all open dialogs; another F12 shows them again.

Within a dialog

Esc	return to the canvas
Ctrl+F4, Ctrl+W	close the dialog
Tab	jump to next widget
Shift+Tab	jump to previous widget
Enter	set the new value

This accepts the new value you typed in a text field and returns focus to canvas.

Ctrl+Enter	in XML Editor, set the attr value

When editing an attribute value in XML Editor, this sets the new value (same as clicking the "Set attribute" button).

Space, Enter	activate current button or list
Ctrl+PgUp, Ctrl+PgDn	in a multi-tab dialog, switch tabs

Controls bar

The Controls bar at the top of the document window provides different buttons and controls for each tool.

Alt+X	jump to the first editable field

Enter	accept the new value
This accepts the new value you typed in a text field and returns focus to canvas.	
Esc	cancel changes, return to canvas
This cancels any changes you made in a text field and returns focus to canvas.	
Ctrl+Z	cancel changes
This cancels any changes you made in a text field but you stay in the field.	
Tab	jump to next field
Shift+Tab	jump to previous field
Use these to navigate between fields in the Controls bar (the value in the field you leave, if changed, is accepted).	
Changing values	
Up arrow, Down arrow	change value by 0.1
PgUp, PgDn	change value by 5.0

Canvas

Zoom	
=, +	zoom in
-	zoom out
The keypad +/- keys do zooming even when you are editing a text object, unless NumLock is on.	
middle click, Ctrl+right click	zoom in
Shift+middle click, Shift+right click	zoom out
Ctrl+mouse wheel	zoom in or out
Shift+middle button drag	zoom into the area
Alt+Z	activate zoom field
The zoom field in the lower left corner of the window allows you to specify zoom level precisely.	
Preset zooms	
1	zoom 1:1
2	zoom 1:2
3	zoom to selection

4	zoom to drawing
5	zoom to page
Ctrl+E, 6	zoom to page width

Zoom history

`	(back quote) previous zoom
Shift+`	next zoom

With these keys, you can travel back and forth through the history of zooms in this session

Scrolling (panning)

Ctrl+arrows	scroll canvas

Scrolling by keys is accelerated, i.e. it speeds up when you press Ctrl+arrows in quick succession, or press and hold.

middle button drag	pan canvas
Shift+right button drag, Ctrl+right button drag	pan canvas
mouse wheel	scroll canvas vertically
Shift+mouse wheel	scroll canvas horizontally

Guides and grid

mouse drag	drag off a ruler to create guide

Drag off the horizontal or vertical ruler to create a new guideline. Drag a guideline onto the ruler to delete it.

|, Shift+\	toggle guides and snapping to guides

If you want to have different values for guides visibility and snapping, set them via the Document Options dialog.

When you create a new guide by dragging off the ruler, guide visibility and snapping are turned on.

#, Shift+3	toggle grid and snapping to grid

If you want to have different values for grid visibility and snapping, set them via the Document Options dialog.

Note that only the 3 key on the main keyboard works, not on the keypad.

Display mode

Ctrl+keypad 5	toggle normal/outline mode

Palette

These keys work both in the floating palette dialog and in the palette frame at the bottom of the window.	
click	set fill color on selection
Shift+click	set stroke color on selection
mouse drag	drag fill color to objects
Shift+mouse drag	drag stroke color to objects
To change fill/stroke of an object by dragging color on it, that object need not be selected.	
You can also drag colors to the Fill (F) and Stroke (S) indicators in the statusbar to change the selection.	

File

Ctrl+N	create new document
Ctrl+O	open an SVG document
Shift+Ctrl+E	export to PNG
Ctrl+I	import bitmap or SVG
Ctrl+P	print document
Ctrl+S	save document
Shift+Ctrl+S	save under a new name
Shift+Ctrl+Alt+S	save a copy
Ctrl+Q	exit Inkscape

Window

Ctrl+R	toggle rulers
Ctrl+B	toggle scrollbars
F11	toggle fullscreen
F10	main menu
Menus can also be activated by Alt with the letter underscored in the menu name.	
Shift+F10, right click	drop-down (context) menu
Ctrl+F4, Ctrl+W	close document window

This shuts down Inkscape if it was the only document window open.	
Ctrl+Tab	next document window
Shift+Ctrl+Tab	previous document window
These cycle through the active document windows forward and backward.	

Layers

Shift+PgUp	move to layer above
Shift+PgDn	move to layer below
These commands move the selected objects from one layer to another.	
Shift+Ctrl+PgUp	raise layer
Shift+Ctrl+PgDn	lower layer
Shift+Ctrl+Home	raise layer to top
Shift+Ctrl+End	lower layer to bottom
These commands move the current layer among its siblings (normally other layers).	

Object

Undo/redo	
Shift+Ctrl+Y, Ctrl+Z	undo
Shift+Ctrl+Z, Ctrl+Y	redo
Clipboard	
Ctrl+C	copy selection
This places a copy of the selection to the Inkscape clipboard. Text from text objects is also placed onto the system clipboard.	
Ctrl+X	cut selection
This works the same as "copy selection" followed by deleting the selection.	
Ctrl+V	paste clipboard
This places the clipboard objects at the mouse cursor, or at the center of the window if mouse is outside the canvas.	
When editing text with the text tool, this pastes the text from the system clipboard into the current text object.	

Ctrl+Alt+V	paste in place
This places the clipboard objects to the original location from which they were copied.	
Shift+Ctrl+V	paste style
This applies the style of the (first of the) coped object(s) to the current selection.	
If a gradient handle (in Gradient tool) or a text span (in Text tool) are selected, they get the style instead of the entire object.	

Duplicate

Ctrl+D	duplicate selection
New object(s) are placed exactly over the original(s) and selected.	

Clone

Alt+D	clone object
A clone can be moved/scaled/rotated/skewed independently, but it updates the path, fill, and stroke from its original.	
The clone is placed exactly over the original object and is selected.	
You can only clone one object at a time; if you want to clone several objects together, group them and clone the group.	
Shift+Alt+D	unlink clone
Unlinking a clone cuts the link to the original, turning the clone into a plain copy.	
Shift+D	select original
To find out which object this is a clone of, select the clone and give this command. The original will be selected.	

Bitmaps

Alt+B	create a bitmap copy
This exports the selected object(s) (all other objects hidden) as PNG in the document's directory and imports it back.	
The imported bitmap is placed over the original selection and is selected.	
Shift+Alt+B	trace bitmap
This opens the Trace Bitmap dialog allowing you to convert a bitmap object to path(s).	

Patterns

Alt+I	object(s) to pattern
This converts the selection to a rectangle with tiled pattern fill.	

Shift+Alt+I	pattern to object(s)
Each selected object with pattern fill is broken into the same object without fill and a single pattern object.	
Group	
Shift+Ctrl+U, Ctrl+G	group selected objects
Use Ctrl+click to select objects within group.	
Shift+Ctrl+G, Ctrl+U	ungroup selected group(s)
This removes only one level of grouping; press Ctrl+U repeatedly to ungroup nested groups.	
Z-order	
Home	raise selection to top
End	lower selection to bottom
PgUp	raise selection one step
PgDn	lower selection one step

Path

Convert to path	
Shift+Ctrl+C	convert selected object(s) to path
Ctrl+Alt+C	convert stroke to path
Booleans	
Ctrl++	union
Union combines any number of objects into a single path, removing overlaps.	
Ctrl+-	difference
Difference works on 2 objects, extracting the top from the bottom.	
Ctrl+*	intersection
Intersection creates a path representing the common (overlapping) area of all selected objects.	
Ctrl+^	exclusive OR (XOR)
XOR is similar to Union, except that it works on 2 objects and removes areas where the objects overlap.	
Ctrl+/	division (cut)

Division cuts the bottom object into pieces by the top object, preserving the fill and stroke of the bottom.

Ctrl+Alt+/	cut path

Cut Path cuts the bottom object's stroke only where it is intersected by the top path, removing any fill from the result.

The result of Union, Difference, Intersection, and XOR inherits the id= attribute and therefore the clones of the bottom object.

Division and Cut path normally produce several objects; of them, a random one inherits the id= of the bottom source object.

Offsets

Ctrl+(	inset path (towards center)
Ctrl+)	outset path (away from center)

The default offset distance is 2 px (SVG pixel units, not screen pixels).

Alt+(	inset path by 1 pixel
Alt+)	outset path by 1 pixel
Shift+Alt+(	inset path by 10 pixels
Shift+Alt+)	outset path by 10 pixels

The actual distance for pixel offsets depends on zoom level. Zoom in for finer adjustment.

All the (,) commands convert the object to path, if necessary, and produce regular path.

Ctrl+J	create dynamic offset
Ctrl+Alt+J	create linked offset

These commands produce an offset object, editable by the node tool, standalone or linked to the original.

Shift+D	select source

Selecting a linked offset and giving this command will select the source path of the linked offset.

Combine

Ctrl+K	combine paths

This is different from grouping in that combined paths create one object.

This is different from Union in that overlapping areas are not affected.

Whether overlapping areas are filled is controlled by the Fill: winding/alternating

switch on the Fill & Stroke dialog.	
Shift+Ctrl+K	break paths apart
This attempts to break an object into constituent paths; it will fail if the object is one solid path.	
Simplify	
Ctrl+L	simplify
This command attempts to simplify selected path(s) by removing extra nodes. It converts all objects to paths first.	
If you invoke this command several times in quick succession, it will act more and more aggressively.	
Invoking Simplify again after a pause restores the default threshold (settable in the Inkscape Preferences dialog).	

Selector

Keyboard select	
Tab	select next object
Shift+Tab	select previous object
These keys pick objects in their z-order (Tab cycles from bottom to top, Shift+Tab cycles from top to bottom).	
Unless you did manual rearrangements, the last object you created is always on top.	
As a result, if nothing is selected, pressing Shift+Tab once conveniently selects the object you created last.	
This works on objects within the current layer (unless you change that in preferences).	
Ctrl+A	select all (current layer)
This works on objects within the current layer (unless you change that in preferences).	
Ctrl+Alt+A	select all (all layers)
This works on objects in all visible and unlocked layers.	
!	invert selection (current layer)
This inverts selection (deselects what was selected and vice versa) in the current layer.	

Alt+!	invert selection (all layers)
This inverts selection (deselects what was selected and vice versa) in visible and unlocked layers.	
Esc	deselect
Backspace, Del	delete selection
Keyboard move	
arrows	move selection by the nudge distance
Shift+arrows	move selection by 10x nudge distance
The default nudge distance is 2 px (SVG pixel units, not screen pixels).	
Alt+arrows	move selection by 1 pixel
Alt+Shift+arrows	move selection by 10 pixels
The actual distance for pixel movements depends on zoom level. Zoom in for finer movement.	
Keyboard scale	
., >	scale selection up by the scale step
,, <	scale selection down by the scale step
The default scale step is 2 px (SVG pixel units, not screen pixels).	
Ctrl+., Ctrl+>	scale selection to 200%
Ctrl+,, Ctrl+<	scale selection to 50%
Alt+., Alt+>	scale selection up by 1 pixel
Alt+,, Alt+<	scale selection down by 1 pixel
The actual size increment for pixel scaling depends on zoom level. Zoom in for finer scaling.	
Scaling is uniform around the center, so that the size increment applies to the larger of the two dimensions.	
Keyboard rotate	
[,]	rotate selection by the angle step
The default angle step is 15 degrees.] rotates clockwise, [rotates counterclockwise.	
Ctrl+[, Ctrl+]	rotate selection by 90 degrees
Alt+[, Alt+]	rotate selection by 1 pixel
The actual angle for pixel rotation depends on zoom level. Zoom in for finer	

movement.

These commands use the rotation center, draggable in Selector (by default it's in geometric center).

Keyboard flip

h	flip selection horizontally
v	flip selection vertically

Mouse select

click	select an object

When you left-click on an object, previous selection is deselected.

Shift+click	toggle selection

Shift+click adds an object to the current selection if it was not selected, or deselects it otherwise.

clickclick	edit the object

For paths, double clicking switches to Node tool; for shapes, to corresponding shape tool; for text, to Text tool.

For groups, double clicking performs the "Enter group" command (the group becomes temporary layer).

Double clicking in empty space swithes to the parent layer in the hierarchy, if any.

Select within group, select under

Ctrl+click	select within group

Ctrl+click selects the object at click point disregarding any levels of grouping that this object might belong to.

Ctrl+Shift+click	toggle selection within group
Alt+click	select under

Alt+click selects the object at click point which is beneath (in z-order) the lowest selected object at click point.

If the bottom object is reached, Alt+click again selects the top object. So, several Alt+clicks cycle through z-order stack at point.

On Linux, Alt+click and Alt+drag may be reserved by the window manager. If you reconfigure your window manager

to not map Alt+click, then it will be free for Inkscape to use.

If your keyboard has a Meta key, you may wish to set your "Modifier key" to use it instead of Alt.

(Sometimes you can also use Ctrl+Alt+click (select under in groups) with the same effect as Alt+click.)

Shift+Alt+click	toggle under
Ctrl+Alt+click	select under, in groups
Shift+Ctrl+Alt+click	toggle under, in groups
Ctrl+Enter	enter group
Ctrl+Backspace	go to parent group/layer

Rubberband

mouse drag	select multiple objects

Dragging around objects does "rubberband" selection; previous selection is deselected.

Shift+mouse drag	add objects to selection

Normally, you need to start from an empty space to initiate a rubberband.

However, if you press Shift before dragging, Inkscape will do rubberband selection even if you start from an object.

Mouse move

mouse drag	select + move

Dragging an object selects it if it was not selected, then moves selection.

Alt+mouse drag	move selected

Alt+drag moves the current selection (without selecting what is under cursor), no matter where you start the drag.

On Linux, Alt+click and Alt+drag may be reserved by the window manager. Reconfigure it so you can use them in Inkscape.

Ctrl+mouse drag	restrict movement to horizontal or vertical
Shift+mouse drag	temporarily disable snapping

This temporaily disables snapping to grid or guides when you are dragging with grid or guides on.

mouse dragSpace	drop a copy

When dragging or transforming with mouse, each Space leaves a copy of the selected object.

You can press and hold Space while dragging for a nice "trail."

Mouse transform

click	toggle scale/rotation handles

mouse drag	scale (scale handles)
mouse drag	rotate or skew (rotation handles)

Scale handles

mouse drag	scale
Ctrl+mouse drag	scale preserving aspect ratio
Shift+mouse drag	symmetric transformation

Holding Shift while transforming makes transformation symmetric around the center of the selection.

Alt+mouse drag	slow movement

Holding Alt while transforming makes transformation lag behind mouse movement, allowing finer changes.

Rotation/skew handles

mouse drag	rotate or skew
Ctrl+mouse drag	snap skew angle

Holding Ctrl when dragging a skew (non-corner) handle snaps the skew angle to angle steps (default 15 degrees).

Ctrl+mouse drag	snap rotation angle

Holding Ctrl when dragging a rotation (corner) handle snaps the rotation angle to angle steps (default 15 degrees).

Rotation center

mouse drag	move rotation center

Moved rotation center remembers its position for (all) selected object(s) until you reset it.

Shift+click	reset rotation center

Resetting rotation center moves it back to the geometric center of the object's or selection's bounding box.

Cancel

Esc	cancel rubberband, move, transformation

Press Esc while mouse button is still down to cancel rubberband selection, move, or transformation of any kind.

CONCLUSION

As we reach the conclusion of "Inkscape Drawing Complete 2024 Guide for Beginners," we pause to reflect on the journey we've undertaken together. From the initial steps of understanding the Inkscape interface to mastering advanced techniques and tools, this guide has aimed to equip you with the knowledge and skills necessary to excel in the realm of vector graphics.

Reflecting on the Journey

Embarking on this journey, we began with the basics of Inkscape, understanding its history, installation, and interface. You were introduced to the fundamental principles that underpin vector graphics, providing a solid foundation upon which to build your skills. Through each chapter, we delved deeper into the functionalities and tools of Inkscape, exploring shapes, paths, colors, gradients, and effects. The progression from basic to advanced techniques was designed to be gradual and comprehensive, ensuring a thorough understanding of each aspect of the software.

Mastering the Art of Vector Graphics

One of the core aspects of this guide was to instill a deep understanding of vector graphics. You learned how Inkscape leverages the power of vectors to create scalable, high-quality designs. The exploration of tools like the Bezier curve tool, the use of nodes and segments, and the manipulation of shapes and paths have empowered you to create intricate and precise artwork.

The Colorful World of Inkscape

Colors and gradients play a pivotal role in design, and Inkscape offers a rich palette to bring your visions to life. We explored the RGB, HSL, and CMYK color models, understanding how each can be used effectively in your designs. The guide also covered the nuances of linear and radial gradients, enabling you to add depth and dimension to your creations.

Beyond the Canvas: Practical Applications and Integrations

Inkscape is not just a tool for creating standalone artworks; it's a gateway to a myriad of creative applications. We explored specialized applications like fashion design, 3D box creation, and even web integration. The guide also emphasized the importance of integrating Inkscape with other software, broadening your toolkit and enhancing your workflow.

Professional Insights and Future Outlook

In addition to technical skills, this guide provided insights into the professional world of graphic design. Understanding the role and responsibilities of a graphic designer, and the current trends and future outlook in the field, prepares you not just as a skilled Inkscape user, but as a well-rounded design professional.

The Path Forward

As you step forward from this guide, remember that learning is an ongoing journey. The field of digital design is dynamic, with new trends, tools, and techniques emerging regularly. Staying curious, experimenting with new ideas, and continuously honing your skills will keep you at the forefront of the industry.

Continuing Your Inkscape Adventure

Inkscape, as a tool, will continue to evolve, and it is essential to keep abreast of these changes. Engage with the Inkscape community, participate in forums, and experiment with new features as they are released. Your journey with Inkscape does not end with this guide; it merely marks the beginning of a lifelong adventure in creativity.

The Essence of Continuous Learning

Your journey with Inkscape doesn't end with the last page of this guide. In the rapidly evolving landscape of digital design, continuous learning is key. This guide has laid the foundation, but the world of Inkscape is vast and ever-changing. Keep exploring new features, updates, and plugins that enhance Inkscape's capabilities. Engage with online tutorials, workshops, and webinars to stay updated and refine your skills further.

Building a Community Connection

One of the most valuable resources at your disposal is the Inkscape community. This vibrant community of designers, artists, and enthusiasts is a treasure trove of knowledge, inspiration, and support. Participate in forums, join Inkscape user groups, and attend meetups or conferences. Sharing your work, seeking feedback, and learning from others' experiences will not only improve your skills but also enrich your journey with diverse perspectives.

The Creative Portfolio: Showcasing Your Work

As you grow in your proficiency with Inkscape, it's important to document and showcase your work. Creating a portfolio of your designs will not only serve as a record of your progress but also as a tool to share your talent with the world. Whether it's for professional growth, freelance opportunities, or personal satisfaction, a well-curated portfolio is a powerful asset.

The Impact of Design in the Digital Age

Reflect on the impact of your work. Design in the digital age is not just about aesthetics; it's a means of communication, a way to convey messages, and a tool for social change. Your designs have the power to inform, persuade, and inspire. As you wield this power, be mindful of the responsibility that comes with it. Strive to create designs that are not only visually appealing but also culturally sensitive and ethically sound.

Embracing Challenges as Opportunities

In your journey with Inkscape, you'll undoubtedly face challenges. Whether it's mastering a complex tool, overcoming creative blocks, or adapting to new trends, view these challenges as opportunities for growth. Each obstacle you overcome is a step forward in your journey as a designer.

The Role of Innovation and Experimentation

Don't be afraid to experiment. The world of design thrives on innovation and creativity. Use Inkscape to experiment with new ideas, blend different techniques, and push the boundaries of conventional design. It's through experimentation that new trends are born, and personal styles are developed.

Preparing for the Future

As technology advances, so do the tools and mediums of design. Stay curious about emerging technologies such as augmented reality, virtual reality, and AI in design. The skills you've developed with Inkscape provide a strong foundation, but being adaptable and open to learning new technologies will ensure that you remain relevant in this ever-changing field.

A Final Word of Encouragement

As this guide comes to a close, take a moment to appreciate your dedication and the progress you've made. The journey of learning and mastering Inkscape is a testament to your commitment and passion for design. Carry this passion forward as you continue to explore, create, and inspire with your designs.

Printed in Great Britain
by Amazon